HINDI IMPERIALISM

HINDI IMPERIALISM

ALADI ARUNA

Translated by R Vijaya Sankar

With forewords by CN Annadurai, M Karunanidhi and MK Stalin

SPEAKING TIGER

SPEAKING TIGER PUBLISHING PVT. LTD
125A, Ground Floor, Shahpur Jat, near Asiad Village,
New Delhi 110049

First published in paperback by Speaking Tiger 2024

ISBN: 978-93-5447-710-2

eISBN: 978-93-5447-711-9

10 9 8 7 6 5 4 3 2 1

Typeset in Adobe Jenson Pro at SŪRYA, New Delhi
Printed at Impressions Printing & Packaging Limited

I place this book as an offering at the feet of the noble martyrs who sacrificed their lives by rising in revolt to resist Hindi imperialism and protect Mother Tamil.

Publisher's Note

This book is the first English translation of Aladi Aruna's *Hindi Egaathipathiyam*. Translated over 2023-24, it has a new foreword written by MK Stalin in 2023 and includes forewords written for previous Tamil editions by CN Annadurai and M Karunanidhi. The first edition of *Hindi Imperialism* in Tamil was published in 1966, followed by subsequent editions in 1993, 2005, and 2017.

Contents

Acknowledgements 11

A Missile in the Anti-Hindi War: Foreword by MK Stalin 13

A Weapon for Tamils: Foreword by Doctor Kalaignar 17

A Fruit of Scholarship: Foreword by Anna 21

Introduction 27

1. A Definitive Purpose in the History of Tamils 31
2. Hindi, Urdu, Hindustani 37
3. The First Language War 51
4. The Satyagraha of 1948 68
5. The Constitution and the Official Language 82
6. The August Agitation 99
7. The Imposition of Hindi 106
8. The Devanagari Script 125
9. Three Language Formula 133
10. The Importance of English 142
11. The Official Language Commission and the Parliamentary Committee 151
12. Black Flag 160
13. The Official Languages Act 171

14. Setting Aflame the Constitution 180
15. Self-immolation 193
16. The January Revolution and a Day of Mourning 199
17. Student Uprising 206
18. Picketing 214
19. The Defence of India Act Invoked 224
20. In Other States... 229
21. After the Storm 238
22. The January Revolution 245
23. The Two Language Formula 253
24. Constitution Burning...Again! 265
25. The 14 Language Formula 287
Afterword: Reflections by a Granddaughter 298

Notes 300

Acknowledgements

I express my sincere gratitude to Mr AS Panneerselvan, a distinguished Fellow at the Centre for Study in Public Sphere, Roja Muthiah Research Library, Chennai. His insightful articles in *The Hindu* always captivated me, and it was his book *Karunanidhi: A Life* that truly inspired me. Our pivotal meeting at the Roja Muthiah Research Library marked the initiation of translating my late father's book on Hindi imposition. Mr Panneerselvan generously devoted several hours to outlining the roadmap for the translation and publication, for which I am deeply thankful.

I am also grateful to Mr R Vijaya Sankar, who has translated the book from the original Tamil into English. Mr Sankar has had a remarkable 36-year journalistic career, during which he served as the editor of *Frontline* for two decades. Currently the Group Editor at AIDEM, he has translated politically significant works and authored several books in English and Tamil. My heartfelt thanks to Mr Vijaya Sankar for his dedication, sincerity, and timely efforts.

A delightful encounter unfolded when I crossed paths with a dynamic twenty-three-year-old student from the Indian Institute of Mass Communication, New Delhi. Despite a significant generational gap, our shared enthusiasm for literature was refreshing. Young Kollappan, through his diligence and commitment, contributed significantly to the making of the English edition of my father's work, for which I extend my heartfelt appreciation.

Special thanks to Mr Ravi Singh and his team at Speaking Tiger Books for their invaluable role in bringing this work to fruition. Their dedication to quality and commitment to sharing meaningful work with readers have made this journey enriching.

I extend sincere gratitude to my daughter, Kavya, whose pivotal role in catalysing the translation of the book into English has helped bring it to a new audience. As the sole grandchild following in his footsteps, Kavya, a law graduate, not only demonstrates a keen interest in politics but also exhibits a profound understanding of my father's journey. During her third year of law school, Kavya's involvement in a project on the JPC probe into the Bofors case facilitated a connection with the first Member of Parliament from Tamil Nadu, recognising her grandfather's legacy and emphasising the importance of preserving his political contributions. Kavya's illumination of my father's political legacy and her unwavering commitment to its continuity are deeply appreciated. Thank you, Kavya!

Finally, my gratitude overflows as I reflect on the immeasurable love and steadfast support generously provided by my husband, Dr V Balaji. Over the entirety of the year, his unwavering commitment has been my source of strength; he has stood by me in every role I embraced, be it personal or professional, without a hint of hesitation or question. The depth of his patience and unshakable belief in me has been a guiding force, propelling me forward in both my personal and professional endeavours. My appreciation for his unwavering presence and belief in my capabilities knows no bounds.

Poongothai Aladi Aruna
Chennai, March 2024

A Missile in the Anti-Hindi War

Foreword by MK Stalin (2023)

'Lovers of Tamil and great Tamil poets rose in revolt against the imposition of Hindi.

They expressed their resentment in fiery words published in newspapers.

The anti-Hindi agitation was everywhere—in towns, villages and hamlets.

Maraimalai Adigal, the man of dignity from Pallavaram, also plunged into the agitation.'

Yes. As passionately described by Kalaignar in the first part of his autobiography *Nenjukku Needhi*, Maraimalai Adigal presided over the conference organised on June 3, his birthday, to mobilise the masses for the first anti-Hindi war of 1938 spearheaded by Periyar.

Starting from that war and concluding with the Dravida Munnetra Kazhagam general council resolution urging the government to 'accept Tamil, the State's official language, which is also the leader of the Dravidian languages, as the Union government's official language and, accordingly, accept all the autonomous languages of the other states also as the official languages of the Union', and the West Bengal Assembly's 1965 resolution on the 'fourteen-language formula', former Minister Aladi Aruna narrates in this volume titled *Hindi Imperialism* the history of the long anti-Hindi struggle. It was like a relay—a struggle led by leaders like Thanthai Periyar, Perarignar Anna and Kalaignar and by movements starting from the Justice Party and ending with the Dravida Munnetra Kazhagam.

This book, which will help the young generation of today to easily understand the fierce, meaningful struggles of the guardians of Mother Tamil, should be on the bookshelf of every soldier of Tamil.

The very fact that the book, since its publication in 1966, has seen four editions and goes into the fifth edition makes us understand its popularity among not only the cadre of the Dravidian movement but also among lovers of the Tamil language.

The 'Save Tamil Struggle' of the Justice Party-Dravidar Kazhagam-Dravida Munnetra Kazhagam was led from the front by Periyar, Anna and Kalaignar. That the reasons for the launch of the 1938 struggle persist even now is clear to every Tamil from the fact that the politics of imposing Hindi, particularly the Union government's brazen move to name criminal laws in Hindi in defiance of the Constitutional mandate that all the laws of the land should be in English, is still in practice. In this context, I think the publication of the fifth edition of *Hindi Imperialism* is timely.

The anti-Hindi struggle succeeded in obtaining Prime Minister Jawaharlal Nehru's assurance on the floor of Parliament that Hindi would not be imposed on non-Hindi speakers, which Perarignar Anna hailed as a promise to be inscribed in golden letters. The anti-Hindi struggle proclaimed that there was an army out there waiting to protect Tamil and led to the Tamil Nadu Assembly passing a resolution that put an end to the three-language formula and adopting the two-language formula. The anti-Hindi struggle announced to the world that the Dravida Munnetra Kazhagam, despite its leaders, including Perasiriyar Anbazhagan, losing their Assembly memberships during the agitation, was a movement that was ready to make any sacrifice in the cause of Tamil. Indeed, many young Tamils laid down their lives during the struggle.

I appreciate Ms Poongothai Aladi Aruna for bringing out the fifth Tamil edition and the first English Translation of *Hindi Imperialism,* which is a treasure trove of information on the struggle. A daughter carrying on her father's service to Tamil symbolises the Dravida Munnetra Kazhagam's tradition of passing on its love and concern for the language from generation to generation. Aladi Aruna, who had attached himself to the Dravidian movement as a student and went on to become a Member of the Legislative Assembly, a member of the Cabinet as Law Minister and later a Rajya Sabha member, was a beacon that shone its light on the principle of federalism. Let the fifth Tamil edition and the first English Translation of *Hindi Imperialism* be a missile that can stop the imposition of Hindi!

With love,

MK Stalin

A Weapon for Tamils

Foreword by Doctor Kalaignar (1993)

The linguistic war of Tamil Nadu, resisting the inherently arrogant Congress empire's relentless frenzy to impose Hindi, pushing aside other national languages—and dismissing the advice of many noble people not foolishly to prefer a raw vegetable over a ripe fruit—has a history that has surprised the world.

There are stone inscriptions that have survived for thousands of years, highlighting the glory of Tamil.

The courageous linguistic warriors of Tamil Nadu have created a new history for those who have been reading and quoting happily only the poems of *Purananuru* and *Kalingathu Parani* that glorify the valour of ancient warriors of the land of Tamils. Seven or eight young Tamils have set themselves on fire, exhibiting their commitment to protecting Tamil. Hundreds of lion-like Tamils have braved the hissing bullets of the police and fallen dead for the sake of Mother Tamil. Tamil Nadu faced unprecedented oppression that felled the young and old alike, like flash floods washing away both tender and ripe leaves in its fury.

An army of students rose in revolt, hoisting the flags of resistance against Hindi and vowing not to allow the attempts to plunge Tamil Nadu into darkness forever to succeed.

Mother Tamil wore a sari dripping with the blood of the sons of the soil.

The nation witnessed the climax of the 20-year war against Hindi.

The sighs of Tamils, wondering whether they should follow the Bihari or kneel before the orders of Uttar Pradesh, turned into the flames of a volcano.

The anti-Hindi revolution has a history and it has many phases—how that volcano came into existence, how it roared, and how it erupted. My dear friend has succeeded in analysing those phases with evidence.

His pen has created this history in a manner that is as inspiring as the anti-Hindi war itself. He deserves high praise for presenting this book like a typical historian without omitting any detail.

The book gives proof of the fact that in history, sometimes heroes become cowards and sacrificers become traitors, and astonishing changes happen in an instant.

When a storm hits land, even particles of dust rise to great heights... then fall and mix with the soil. Nobody spends time worrying about it. Similarly, there were some people in the anti-Hindi agitation who later became something else. But that did not bring down the war's intensity, nor did it lose sight of its objective. The upsurge in Tamil Nadu continued like the restless sea. Comrade Aruna writes the story of this battlefield in his characteristically evocative style. The book is not just rhetorical. It has explanations that will give fitting replies to the empty claims of the supporters of Hindi.

This book kindles the hope that many such works will be published and that people with some time to spare will make special efforts to write them.

The number of people eagerly reading books of knowledge is going down. I hope this book, titled *Hindi Imperialism*, will put an end to this pathetic situation by creating a renewed interest in reading.

This is a book of knowledge that records a history which will serve as a weapon in the arsenal of the linguistic war. Had such a weapon containing the sentiments of Tamils not come out, by now, many people would have spent numerous days pledging their self-respect to Hindi fanatics.

Peace is not yet restored fully. The dark clouds have not dispersed; in fact, they seem to be expanding. Neither the flashes of lightning nor the roars of thunder have stopped. The ghostly dance of trees is on.

Another deluge?

Tamil Nadu stands like a question mark! The rulers have to answer. If they don't respond, Tamils will give the answer.

This is the feeling I had while reading this book, and it gave me goosebumps.

One who opposes Hindi dies as a Tamil. One who supports it lives like a broker.

With love,

M Karunanidhi

A Fruit of Scholarship

Foreword by Anna (1966)

My friend Aladi Aruna is an ideologically agile youth—a lawyer who has earned the goodwill of the people of Tamil Nadu from his student days.

Today's Tamil youth have developed a special liking for Tamil, and they expect the government to realise that it is a classical language and strive to enhance its prestige. The feeling that Hindi's dominance would harm the Tamil language and the Tamil race as a whole has fuelled this passion further.

The Congress government has not only refused to respect this sentiment but also tends to ridicule it, describing it as a result of confusion, vain fear and unnecessary frenzy and showing an imperialistic attitude that brushes aside the real fear of Tamils. There is none who is not anguished by this attitude except those who have sold their souls for personal gains.

It is these anguished people who have been trying to stall the invasion of Hindi imperialism through agitations and sacrifices of their lives.

In order to show and explain that love for one's language is not bigotry and that Hindi's dominance would be harmful, linguists, poets, veteran administrators and the leaders of various political parties have been doing serious work consistently and relentlessly in the hope that justice will prevail one day.

This upsurge has been growing not only in Tamil Nadu but also in Bengal. Some people—those who are in touch with the government and those who have embraced slavery—have been going around saying vacuously that this is an empty, orchestrated sentiment.

This is not an empty, orchestrated sentiment. Through this book, Aladi Aruna tells the nationals that it is a perspective built on irrefutable reason.

A stormy orator, Aruna has proved in these pages that he is an excellent, clear-minded writer and a lawyer who can present his arguments and evidence in such a way as to bring out the truth inherent in his case. I am very, very happy and proud to note this.

Aruna has made me happy by creating something I expect from educated youth in the Dravida Munnetra Kazhagam. It is easy to write a hot and spicy book condemning Hindi imperialism. But this book doesn't do that. It records an explanation, a history that narrates to the nation the origin, aim and evolution of Hindi imperialism and the increasing resistance to it.

At the outset, I said Aruna is an ideologically alive youth. However, in this book, he proves not only his agile mind but also his interest and skill in digging out facts and analysing an issue. The distinction of the book lies in the fact that it creates a new awakening, not only among people who have linguistic pride but also those who refuse to acknowledge linguistic rights as a serious issue. Although many books have been brought out on the anti-Hindi war of Tamil Nadu, Aruna's book stands apart, presenting in a coherent way arguments and proofs from various books, incidents and opinions of many people.

The nation knows that our peaceful struggle against Hindi imposition has not yielded the desired results and that it must continue. We have no other weapon than the belief that we've been fighting for an honest objective with proper reason. That has the potential to give us the courage to face oppression and atrocity, however horrible they may be. Being armed with just a belief might dishearten us sometimes. That belief should have been built on proper reasons and proofs. Aladi Aruna has done just that in this book.

Its style brims with enthusiasm. Its scholarship shines bright. It is clear that he has worked very hard to write this book.

I laud this young man affectionately for his serious effort to contribute to the struggle for a noble cause.

I wish this fruit of his scholarship reaches the homes of good people and inspires them to love their language. I appeal to the Tamil community to read the book that will help them to march on the right path.

Long Live Tamil!

Let Tamil Win!

With love,

Annadurai

HINDI IMPERIALISM

ALADI ARUNA

Introduction

'Thamizhagam, with a roaring sea as its boundary.
The Tamil-speaking great world lying between
the Vengada Hills in the north
and Kanyakumari in the south.'

—Payiram by Panamparanar, verse in the
ancient Tamil grammar work, *Tholkappiyam*.

'Oh Sweet Tamil! I live because of you;
even if gods offer me the nectar of immortality,
I won't take it.'

—From *Madurai Sokkanathar Viduthoothu*
by T Sangu Pulavar.

The greatness of Tamil expressed by poets in these lines explains why Tamils have consistently fought against the dominance of Hindi.

Tamils had a heightened consciousness of Tamil language and Tamil Nadu, their land, even before the era of Christ, when belief in God and adherence to religion were intense.

The Congress won in the Madras Presidency in the general election of 1937. Rajaji, the great scholar, assumed office as Chief Minister. He imposed Hindi as a compulsory subject in schools. The Dravidar Kazhagam launched an agitation against it in 1938 under the leadership of EVR Periyar. The struggle continues even today. Leaders of the Dravidian movement like Periyar, Arignar

Anna and Kalaignar Karunanidhi led the agitation, and an army of Tamil scholars and students rallied around them. The language war still goes on. It will certainly continue until Tamil becomes an official language at the Centre.

The sacrifices made by the Tamils to protect their language and defeat the domination of Hindi occupy a higher place in the history of the world than their sacrifices in the non-violent independence movement led by Gandhiji. I am proud of having written a book recording the history of the sacrifices made by the people of Tamil Nadu and the Dravidian parties, especially the Dravida Munnetra Kazhagam, in their struggle for acceptance by the Centre of Mother Tamil as an official language.

The first edition of this book came out in 1966, a year after the language revolution of 1965. When I gave a copy of the book to Anna, I was surprised to see his extreme joy. Uncontrollable tears welled up in my eyes. Anna was overjoyed like a mother who saw for the first time the infant that she had given birth to. I requested him to write a foreword. He promised to do so in a week. That foreword shines like the crown of this book.

My experience as a student who assisted my college mates when the language revolution broke out in the Madras Law College in 1965 helped me describe that struggle without omitting any incident. This book has already earned the distinction of being the first written record of that revolution.

In 1986, when the DMK launched the agitation by burning copies of the constitutional provision on the official language policy of the Union government, the frontline leaders of the party, including Kalaignar Karunanidhi, and its legislators participated in it. They went to jail smiling. The MGR government's oppressive act of disqualifying seven DMK legislators was a great betrayal of Tamil and Tamils.

In the second edition, which was brought out in 1986, four chapters were added detailing the struggle and the manner in which a section on the official language was incorporated into the Constitution. They enriched the book further.

This is the third edition of the book. Since the anti-Hindi struggle was a historic mission of the Tamils to achieve a noble goal, I have added as many photographs of the martyrs as possible in this edition. New details and statistics have also been added to it. Many facts mentioned in the Official Language Commission surprise us. The reports of the commission show how the Union government tottered and wavered in its serious efforts to impose, develop and propagate Hindi.

Among the Dravidian movement's unique ideals, two are primary and very important. One of them is the ideal of 'collective rule at the Centre, autonomy for the states'. The second one is: 'Permanent opposition to Hindi imposition'. I am proud to have researched these ideals and published two books—*Unfederal Features of the Indian Constitution* and *Hindi Imperialism*. I consider these two books major achievements in my public life.

[...]

With love,
Aladi Aruna
Chennai, 9.7.2004

Chapter 1

A Definitive Purpose in the History of Tamils

'I'll tell you something with all humility. This is not a language issue. This is nothing but an issue of domination. To know how submissive we are, political supremacists, political conspirators and fanatic imperialists impose their language and tell us:

"You must accept only this as the official language, exams will be conducted only in this language, laws will be written only in this, only in this language will they speak in Parliament. You come here only if you know this. If you don't know this, you go and lie submissively in your country, in your nest, as a second-class citizen, as a degraded human being, as an indifferent person, as a lackey of all and sundry."'

—Arignar Anna

The question of the official language in India has disappointed intellectuals, betrayed the trustful, and made neutral observers hang their heads in shame while provoking non-Hindi-speaking people to rise in revolt with a war cry and triggering a great revolution. It has now become obvious that any decision taken on the issue of official languages without the unanimous support of non-Hindi-speaking people will not be sustainable. Any decision contrary to their wish will have adverse consequences, disrupt peace in the country, put to test law and order, impede progress and hamper national unity. Objective researchers know very well that India's future, its political situation, social reforms, industrial progress, and economic equality depend on finding a just solution to the language issue, which is deeply embedded in people's hearts.

The number of spoken languages in the Indian subcontinent is 1,652. After analysing these languages in terms of their literary wealth, cultural background, written form and the number of their speakers, members of the Constituent Assembly recognised only 14 as national languages. This number was increased to 22 later. Most of these were official languages before British rule. Kings and regional chieftains encouraged and nurtured them. These languages, which reached great heights owing to the support of their patrons and whose fame spread like fragrance thanks to the works of writers and poets, lost official recognition during British rule and became marketplace languages.

Scholars of Thirukkural were not respected, but those well-versed in Oliver Goldsmith's poetry were hailed as men of sharp intellect. Those who researched *Silappadhikaram* were not honoured, but those who pronounced the name of Shakespeare were glorified as master playwrights. There was none to appreciate Kamban's immortal poems, but they praised Milton's poetry, which was no match for even a single verse of Kamban in terms of poetic excellence and imagination.

Love for the mother tongue withered while English roared. This was not the fate of Tamil alone. It was a darkness that engulfed all parts of India.

The British, who brought the entire Indian landscape under one umbrella for their convenience, used English as the official language. The Congress movement, which beat the drums of freedom against the rule of the British, decided that India should have one of the Indian languages as the common language of the country and chose Hindi. This was the origin of the problem.

And it was the beginning of the phase that laid the foundation of Hindi imperialism.

The importance of English could not be ignored even at the height of the valiant struggle against British rule, which saw brave protesters setting foreign goods aflame and opposing the ways of the alien forces. The Congress was unable to justify its support of Hindi and make it acceptable to all. Right from the outset, Congressmen in the South understood the motive behind the statement that choosing one of the Indian languages was an act of patriotism. The Congress' language policy worried them. However, Hindi fanatics decided to get the stamp of popular approval for Hindi when the freedom movement was at its peak and acted systematically and aggressively towards that end.

At the Congress' all-India session in Gaya in 1922, the leaders spoke only in Hindi. The delegates from the South stood perplexed like new apprentices of a magician unable to understand his chants. This, even though Rathinagopalakrishna Ramayya of Andhra was the organising secretary of the session. Disturbed by the attitude of the Hindi fanatics attending the session, he issued a statement explaining the dangers of accepting Hindi as the official language:

'All the leaders at the Gaya session waxed eloquent in Hindi. Giving Hindi a dominant position will only end in establishing our slavery in another form. It sounds nice to say that we need a common language and that it should be Hindi. But we can't tolerate a situation where we become the slaves of Hindi from today itself. If Hindi takes the place of English, it will be very harmful to us, the South Indians. The mother tongue is the lifeline of people. If we are forced to learn a different language and express our views only through it, it will not only hamper our real progress but also lead to the erosion of our mental abilities. So, the time has come to warn our politicians that they have to be very cautious about making Hindi the common language of India.'

The issue of language does not change with time as economic, social and political issues do. It cannot have new justifications. A language retains its basic characteristics since the time of its birth. People who once worshipped the rule of kings now respect democracy. People who accepted zamindary later rose in revolt against it. People who accepted caste divisions in the past now fight against its atrocities. But those who supported their mother tongue in the past do not oppose it now. They do not ignore its essential place in their lives.

The basis of one's mother tongue cannot change with the advent of new political philosophies. Scientific progress cannot disrupt its life force. Every language remains an inseparable part of the people who speak it.

The love for one's mother tongue is an emotional issue. None, however great he or she may be, can elude or escape its grip. Whatever justification is preached to the world in defence of one language, the heart and consciousness revolve around the mother tongue. That is why Irish freedom fighter Éamon de Valera said[1], 'I'd give up Ireland and choose the Gaelic language' when asked to choose between the two.

That is the reason why Pavendar Bharathidasan wrote this immortal verse[2]:

'Engal vaazhvum engal valamum
Mangatha thamizhendru sange muzhangu'
[Let the conch proclaim that the vibrant Tamil language
is the source of our life and our wealth.]

The national consciousness of people is not formed through geography. It does not gain strength by political unity. It is not reinforced by the glories of tradition. It is the mother tongue which creates and sustains patriotism. National consciousness is formed through it.

International historian Arnold Toynbee[3] says: 'Growth of patriotism does not depend on traditional boundaries or new geographic positions. It is entirely based on the love for the mother tongue.' Destroying the mother tongue, which forms, nurtures and emotionally protects patriotism, or snatching away the right over the mother tongue will greatly endanger nationalism itself. An alien language will never develop nationalism. Some who accept this truth as far as English is concerned deny it when it comes to Hindi. Some irresponsible people say callously, 'Why so much extremism and intensity in the language issue? Isn't language just an instrument to express and explain one's opinion? So, why should one differentiate between one's own language and an alien language and fight over it?'

Stone Age man learnt to make sounds through irregular lip movements when he had to deal with wild animals and birds. Properly arranged sounds became language. But language was not just an instrument of communication for a community to attain maturity by producing literary wealth and studiously developing cultural values. Had the world considered language just an instrument, in this time and age when printing presses, typewriters and other technological gadgets are aplenty, humanity would have chosen an easily learnable language as its medium of communication. No civilised community is prepared to give up its uniqueness. It protects that uniqueness through its language.

If the Indian government considers language just an instrument, then why should it plan to use Hindi, which lacks the shape and strength to serve as an instrument? Why should it ignore English, which is excellent and useful? As Anna said, 'Language is not an instrument. It is a way of life.'

A noted English historian once remarked: 'Do you want to enslave a race? You destroy its language.' An examination of the truth of this statement will make one realise that the government's official language policy is a sign of the invasion of a new imperialism. Therefore, the official language policy is not about language. It is about domination. It is a terrifying conspiracy to enslave a section of the people of a free country. But the people have woken up, risen in revolt and are determined to win their fight against Hindi imperialism.

Thus, the language issue has become a struggle to achieve an extraordinary goal.

Chapter 2

Hindi, Urdu, Hindustani

> *'I may be alone today in my belief, but it is obvious that ultimately it is neither Sanskritised Hindi nor Persianised Urdu which will win. It is Hindustani which will win ultimately. All these disputes will vanish when the bitterness among us goes away. We have to feel ashamed of this.'*[4]
>
> —Mahatma Gandhi

The decision of the Congress to embark on a chauvinistic path, burying the ideals and strong beliefs of Mahatma Gandhi, who built and nurtured it, has led to a long chapter in its history filled with bloodshed and dead bodies.

The Congress, which fought the domination of the British in pursuit of national freedom, not only boycotted foreign goods, but also raised its voice against English. Congressmen strongly condemned practices such as writing, speaking and communicating in English and following alien customs. They nurtured the same kind of hatred against the English language as they did against the British. They wanted to replace English with an Indian language.

Gandhi believed that it was his foremost duty to prevent any new problem from arising in the attempt to choose an Indian language in place of English. He also thought that a solution must be found in a way that would not exacerbate the Hindu-Muslim conflict, which was already deep-rooted in North India and was destroying nationalist feelings. In his belief that Hindus and Muslims interacting with fraternal love will alone help build stability in the Indian subcontinent, Gandhi thought that any national language should be acceptable to both sides and proposed Hindustani. Initially, the Congress wholeheartedly accepted his proposal.

In 1925, the Congress declared Hindustani the national language[5]. In line with this declaration, it reformulated its organisational rules. The following were the changes made in Rule 25: (a) The proceedings of the Working Committee, the All India Congress Committee and the Congress' all-India session will be conducted in Hindustani. Members who cannot speak Hindustani can speak in a regional language or English after seeking and getting due permission from the president of the session; (b) The Pradesh Congress Committees' proceedings will be conducted in their respective languages as usual.

Under this rule, Hindustani became the administrative language of the Congress' central bodies. It silenced the opposition of the non-Hindi-speaking representatives with the condition that they could speak in a non-Hindustani language, though only with the permission of the president.

Whether the Congress followed or was able to follow this rule is a different matter. But the Congress' national language policy and its practices created a fissure in the Indian subcontinent.

Once the Congress accepted Hindustani as the national language, Muslims, whose mother tongue was Urdu, raised the following questions: What is Hindustani? Which language does it refer to? What is its script? Who are its owners? Why is it necessary to accept Hindustani alone as the national language? The answers given by Congress leaders, including Mahatma Gandhi, did not satisfy the Muslims.

On several occasions, Gandhi clarified that there was no separate language called Hindustani and that it was a mixture of

Urdu and Hindi. However, the Congress, which was in the grip of Hindu religious fanatics, acted in a manner that ran contrary to Gandhi's ideas and explanation. It removed Urdu words from usage, ignored Urdu literature, refused to respect Urdu scholars, replaced Hindi words with Sanskrit words and encouraged only Hindi writers. Hindustani existed only in its organisational rule, while in practice, a pro-Hindi campaign was carried out systematically. Under the patronage of Congress leaders who were Hindu religious fanatics, institutions such as the Bharatiya Sahitya Parishad and the Hindi Sahitya Sammelan were set up. Through these bodies, crores of rupees were spent for the development of Hindi. Leaders like Gandhi, Rajendra Prasad[6], and Purushottam Das Tandon[7] participated in these campaigns.

Gandhi tried to achieve a balance between Hindus and Muslims; however, the activities of the Hindi fanatics in the Congress created strong resentment against its language policy. Gandhi, who believed that the national language policy would not succeed without the cooperation of Muslims, spoke and wrote on several occasions about respecting their sentiments and doing justice to them. He said:

'Hindi + Urdu = Hindustani.'

'Hindi, Hindustani and Urdu... these three words refer to the language spoken by the Hindus and Muslims in Northern India.'

'Before the word Urdu came to be used, Hindus and Muslims used the word Hindi to denote that language.'

'If the word used by you consciously denotes a common language, there is no harm calling it by any name.'

Gandhi said Urdu itself was earlier known as Hindi, that both Hindi and Urdu referred to the same language, and that a national language was important and not its name because he desired that the national language should be adopted by consensus, and the issue should not cause a rift in Hindu-Muslim relations.

Hindi fanatics, and Congress leaders who were Hindu religious fanatics, had none of Gandhi's concern for taking Muslims along. And it was for this reason that Gandhi's views and decisions on the language issue were made impractical and lifeless.

The Muslims asked Gandhi to rename the Bharatiya Sahitya Parishad as the Hindustani Sahitya Parishad in the hope that it would help the growth of Hindustani, a blend of Hindi and Urdu. But Congress leaders refused to accept their suggestion. The Congress, which had accepted Hindustani as the common language, could have accepted their just demand. However, those Congress leaders who were systematically trying to develop Hindi and encourage the practice of Hindu dharma would not accept it.

To counter the Hindi fanatics' attempts to establish their dominance in the name of Hindustani, Muslims started referring to the national language as Urdu-Hindi or Urdu-Hindustani. Intellectuals tore apart the pretence of a two-language drama enacted by the Hindi fanatics in the Congress.

The Congress, which initially spoke of Urdu-Hindustani as the common language, slowly but firmly removed Urdu from that reference and started saying that Hindi-Hindustani was the common language. Muslims strongly objected to this shift. Later, the Congress leaders even changed the term Hindi-Hindustani and said that Hindi was the common language and the national language of India. By explaining that Hindi was not the name of the original language and that it was the name given by Muslims, they tried to turn the accuser into the accused. They sought to mobilise support for the dominance of Hindi by spinning a new theory that Hindi was inclusive of Urdu.

Opposition to the Congress' common language policy grew. In the Indian subcontinent, unity was, at best, patched together. The opposition to the language policy threatened to tear up even that patchwork.

The letters that Mahatma Gandhi received pointing out the

betrayal of Hindi fanatics and their chauvinism serve even today as warning signals for the people of the great Dravidian community, who are in danger of being reduced to second-class citizens. These letters said:

* 'By using the word Hindi in the place of Hindustani, they change the beauty of the word and its political and religious connections.'
* 'It is obvious that those who wish to spread the use of Hindi are openly trying to Aryanise Indian life instead of spreading its spoken form.'
* 'Hindi has Hindu religious and cultural characteristics. Seeing the issue in its totality, Muslims would not want to identify themselves with that language.'
* 'Hereafter, those who know only Urdu may not be able to understand Hindi.'
* 'If a language harms the Mother Tongue, none should study it even if it happens to be God's language.'
* 'Though you say Hindi is the common language of India, you wrote your autobiography or the story of your satyagraha in South Africa in Gujarati, not Hindi. Had you written it in Hindi, a large number of people would have been able to read and appreciate it. But you were more interested in writing in Gujarati than in Hindi. So, I want people to follow what you did rather than what you said.'

Gandhi published these letters in his *Harijan*.

Unlike Muslims, non-Hindi-speaking Congressmen did not raise their voice against linguistic chauvinism.

In those days, getting the British out of the country was the sole objective before the Congress. Those who spoke against the white rule were considered heroes. Those who fostered the spirit of freedom in people through their words and deeds were treated like nobles. People considered the respect and reception accorded to nationalist leaders the rewards for freedom. Some even thought that opposing the nationalist leaders or hurting their sentiments was not only wrong but seditious.

Taking advantage of this nationalist upsurge, the Hindi fanatics in the Congress laid the foundation for Hindi dominance. They said that acceptance of a national language would destroy the dominance of English and, along with it, the propaganda machinery, the administrative institutions, the education methods, and the political, social and literary ideas of British imperialism. As a result, they said, British imperialism would be uprooted from Indian soil.

The Hindi fanatics used people's opposition, hostility, hatred and resentment against the British not only to create a nationalist upsurge but also to cleverly pave the way for the crowning of Hindi as the national language.

Due to the hatred of British imperialism, the language issue did not create any major fissure within the Congress.

When the Congress accepted Hindustani as the national language in 1925, there was no leader of stature in the South who was respected by the national Congress leadership and could advise them on the injustice that would be meted out to non-Hindi-speaking people. Nor did the few South Indian leaders come forward to persuade the national leadership to give importance to the language issue and make a just decision after deliberating on it since the most serious objective before them at the time was the freedom of the country.

This does not mean that credit for recognising the deception, chauvinism and fanaticism inherent in the Congress' language policy and rising in revolt against it should be accorded to the Urdu-speaking Muslim community. Highlighting the fertility and richness of Urdu, they demanded national language status for it, arguing that:

* 'Non-Muslims also speak Urdu.'
* 'Urdu is a colloquial language. It is simple, rich and sweet. Urdu alone has the eligibility to be the national language.'
* 'If Hindu and Urdu are taught to people, Urdu has the potential to drive away Hindi.'

Had the nationalist leaders living in Dravidam understood the chauvinistic attitude of the Hindi fanatics and raised their voice in support of their mother tongue like the Urdu speakers, the idea of Hindi dominance would have died in its womb. Hindi is a challenge to non-Hindi speakers even today because of the leaders' failure or refusal to address the issue.

Because Gandhi accepted Hindustani as the national language common to both sides and wanted to develop it, he said: 'Some people are dreaming of making Hindi the national language while others are dreaming of making Urdu the national language. This will remain only a dream forever. It is also an unholy dream.'

Gandhi knew very well that Hindus would oppose Urdu if it became the national language, and Muslims would oppose Hindi if it became the national language. As both sides wanted their respective mother tongues to be the national language, he said, it would only be a dream and an unholy dream at that. At no point in time did Gandhi waver from his position that Hindustani would be the national language and he reiterated it until the end.

He spoke and wrote only in Hindustani. He never eliminated Urdu words from his language. Nor did he impose Sanskrit words. He spoke in a simple language that people could understand.

At the Hindi Sahitya Sammelan, Urdu speakers demanded that the Urdu script be used for Hindustani and Hindi speakers argued in favour of the Devanagari script. Only after the Sammelan accepted Gandhi's idea that the word 'Hindi' was inclusive of Urdu did he agree to assume its presidency. He worked for the growth of Hindi and Urdu simultaneously. He published *Harijan,* his weekly newspaper, in both Hindi and Urdu. When he had to stop publishing the Urdu version of the paper owing to financial losses, he stopped the Hindi version as well.

At no juncture did Gandhi say that Hindi should be given special preference and enthroned. He said that if we approached the issue scientifically, ignoring its social dimension, we would only make Hindustani the national language. Hindustani, according to him, is neither Sanskritised Hindi nor Persianised Urdu; it is a blend of Hindi and Urdu.

Gandhi hated Sanskritised Hindi. Not only did he refuse to accept it as the national language, he was against referring to Hindi as the national language. He explained all these ideas in the Hindi Prachar Sabha, which was set up to propagate Hindi. Addressing the Silver Jubilee meeting of the Dakshina Bharat Hindi Prachar Sabha in Madras, he said: 'The name of our institution is Hindi Prachar Sabha. Hereafter, it should not be called Hindi Prachar Sabha. We should use the word "Hindustani" in the place of "Hindi".' Two days later, he said at the same venue: 'I want to tell you another thing. I've also asked Sathyanarayan to convey that to you. When you take oath in the name of the national language, you should mention Hindustani, not Hindi.'

Gandhi recognised that Hindi was supported by Hindu religious fanatics with an ulterior communal motive and that they were systematically trying to establish the dominance of one language in the Indian subcontinent. In order to save people from the dangers of Hindi supporters propagating Sanskritised Hindi, he attached himself to the Hindustani Sabha and worked for its development.

Gandhi's language policy had received the full support of the progressive sections of the Congress. Its North Indian leaders, who did not succumb to communal bigotry, stood by Gandhi. In an article, Pandit Jawaharlal Nehru said: 'Hindustani should be accepted as the national language. Any man in India should have the right to use Hindustani in courts and government offices across India without having to present a translation or a copy.'

The Congress should have accepted Gandhi's language policy. However, despite the support of progressive people in the North, it was not accepted. Although the Hindi fanatics did not oppose Gandhi openly on this issue, they worked tirelessly to defeat his idea. They did not accept Gandhi's view that Hindustani, which had been accepted by the Congress as the national language, could be written in Urdu as well as Devanagari scripts. They feared that if the Urdu script were accepted, Hindi, which was sustained by borrowing from Sanskrit, would be destroyed. Realising that if people started reading Urdu literary works, they would not respect Hindi literature, they insisted that Hindustani should be written only in the Devanagari script and not the Urdu script. Gandhi believed that acceptance of both scripts would enrich Hindustani and strengthen Hindu-Muslim relations. He made it clear that if a State decides to give recognition only to the Devanagari script in inter-state communications, it will be an injustice to Muslim brothers. Considering that they are a minority community, that will be a big crime. He also said that if only the Devanagari script were used, it would be understood by a very small section of people. By saying this, he reiterated the fact that a majority of the people did not know the Devanagari script.

Gandhi also explained his position clearly in these words: 'I communicate with Muslims and Hindus in Delhi every day. The spoken language of a majority of them has very few Sanskrit words and a large number of Persian or Arabic words. They do not know the Devanagari script.' Jawaharlal Nehru supported and encouraged Gandhi's views.

Gandhi's policy on language and script greatly disturbed and worried the Hindi fanatics. They did not like his efforts to satisfy Muslims. They were also highly disappointed by his insistence on Hindustani and his efforts to develop it.

The Hindi Sahitya Sammelan did not follow Gandhi's advice. On the contrary, it was keen on developing Hindi and stoking communal passion. Its attitude distressed Gandhi. So, he concluded that being part of the Sammelan was wrong, unnecessary, and tantamount to supporting injustice and wrote to PT Tandon expressing his wish to dissociate from it. He said: 'I've been getting letters written in Hindi, Urdu and Gujarati asking me how I could be part of the Hindi Sahitya Sammelan and the Hindustani Sabha. According to the policy of the Sammelan, Hindi written in Devanagari script alone should be the national language. According to my policy, the language that uses both Devanagari and Urdu scripts should be the national language. It should not have a large number of either Sanskrit or Persian words. When I do not like to accept the language propagated by the Sammelan as the national language, it is my duty to leave the organisation[8].' This, he said, would remove people's confusion about the national language policy, besides clarifying his position.

In his reply to Gandhi, Tandon said that there was a change in Gandhi's attitude and that the Sammelan had been functioning properly. He did not express any regret about the chauvinism of the Sahitya Sammelan and its rejection of Urdu and Hindustani. Tandon's reply upset Gandhi. He thought that the Sammelan, after announcing its acceptance of his language policy, had betrayed him in practice. He believed this would affect the national interest. He wrote again to Tandon, asking him to accept his resignation:

'I regret that the Sammelan has not accepted my explanation about Hindi. My views on this issue have grown stronger. My explanation about the national language is that it should be a combination of the knowledge of Urdu and Hindi languages and the Devanagari and Urdu scripts. I will be happy whenever it happens. I regret to know that the Sammelan has not accepted this explanation of mine. So, I request you to accept my letter of resignation. While working in support of Hindustani, I will cooperate for the development of Urdu and Hindi.'

The Sammelan accepted Gandhi's resignation with crocodile

tears. In reality, Hindi fanatics were happy that the biggest obstacle to the propagation of Hindi had been removed. They were also delighted that his resignation had paved the way for propagating Hindi freely and fearlessly.

After the general election in 1937, the Hindu-Muslim problem heated up in North India. Hindi fanatics used this hostility born out of socio-political issues to turn Hindus against Urdu and crown Hindi as the national language; in this effort, they succeeded to some extent. They ignored the advice of Gandhi, who acted as an arbitrator, and fought for Hindi with communal fanaticism.

When the Indian political situation worsened leading up to the India-Pakistan partition, the tactics and propaganda methods they employed would have been beyond the imagination of even Machiavelli.

The fact that many Hindu fanatics were front-ranking leaders of the Congress was helpful to the Hindi propagators. As nine crore Muslims became part of a separate country following Partition, the number of people supporting Hindustani and opposing Hindi came down considerably. This fact also worked in favour of Hindi fanatics. Congress leaders started saying that supporters of Urdu were Pakistan's slaves[9] and supporters of Hindustani were not patriotic.

The Hindi fanatics in the Congress succeeded in turning the post-Partition hatred against Muslims into a hatred of Hindustani and Urdu.

Many Congress leaders spoke openly against Gandhi's wish to the extent of pushing the movement towards the decision that Hindi was India's national language. Those who toiled for the development of Hindustani and Hindu-Muslim unity were upset by the attitude of these Congressmen.

Dadabhai Naoroji's granddaughter Perin Ben wrote a letter to Gandhi expressing anger against Congress leaders who were working in favour of Hindi:

'The efforts of the so-called great leaders to bring down Hindustani from the status of the national language, for which we toiled as one for many years, and keep Hindi in its place is regrettable, deceptive and shameful,' she wrote.

Only the few who had the noble intention of saving the Indian subcontinent with the cooperation of Muslims followed Gandhi's language policy after Partition. Leaders like Dr Rajendra Prasad, PT Tandon, Govind Ballabh Pant[10] and Govind Das[11] urged the Congress to make Hindi the national language. What worked in their favour was the majority of communal-minded Hindi supporters, the minority status of Muslims and the irresponsible and callous attitude of some Southern leaders of the Congress, who were willing to accept any language as the national language.

A resolution was brought with the support of the Congress to introduce Hindi as the national language in the Constitution. Its intent was to assign to Hindi the broad sense implied by the word Hindustani.

Abul Kalam Azad portrayed the linguistic fanaticism of Hindi supporters in the following words:

'Finally, this issue was left to a separate committee with the brief to come to a new decision on the basis of all the resolutions. I was a member of that committee. I went to its first meeting. I realised that a majority of its members had already come with a decision. They were not prepared to accept Hindustani in the place of Hindi. In this situation, I was unable to cooperate with that committee. Hence, I distanced and dissociated myself from it. As far as the language issue is concerned, I have explained my position. I regret that it was not resolved in the way it should have been resolved.'

When Azad explained step by step how Hindi fanatics worked unitedly and systematically at every stage and how the Congress leaders cowed down to them, his views, arguments, and facts moved those with a conscience, perplexed those who strayed, made the betrayers hang their heads in shame and shut the mouths of those who hailed the new decision.

Describing how Gandhi strove to develop Hindustani[12], Mr Mohammed Hifzur Rahman regretted the Congress' betrayal with a heavy heart. He said: 'He worked hard for the development of Hindustani. I still remember it. On January 30, three days before Yama took Gandhiji away from us, I met him in Birla House. It was about 10 or 11 in the night. He told me that I should help propagate the importance of Hindustani among the people!'

Congressmen had no intention of examining, in a non-partisan manner, the suggestions that came from various sections of people. They dared to throw Gandhi's policy into the dustbin, so it was foolish to expect them to pay heed to the views of Hindustani supporters such as Maulana Abul Kalam Azad, Mohammed Hifzur Rahman, Mohammed Ismail and Naziruddin Ahmad.

When we realise that even a rationalist like Jawaharlal Nehru succumbed to the wild claims of Congressmen who were Hindu religious and Hindi language fanatics, we can understand how strong their influence was. The fact that Nehru, who had been speaking and writing in favour of Hindustani, paid heed to Hindi fanatics gave them an opportunity to garland themselves with victory in a very short time.

In the Constituent Assembly, Hindi fanatic RV Dhulekar[13] expounded the reasons why Hindustani was given up and Hindi was accepted. He said: 'It is with the greatest unhappiness that I have to say that in spite of our honest efforts to solve the problem of this country on a non-communal basis, the result has been that we are suffering still [he refers to the separation of Pakistan]. Hence, I wish that my friend Maulana Hifzur Rahman may take it from me that it is only a reaction to our honest efforts, which did not succeed, which caused the pendulum to go over to the other side.' When he said this aggressively, Pandit Nehru shouted, 'hear, hear'. On hearing the encouraging words of Nehru, Dhulekar said:

'I am very happy at the thought that I have spoken the mind of my honourable friend, Jawaharlal Nehru.'

This is one more evidence that Pandit Nehru also cooperated with the Hindi fanatics in introducing Hindi as the national language in the Constitution.

Thus, Hindi found a place in the Constitution as the national language with the full cooperation of the Congress party. Its refusal to recognise the extent of the adverse impact on non-Hindi-speaking people and on India's politics goes to prove that India's unity, which breaks apart again and again, does not have a sustainable life.

Gandhi wanted to find a solution to the language issue in a way that would safeguard the unity of the Indian subcontinent. But the Congress was not willing to give up Hindi even if it created enmity, even if the party had to take the blame, even if blood was shed, and even if Bharat Mata was dismembered. As a result of this attitude, they not only defeated Gandhi's policy but also cut India into two pieces.

Initially, Hindi fanatics believed that it was only the Muslims who opposed Hindi. They hoped to celebrate the crowning of Hindi in the heady days of freedom after Partition. Historians, however, could see clearly where the opposition to Hindi would take India in the future. They were agitated by the doubt that Bharat Mata would have a very short life.

Chapter 3

The First Language War

'The world will never get another opportunity like this one to realise how many pure Tamils with a sense of honour live in Tamil Nadu. Never! A war between Aryan conspiracy and Dravidian courage has begun. So, people and youth of this country, get ready, come forward and take part in it. Be ready! Be ready! Victory is certain.'

—EVR Periyar

The Congress, which had initially decided that among all the Indian languages, only Hindustani will be the national language, believed it could establish Hindi as the national language once it managed to overcome the opposition of the Muslims. So, the party wore various disguises from time to time to mollify them. The disputes within and outside the Congress in the North over the national language did not arise because of their love for the language; rather, it was based on communalism and religious fanaticism. These were given the colour of 'linguistic affinity'.

The ones who demanded that Hindi be made the national language had this rationale: Hindi was the language of the Hindus, and India belonged to the Hindus, and hence, Hindi should be the national language. But the Muslims said: India does not belong only to Hindus. It is the land of Muslims also. Urdu is their mother tongue. So, Urdu, too, should be the national language. It was to unite these two sections of people that Gandhi chose Hindustani as the national language.

The Congress made no attempt to ascertain the opinion of the Dravidian language speakers—the third section of people who were completely different from the other two—and satisfy them. They fed the people with Hindu religious fanaticism to foster the freedom movement.

Initially, many Congress leaders spoke of religion, aiming to encourage Hindus to propose that India would be a Hindu country once it became free. They believed that if the religious sentiment of Hindus became dominant, it would help them propagate Hindi and suppress Muslims. The Congress hoped to take advantage of the upsurge of the freedom movement to easily win over the Hindus among Dravidians to their side on the language issue, using the religion card. However, the intense reformist propaganda of the Self-Respect Movement and the patronage of the Justice Party saved the Dravidians from falling prey to religious fanaticism.

The Congress could not succeed in wooing South Indians to take a pro-Hindi stand in the name of Hinduism. However, taking advantage of the upsurge in the freedom movement, it took care to ensure that they did not join Urdu supporters in opposing Hindi.

Some Southern Congressmen with a sense of self-respect did oppose the Congress' language policy. However, they withdrew their opposition, fearing that it would harm the passion for freedom and help Muslims gain the upper hand. As a result, the Congress concentrated on satisfying Muslims and ignored the sentiments of South Indians.

In the elections held in 1937, the Congress captured power in most provinces, including Madras. In the Madras Presidency, a Ministry led by C Rajagopalachari [Rajaji] assumed office. In line with the Congress plan, Rajaji tried to impose Hindi in the presidency. At a meeting held at the Ramakrishna Mutt in Chennai, he spoke about making Hindi compulsory for the first time. His speech created a sensation. The Justice Party and the Self-Respect Movement strongly condemned his move to make

Hindi compulsory in schools and warned that it would ruin the lives of non-Hindi speakers. Tamil litterateurs said that the Tamil language would become extinct.

Religious-minded lovers of Tamil were afraid that Aryan culture was invading the Tamil region and conspiring to destroy Tamil culture. A popular rhyming slogan then was: *Hindikku ini ingu enna velai? Kurangukku malar solayil idamundo?* (Hindi does not have a place here, just as a monkey does not have a place in a flower garden).

The Karanthai Tamil Sangam raised its voice against these attempts. The Senthamizh Kazhagam in Thiruvaiyaru passed a resolution in this regard and sent it to the Madras government. A protest meeting under the leadership of Navalar Somasundara Bharathi[14] was held in Soundarya Hall in Madras. The speeches of Annadurai, Maraimalai Adigal and KM Balasubramaniam[15] awakened the people of Madras. District-wise meetings of the Self-Respect Movement adopted and passed condemnatory resolutions against the Madras government's decision.

A conference of Tamils was held in Trichy on December 26, 1937, to stop the imposition of Hindi. Advocate K Subramania Pillai presided over the meeting, and Navalar Somasundara Bharathi delivered the welcome address. TV Uma Maheswaran[16] inaugurated it, and Periyar EVR delivered a special address. The meeting passed a resolution against compulsory Hindi learning. It was also in this conference that a resolution was passed demanding Tamil Nadu's secession from India. A three-member committee comprising Periyar EVR, Navalar Somasundara Bharathi and TV Uma Maheswaran was constituted to meet the Governor and explain to him the unanimous opposition of the people of Madras Presidency to the imposition of Hindi. The Trichy conference was the first step in the movement against Hindi. It created a stirring among the people.

The Congress government refused to accept the resolution

of the conference of Tamils, describing it as the howl of an anti-Brahmin minority. To strengthen the opposition of South Indians to Hindi, another conference was convened in Kanchipuram, presided over by KV Reddy Naidu, former chief minister of the Madras Presidency. Addressing the conference, Reddy Naidu said: 'Not only the Tamil, but all whose veins carry Dravidian blood will oppose the imposition of this unwanted Hindi on children who are already heavily burdened and families that live in peace. One who does not appreciate his mother tongue is a cowardly traitor to it. These traitors to the mother tongue will be called Judas Iscariot, after the one who betrayed Jesus Christ for the sake of a small amount of money. Jesus was killed because of Judas' deceit. But Christianity lives on. Similarly, let the Dravidian languages escape from the modern-day Judas Iscariots and live on.'

As a result of this conference, those who had earlier held back now spoke up. Those sleeping were woken up. The Kanchipuram conference served as a warning signal. The Congress government ignored the opposition and condemnation expressed in democratic, peaceful ways. It made fun of the voices of protest. It mocked the warning of the educated. On April 21, 1938, the order making Hindi compulsory in schools was passed. It made learning Hindi mandatory for students in the first to third forms (sixth standard to eighth standard). In the first year of its implementation, Hindi was imposed on 125 schools—60 in Tamil Nadu, 54 in Andhra, four in Kannada-speaking areas and seven in Kerala. Congress supporters—lovers of the Aryan culture—supported the government's move. The Tamil weekly, *Ananda Vikatan*, asked sarcastically, 'Why only Hindi? Even Sanskrit can be imposed above the third form.'

The imposition of Hindi triggered a revolt among the Tamils. They realised that unless this was resisted, there would be no life for the maiden known as 'Tamil', nor would Tamilians hold their heads high. 'Death comes only once, whether you are six years old or a hundred years old. Let us protect Mother Tamil.' With this vow, they began preparations for a do-or-die battle.

On May 28, 1938, a camp was held in Trichy under the leadership of Prof Somasundara Bharathi to find ways to defeat the attempt to impose Hindi. The participants decided to oppose it at any cost. To save Tamil and defeat Hindi dominance, they decided to constitute an anti-Hindi forum to conduct campaigns in places where Hindi was being taught compulsorily, form similar anti-Hindi forums in those places, collect funds and carry forward the movement. It appointed Prof Somasundara Bharathi as the president, KAP Viswanathan[17] as the secretary of the forum and EVR Periyar, TV Uma Maheswaran, WPA Soundarapandian[18] and KM Balasubramanian as its members. They passed the following resolutions:

1. To appeal to parents and patrons to not send students to the first three forms of the schools where Hindi is compulsory.
2. To picket schools to prevent students from entering these schools.
3. To make arrangements to boycott Hindi teachers in every possible way.
4. To observe an anti-Hindi day all over the Madras Presidency.
5. To express people's hatred for Hindi through protests such as showing black flags to ministers whenever possible.
6. To conduct a civil disobedience movement until all the above efforts succeeded.
7. To campaign against making Hindi an elective subject—as we understand that ministers are trying to make Hindi learning compulsory for public posts in the province.

Tamils were overjoyed because they thought these resolutions were the weapons that would defeat the enemies—the spears that would attack the enemies, the arrows that would tear Hindi to pieces and make it scurry for its life. They hoped the enemy camp would be destroyed, that Tamil would live on, the traitors to the mother tongue would be defeated, and Tamil would get a new lease of life.

This is how poet Bharathidasan[19] described the fight:

An army is needed.
A big army is needed.
To save the rich Tamil language
An army is needed.

Periyar EVR published many passionate articles in *Viduthalai* to make people rise in revolt. The articles he wrote on the necessity of the anti-Hindi war, the duties of Tamils, and the protests to be conducted were like bombs that would reduce the enemy camp to ashes. These were the clarion calls that would make the government, which was dependent on oppressive methods, die of fear.

At the beginning of this chapter, I referred to a message given by Periyar asking people to get ready for war. He also asked them to be prepared to shed blood and die in the war. He wrote: 'Nobody should think that going to jail to achieve what one wants is a very ordinary thing. Acharyar (Rajaji) will not make it easy for you. So, you should not think that it is enough to be prepared to go to jail. In fact, going to jail is a petty thing indeed. It should be left to ordinary people. But famous personalities and office-bearers should be prepared to get beaten up and die.' These words reflected Periyar's determination. The government was shocked to learn that Periyar was prepared to fight to death against the imposition of Hindi.

Around the time of the Trichy camp, an anti-Hindi conference under the leadership of Maraimalai Adigal was held in Kodambakkam (Chennai). It was a great show of unity by Tamils from different sections—politicians, religious leaders, atheists, believers, members of the Self-Respect Movement, the Justice Party and so on. Maraimalai Adigal's speech turned the participants into warriors who took the following vow:

'Dear Tamil, I exist because you exist. If you are not there, I do not want to live.'

While the conference was on, the news of the arrest of Palladam Ponnusamy[20], who was on fast unto death in front of Rajaji's residence, reached the venue. The participants rose in anger and marched towards the Chief Minister's residence, raising anti-Hindi slogans. A huge demonstration was held in front of his house, followed by a meeting that continued late into the night.

The police arrested Shanmugananda Adigal[21] and CD Nayagam[22] and filed a case against them for having held a demonstration in front of the Chief Minister's residence. Shanmugananda Adigal was sentenced to four years' rigorous imprisonment. The court sentenced Nayagam to a month's simple imprisonment and slapped a fine of Rs 200 on him.

Palladam Ponnusamy, who went on a fast on June 1, 1938, was a Congressman. To disrupt his fast and create confusion, other Congressmen let a snake into the venue. They threw stones at him. But he continued his fast, ignoring the traitors' despicable acts. On the third day of his fast, he was arrested and sentenced to rigorous imprisonment for four months.

The anti-Hindi agitation, which began on June 3, 1938, lasted until February 21, 1940. The Congress government was shocked that religious leaders, Tamil teachers, the general public and the youth had joined the agitation, while Congress leaders were busy climbing the ladder of success and accepting new honours. The Chief Minister's residence and the Theological Society in Madras became the venues of protest. Various groups took out big processions and resorted to picketing at every opportunity.

The methods adopted by the Congress government to suppress the agitation appeared to the people to be worse than those of the

British. The police beat up the agitators brutally. Legislators like AT Panneerselvam[23], Diwan Bahadur Appadurai and Raja Sir Muthiah Chettiar[24] condemned the government for beating and torturing people who were agitating peacefully.

The Congress was not content with letting loose a reign of terror. It filed cases against agitators and imprisoned them for years together. But the army of Tamils continued to fight despite the punishment. A total of 1,271 people were arrested. When the first leader of the agitation, CD Nayagam, was arrested, his second in command, Eezhathadigal[25], jumped into the fray. He was sentenced to nine months rigorous imprisonment. Arignar Anna was imprisoned for four months. Other leaders who had to undergo rigorous imprisonment were advocate KM Balasubramaniam (six months), SK Swami of Kumbakonam and Swaminathan of Chennai (one and a half months), Arunagiri Adigal[26] of the Saadhunarayana Desigar Madalayam (two years), and the poet, Tiruvarur Balasundaram[27] (three years).

Action was taken against the Dravidar Kazhagam's daily, *Viduthalai*. The government, which had already collected Rs 1,000 as surety from it, asked the newspaper's proprietor to pay Rs 1,000 more as surety. It filed cases against its manager, EV Krishnasamy, the elder brother of EV Ramasamy, and editor S Muthsamy Pillai. They were sentenced to six months of rigorous imprisonment.

The opposition leaders in the Assembly condemned the government for filing cases against anti-Hindi agitators under the Criminal Law Amendment Act of 1935 with the intention of keeping them in jail for a long time and oppressing them ruthlessly.

Speaking in the Assembly, Diwan Bahadur A Appadurai Pillai reminded Congressmen that before coming to power, they had described the Act as a measure of 'political fraud,' an 'instrument of oppression' in the hands of chauvinists and a foolish law that is both petty and dangerous and criticised them for using the same law to punish anti-Hindi agitators unjustly. He cited some examples in support of his argument.

Condemning the government for imposing Hindi against the people's will, Khan Bahadur Khalifullah[28] Sahib challenged the Congressmen: 'I give this call in this honourable Assembly. If any member of the House is prepared to resign, I am also ready to resign. I call upon that member to contest the election again from his own constituency. I will defeat him by winning 99 per cent of the vote in that constituency. (At this point, a Congress member shouted 'oho'). There is no point shouting "oho". I have given this call. If you are brave, you accept this challenge. Resign from your positions. I am ready to quit at this moment.' No Congress member was man enough to accept his challenge.

In his address, Rao Sahib AT Panneerselvam explained the harm that would befall Tamils if Hindi was imposed on them. He concluded his speech with this warning: 'If you want to ignore the people's opposition with oppressive measures, please go ahead. Resort to whatever oppressive measures you can take under the Criminal Law Amendment Act. Stifle people's opinion. But the day is not far off when you will regret your actions.'

Chief Minister Rajaji responded callously to the opposition's voices of protest. He ridiculed the charges against the government. He pontificated on parliamentary democracy, saying that the minority should go along with the decision of the majority. He said he would not tolerate attempts to stop the government's actions. It was a different matter altogether to oppose the moves of an alien government, he said. Moreover, after agreeing to make an allocation for the propagation of Hindi during the discussion on the Budget, he said later that the opposition does not have the right to oppose it. He also made fun of the sacrifices of the anti-Hindi agitators.

People were disappointed with the Chief Minister's reply to the charges against the government and his defence. His sarcastic remarks and irresponsible responses angered many of them. The anti-Hindi sentiment exploded like a volcano. As a result, people across Tamil Nadu observed an anti-Hindi day.

The sacrifices of religious leaders and women in the anti-Hindi struggle of 1938 were outstanding and a matter of pride for the Tamils. Religious leaders not only opposed the imposition of Hindi openly, but also participated in the protest marches. They withstood the government's oppression and entered the horrendous jails with a smile. The sacrifices of the family of Maraimalai Adigal will thrill one even now. His entire family dedicated themselves to the cause of saving Tamil. His elder son, Manikkavasagam, was active in the anti-Hindi movement. His younger son quit his job, joined the movement and went to jail. His only daughter, Neelambigai Ammaiyar, encouraged women to participate in the agitation. His daughters-in-law Sarojini and Gnanammal were jailed for joining a picketing programme.

Women played a very courageous role in the agitation. Their huge participation in the struggle was unprecedented. On November 13, 1938, women convened a conference of Tamils at Ottraivaadai in Chennai. In her welcome address, Thamarai Kanniyar said:

'Things have come to such a pass that we, like Kannagi (in the Tamil epic *Silappadhikaram*), have to lament that no noble person is around, no god is around. Today, our Mother Tamil is being harmed. It means that the entire community of Tamil women is in danger. If you rise in revolt against this...'. As soon as she said these words, the applause from the crowd was, in effect, a challenge to the government.

Delivering the presidential address, Neelambigai Ammaiyar said to Tamil women: 'The government thrusting Hindi, a maid from another country, into our homes is like providing food and shelter to another woman when our own mother is crying from hunger. This must be resisted by us, the children of Mother Tamil.'

On November 14, 1938, the first batch of women fighters got into action. Dr Dharmambal[29], Ramamirtham Ammaiyar[30], Malarmugathammaiyar[31], and Seethammal picketed the Hindu

Theosophical School and were arrested. This imprisonment of the women further strengthened the resolve of the anti-Hindi agitators. Some women participated in the picketing programme and went to jail with their infants. A total of 73 women and 32 infants were jailed. What was the wrong committed by the newborns? They had drunk the milk of mothers who had bravely raised the slogan, 'Hindi down down'. Isn't that milk filled with anti-Hindi sentiments?

The agitators employed various methods to spread and intensify the protests. They decided that an army of Tamil lovers would march from Woraiyur (Trichy) to Madras. They chose I Kumarasami Pillai and Ramamirtham Ammaiyar to lead the army. They also chose Braveheart Alagirisamy as their 'general' and Thirumalaisami, editor of the journal *Nagara Thoodhan* (City Ambassador), as the convenor. This was called The Great Army of Tamils. Over 500 youth expressed their wish to join this army, but the leaders chose only those who were physically and mentally strong. The army began its journey from Woraiyur on August 1, 1938. Periyar greeted the participants and inaugurated their march. They walked through villages raising slogans like 'Long live Tamil' and 'Hindi down down'. They held public meetings at important places. Alagirisamy addressed these meetings, setting the listeners' hearts on fire and bringing tears to their eyes. In all, they held 87 meetings as they marched through 234 villages and towns. They pitched camps at 60 places. It took them 42 days to reach Madras. They crossed rivers, surmounted hillocks and walked under the hot sun. They trudged on, unfazed by heavy rains and howling winds. Some fell ill but continued their march after medical treatment.

On September 11, the army reached Madras. A massive rally was held under the leadership of Maraimalai Adigal. Periyar spoke in praise of their great achievement. A report prepared on behalf of the marchers read: 'No other army has traversed as many miles as this Tamil Army has done. Gandhi's Dandi March and Rajagopalachari's Vedaranyam March did not cover even one-fourth of this distance. So, the incomparable Tamil Army has achieved the highest ever stature in Indian history.'

The first martyr of the anti-Hindi war was Natarasan. The second was the great warrior Thalamuthu. It was on the basis of their martyrdom that the foundation of the Save Tamil Movement was laid. Their incomparable sacrifice continues to inspire Tamils.

Natarasan was jailed on December 5, 1938. A pimple led to the swelling of his face. He was admitted to a hospital. The government refused to release him even when he was on the verge of death. On January 15, 1939, he died as a political prisoner. Even before Tamils could recover from the shock of his death, on March 12, 1938, Thalamuthu died in jail. On hearing this news, the entire city of Madras wept. Tears of blood rolled down the cheeks of Mother Tamil. Raja Sir Muthiah Chettiar and C Basudev, former Mayor, carried his body on their shoulders to the graveyard. When Arignar Anna recounted Thalamuthu's outstanding contributions, mourners at the cremation ground wept inconsolably. He said in a choked voice: 'When Comrade Natarasan was put to rest, I thought Tamils will not go through another such tragedy. But I am distraught by the death of Comrade Thalamuthu, who was a star from the Nadar community. When his funeral procession wound its way to the cremation ground, thousands of Tamils lined up on the roadside and wept. I consider the death of Natarasan and Thalamuthu as the death of my brothers.'

The ultimate sacrifice of Natarasan and Thalamuthu gave a new lease of life to the anti-Hindi struggle. Their glory will remain as long as Tamils live on this earth.

Tamils were beaten up, kicked, tortured, imprisoned; they shed blood and sacrificed their lives. Yet, the Congress government did not scrap its language policy. Rajaji said, insolently: 'Who are opposing Hindi? One Ramasamy and one Bharathi. Ramasamy is a Brahmin hater. Bharathi is a scholar. Should I abandon Hindi just because a Brahmin hater and a scholar oppose it?'

The government did not relax its oppressive measures and brazenly declared: 'We will suppress the agitation... you have to accept Hindi.' But Periyar continued to fight, dismissing the Chief Minister's threats, the bureaucrats' warnings, and the abuses of the betrayers of Tamil. When the government's oppression intensified, Periyar's speeches unleashed a storm. His words emitted fire. He became a lion whose roars challenged the government.

Fearing that Periyar would ignite a revolution, the government filed a case against him, taking his supporters by surprise. Periyar did not want to fight the case in court. It was not because he thought justice was not on his side; it was because he believed that he would not get justice in the prevailing circumstances. After the prosecution witnesses had deposed before the court, he read out a statement expressing his views. Every sentence in that statement should be imprinted on the minds of idealists forever.

He said: 'This court comes under the administration of Congress ministers. You [the judge] also belong to the Brahmin community. Moreover, the Congress ministers are bent on suppressing the anti-Hindi agitation. The respected Premier [Chief Minister Rajaji] said at a public meeting on the beach that one need not look at what is just and what is unjust in this matter; one should compare the anti-Hindi agitation to a sudden act of robbery. So, in my opinion, the steps taken by the ministers against the anti-Hindi agitation are nothing but acts of oppression.

'It is madness to expect justice from such courts during this time of oppression. So, I don't have faith in this court and the justice it will administer. I request the honourable court to give me the maximum possible punishment that will satisfy them [the government] and the lowest possible prison class and bring an end to this drama. To achieve an ideal that is just, one has to suffer all kinds of hardships. So, I request you to heed my request.'

His statement is an excellent guide to all those fighting to uphold justice. His heart was brimming with fearlessness and courage.

Very few in the world have spoken so strongly in court as Periyar did. He was willing to accept any punishment for the sake of his ideals. His sacrifice can instil hope in the hearts of all those who fight for their ideals.

Justice Madhav Rao, the judge of the fourth court in George Town, Chennai, awarded Periyar a prison sentence of two years and imposed a fine of Rs 2,000. His judgment said that if he failed to pay the fine, he would have to spend six more months in jail. Periyar smiled when he heard the verdict. But those who had gathered in the court were in tears. Even Congressmen were sad. Many journals condemned the government's vindictive action. Periyar refused to pay the fine and was imprisoned for two and a half years in the jail at Bellary. They also confiscated his car, worth about Rs 4,000, in lieu of his fine.

The police secretly took Periyar to Bellary Jail in a train. His supporters observed each day of his incarceration as anti-Hindi day. Later, he was shifted to the Coimbatore jail. Meanwhile, a new army came up to demand his release. Women also came forward to join this force. They picketed the Premier's residence under the leadership of Mrs R Narayani Ammaiyar[32]. She was sentenced to six years of rigorous imprisonment.

The resentment of Tamils, the criticism in newspapers, the relentless struggle against the imposition of Hindi, led to a volatile situation in the country. Things came to such a pass that releasing Periyar became the only way to restore peace. On April 22, 1939, Periyar was released from jail without any prior announcement. The agitators were overjoyed. But Periyar was not happy. This became evident in his speech at a meeting organised to celebrate his release. He said: 'The task I had undertaken is not over. Hindi has not gone away. Why did I come out? I think that I should have died in jail. That would have galvanised the movement. Senthamizh would have won.' These words affected people deeply. They realised how completely committed Periyar was to the cause of Tamil.

Periyar spent only 164 days in jail. Within five months of his release, the Congress Ministry resigned for another political reason. The interim government released all the agitators on November 11, 1939, hoping to earn public goodwill. But Periyar did not lower the banner of revolt just because his followers were released.

In a joint statement, Periyar, Sir Selvam and Kumara Raja said: 'On behalf of Tamil, we thank you for releasing them. But the ideal for which they went to jail has not been achieved. Abandon your plan to impose Hindi and facilitate the withdrawal of Tamils' agitation. Tamil people will not be calm, peaceful or satisfied until the mandatory learning of Hindi goes away.'

The government was forced to bow before Periyar's determination. However, it was not willing to accept the adverse impact of its policy openly and give it up fully. It promised that Hindi would not be made compulsory in the remaining schools but would continue to be taught in schools where it had already been introduced. The government's plan was to impose Hindi in 100 schools every year.

Periyar did not accept this assurance. He decided to agitate tirelessly until Hindi was abolished in schools. Anti-Hindi agitators met in Kanchipuram and formed another agitation committee comprising 14 members, with Periyar as president and Anna as secretary. The anti-Hindi campaign intensified again. Anna's speeches terrified the government. His oratory attracted waves of youth into the movement.

Addressing a meeting at the Gokhale Hall, Madras, Periyar said: 'This is the last warning. No words hereafter. Only action. The job now is to shatter the Hindi policy. What does this ruler say? Will they abandon this policy or not?'

The government was scared. It realised that another agitation would lead to a national uprising, and if it resorted to oppression again, it would lose the goodwill of the people.

On February 19, 1940, Periyar gave the final warning to the government from Gokhale Hall. On February 21, 1940, the government announced that it would not impose Hindi on the people. Its official statement said: 'The policy of compulsory Hindi has caused anger and resentment among the majority of the people. The government feels that teaching Hindi as a compulsory lesson without exams in the first three forms will give students sufficient knowledge and proficiency in that language. So, the government has decided to withdraw the policy of compulsory Hindi with immediate effect.'

Tamils celebrated their victory with poet Bharathidasan's song:

Engal vaazhvum engal valamum
Mangadha Thamizhendru Sange Muzhangu!
Engal pagaivar engo maraindhaar
Ingulla Thamizhar ondraadhal kande!
[Let the conch proclaim
that Tamil is the source of our life and prosperity;
At the sight of Tamils uniting,
our enemies disappeared!]

There were celebrations in every nook and corner of the Presidency. Muhammad Ali Jinnah sent Periyar a telegram: 'You have won the anti-Hindi war. My hearty congratulations to you.'

The struggle that lasted from 1938 to 1940 was the first language war. The credit for winning this war goes to Periyar EVR.

Arignar Anna remarked: 'Only two satyagrahas have succeeded in India. The first one was at Vaikom[33], and the second one is today's anti-Hindi struggle. It was Periyar who fought relentlessly in both.'

Had Periyar not led the agitation, Hindi would have entered

unchallenged into Tamil Nadu. If Hindi is unable to dominate again in Tamil Nadu even now, it is because of the victory achieved by Periyar. All Tamils must be grateful to him.

History is mischievous. The history that made Periyar the hero of Tamils made him a behind-the-scenes player in the enemy camp during the anti-Hindi struggle of 1965. The same history that identified Rajaji as the traitor in 1938 turned him into a hero of the anti-Hindi struggle of 1965.

Chapter 4

The Satyagraha of 1948

Hindi is dominant in Tamil Nadu,
Oh, my countrymen, come forward.
When Tamil is put in harm's way,
What is the purpose of having this body?

—Revolutionary poet Bharathidasan

It was the time when the Congress was at its peak, when people, from a schoolboy to Pandit Nehru of global fame, were marching in every street singing the song of freedom, praising the Salt Satyagraha, extolling the greatness of the Civil Disobedience Movement and the fervour of the Quit India Movement and the brilliant leadership of Gandhiji.

It was the time when the ruling aliens had run away, when those who had faced lathis and bullets, had lost limbs, spent years together in jail had finally won the right to rule. They assumed office as ministers and earned new identities as the heroes who would rule the nation.

It was the time when Congressmen reaped the fruits of their sacrifices—fruits such as the approbation of the masses, receptions organised by clubs and by the rich in their bungalows, encomiums of poets, special pujas of purohits, feasts offered by business barons, innocent people's love-laden praises and doctorates conferred by universities.

It was also the time when the Dravidar Kazhagam had as its members the strong-willed, the clear-minded and those who saw religion as evil. In their view, religion was the selfish creation of pretenders and the mischievous centre of Vedic believers; the Vedas were the magic wand of conspirators and the selfish texts of exploiters; God was man's creation, fools' belief and the source of livelihood for big sinners; religious leaders were ignominious people who indulged in sexual acts and cheats who lived by hoodwinking people.

It was the time when the Kazhagam propagated sharp reformist ideas that religious leaders, adherents of shastras, and the weak-willed and servile could not countenance even from a distance.

It was the time when leaders like Periyar, Arignar Anna, revolutionary poet Bharathidasan, Navalar Nedunchezhiyan, Kuthusi Gurusamy[34], Kalaignar Karunanidhi, EVK Sampath, NV Natarajan[35], KK Neelamegam[36] and TM Parthasarathy[37] worked tirelessly, unmindful of abuses and accusations.

The power-drunk wearers of the crown had grown arrogant with the thought that they were proud rulers, they had political power, they had the armed forces under their command, they were growing richer, and their influence was increasing. They were so arrogant that they believed they could do anything they pleased and no one would oppose them.

The Ministry led by Omandur Ramasamy Reddiar[38] decided to impose Hindi again. It refused to accept the recommendation of an expert committee on education that Hindi learning should not be made compulsory. On June 20, 1948, the Madras government issued an order imposing Hindi. It had not forgotten the anti-Hindi agitation of 1938. Keeping in mind the Tamil people's brave resistance against the imposition of Hindi and the predicament of Premier Rajaji and his Education Minister P Subbarayan, its order made Hindi a compulsory subject in the Andhra, Kerala and Kannada regions of the Presidency and an optional subject in the Tamil areas. National dailies, Indian nationalists and the Hindi Prachar Sabhas condemned this partial move. 'Should the government refrain from making Hindi compulsory for fear of the response of a few people? Shame on the government. This is a sign of the ruling party's weakness,' they said. Scared by this internal hostility, the government issued another order making Hindi compulsory all over the Presidency. It declared Hindi, Sanskrit, Arabic, Telugu, Malayalam and Kannada as second languages and made it compulsory for students to study one of them and pass the relevant exam.

Although Hindi appeared to be an elective language in this scheme of things, the government made no effort to help those who opted to study the non-Hindi languages. It forced students to learn Hindi as a second language.

Periyar strongly condemned this sly attempt to impose Hindi. He met Chief Minister Omandur Ramasamy Reddiar and urged him to withdraw the order. Feeling intimidated by the threats of the newspapers, the pressure from the Brahmins and the opposition of some Congressmen, the Chief Minister refused to accede to Periyar's demand.

The government, which did not have the courage to declare that learning Hindi was compulsory, issued the following deceptive statement: 'Some people, who have not properly understood the government's plan, have wrongly assumed that Hindi has been made a compulsory subject. We have included Hindi in the group of second languages. This group also has Hindi, Sanskrit, Arabic, Telugu, Malayalam and Kannada languages. Students can learn any one of these languages. There is no compulsion to learn a particular language.'

The truth was that the government did not create facilities to teach Telugu, Malayalam or any other second language in any school. When Education Minister Avinashilingam Chettiar visited the Tirunelveli district, a teacher asked him, 'What do we do when a student does not want to learn Hindi as either a compulsory language or an elective language?' The Minister did not say that the school could teach him either Malayalam or Telugu. Instead, he said: 'Such a student should be thrown out of the school.'

The Dravidar Kazhagam then issued the following statement: 'Hindi has entered the State again with the support of the rulers and the blessings of Indian nationalists. The injured tiger rises again. The dismembered demoness cackles again. Oh, dear Tamils, you, who ruled the world through your flag; they say Hindi is dominant again in Tamil Nadu. Come together again to stop this.'

On July 17, 1948, a conference of the opponents of Hindi was held in St Mary's Hall in Chennai. Leaders like Periyar, Arignar Anna, revolutionary poet Bharathidasan, Dr Dharmambal, Thiru V Kalyanasundaram Mudaliar, Thamizharasu Kazhagam leader MP Sivagnanam and Arunagiri Adigal spoke of the importance of launching another satyagraha against Hindi. This conference was a milestone in the history of the anti-Hindi movement.

The executive committee of the Dravidar Kazhagam met in Madras to decide on the methods of the struggle. Representatives from all districts participated and shared their ideas. The committee passed the following resolutions unanimously:

'This committee condemns the government's decision to impose Hindi in classes one to three at the instigation of some people after having promised that Hindi will not be compulsory in classes one to six. It resolves that Hindi should not introduced in these classes as either a compulsory language or an elective language.

'By refusing to accept people's opinions expressed through conferences and public meetings in the past one month, holding on to its opinion and cheating people through various interpretations of its policy, the government has forced the Dravidar Kazhagam to resort to direct action. The Kazhagam has chalked out the following programme in line with its action plan: 1. Picketing schools 2. Taking out processions and conducting public meetings and boycotting Minister's programmes to convey the people's resentment against the government 3. Defying any governmental move to ban such activities 4. Forming a working committee to coordinate effectively these agitations.'

As the first step in this direction, the committee decided to picket either the Thondai Mandalam High School or the Hindu Theological High School in Chennai from August 10 onwards and appeal to the students not to attend classes. It appointed Comrade CN Annadurai as the leader of the first batch of picketers.

Tamil society was overjoyed that such an agitation had been planned. The people rose up in revolt. They sounded the drums of war, announcing that they were ready to sacrifice their lives for the sake of Tamil. Anna, the lion of the Pallava country, the general of the rationalist camp, the architect of the Tamils' intellectual world, the protector of Tamil language, the veteran of many a battlefield, the winner of many hearts, the pearl yielded by Kanchipuram and the wealth of the Kazhagam, assumed the leadership of the agitation. Every nook and corner of the Tamil country rejoiced that Tamil would live on and that Hindi would die.

Anna declared, 'August 10 will go down in history as a red-letter day. The righteous struggle to save Tamil will begin on this day. This is the day that will make people realise how traitors tried to ruin our world-renowned language, which is our life. August 10 will be the day when the world will know and will have to accept the demand for a separate Dravidian republic. On that day, the world will realise how August 15 (the day of independence) gave birth to August 10, the day our protests will begin.

'Our Dravidian comrades have received the invitation that they were eagerly waiting for. The scars inflicted on us by our oppressors and the blood we are going to shed should become the ambassadors that will bring back to our camp those Dravidian comrades who have forgotten Dravidam and joined the oppressors. I have accepted the leadership of this righteous struggle because I have faith in you. I invite every one of you to join the ranks of our army. The battle has begun. Come and join us and taste victory.'

The picketing began in front of the Muthialpet High School. As the volunteers marched towards the school, thousands of people lined up on both sides of the road and raised slogans such as, 'Long Live Tamil!' 'Hindi down down!' 'Long Live the satyagrahis!' 'Long Live Periyar!' 'Long live Anna!'.

Under the leadership of Arignar Anna and his lieutenant CTT Arasu, volunteers Dhanalakshmi Ammaiyar[39], her son Dravida Mani, N Subramanian, M Anandappan, TT Pandian, N Krishnan, S Natarajan, Kalaichelvan and N Mariappan picketed the school. They appealed to the students not to study Hindi. They picketed the school again in the evening. This continued for 22 days. Although there were no arrests, violence, police beatings or teargas attacks, support for the agitation grew by the day. Thamizharasu Kazhagam leader MP Sivagnanam issued a statement in support of the satyagraha.

At their State-level conference in Madras on August 14, 1948, teachers, who knew the minds of the students and the sentiments of the people at large very well, passed the following resolution: 'As this conference is of the opinion that the government's decision to make this unwanted Hindi compulsory or elective for students who cannot comprehend it is tantamount to destroying the country, its people and the Tamil language, it urges the rulers to remove Hindi from the high school curriculum.'

On August 22, 1948, the executive committee of the Dravidar Kazhagam met at Periyar's house in Madras. They wanted to give the increasingly popular agitation a new direction. Leaders like Periyar, Arignar Anna, CTT Arasu, KK Neelamegam, CVM Annamalai, KA Mathiyazhagan, NV Natarajan, EVK Sampath, KVK Sami and AP Janarthanam participated in this meeting. Even as they were deliberating on the future course of action and discussing a plan to wave black flags during Governor-General

Rajaji's visit to Chennai on the following day, the government, which had so far lacked the courage to confront the agitators on the battlefront, arrested and jailed the 93 participants.

The agitation now took place on two fronts. The first one was the satyagraha and the second one was to show black flags to ministers. Black-shirt volunteers waved black flags at all their functions as a mark of protest against the policy of giving life to an alien language and ruining their own language. Black flags greeted Governor-General Rajaji and the Governor, Krishna Kumarsinhji Bhavsinhji, who was also the king of Bhavnagar (Gujarat). Dravidar Kazhagam volunteers also showed black flags to Local Administration Minister K Chandramouli in Dindigul, Education Minister Avinashilingam Chettiar in Dharmapuri, and Agriculture Minister Madhava Menon in Alandur. In Kanchipuram, a black flag demonstration was held against Chief Minister Omandur Ramasamy Reddiar.

When black flags greeted every Minister whenever he participated in public functions, the police lathi charged the agitators. They were not allowed on the streets, and those who defied the police were chased and brutally beaten up. Hundreds of Tamil volunteers will never forget the lathi charge that they were subjected to when they waved black flags at Rajaji in Chennai. Among those mercilessly beaten were K Appadurai[40] and his wife. Both were pushed onto a barbed fence. Appadurai was left bleeding. Not content with beating up the agitators, the government arrested them and filed cases against them.

Showing black flags as a symbol of protest is not only a democratic right but also a basic right that should be respected by every humane person. The oppressive government refused to accept even this basic right, tortured the courageous Tamil agitators and took pleasure in lodging them in jails. But the Kazhagam was not rattled. On the contrary, it intensified the agitation, asking the government to beat the volunteers as long as it had the lathi in its hands and shoot them until its guns ran out of bullets.

Volunteers were advised to resort to a token picketing programme in front of all the schools in the State on September 15, 1948. The government beefed up security outside all the schools. The protectors of the ruling lords went around the streets, wielding rifles and threatening the public. The picketing programme was conducted successfully in the important towns of Chennai, Trichy, Madurai, Salem, Vellore, Tiruvannamalai, Kanchipuram, Virudhunagar and Thoothukudi. Schools were picketed in more than 300 places across the State.

The agitation at Thoothukudi was dramatic. Citizens participated in the agitation with an enthusiasm unmatched by people of any other town. A total of 91 volunteers participated in the picketing programme in batches led by KVK Sami, the honest comrade with an unwavering ideological commitment who was hailed as the Pandiyan king and Dravidian hero.

That day of token protest happened to be the wedding day of Kalaignar Karunanidhi. Clad in his wedding clothes, he was sitting in the shamiana in Tiruvarur, his hometown. He heard the anti-Hindi agitators' slogan, 'Hindi down down; long live Tamil,' on the street outside. Unable to keep sitting in the shamiana, he rushed out and joined the procession in his wedding finery. When the wedding party came in search of the groom, they saw a slogan-shouting Karunanidhi picketing a school. Fortunately, none of the agitators were arrested on that day. The wedding took place after the picketing programme ended. Kalaignar's participation, unmindful of the special occasion in his life, added glory to the Tiruvarur agitation.

The police arrested the agitators only in a few towns and filed cases against them. This was done to satisfy the bosses at the Centre because they were afraid that if they arrested all of them, the agitation would be intensified, posing a serious law and order challenge.

On September 16, 1948, just a day after the token protests, when a larger number of people had begun to come out on the streets all over the State, Periyar suspended the agitation. Everyone was surprised and shocked. It was as if a scorpion had stung the volunteers, leaving them writhing in pain. To pacify the heart-broken cadres and explain the reason behind Periyar's decision, Anna wrote a letter: 'The token protest happened very successfully in all the places on September 15, 1948. Had the struggle continued, a quick victory appeared possible. The temporary suspension of the agitation at this juncture might have disappointed and worried many people. But our Kazhagam comrades should look at the reasons for its suspension with a broad mind. Even before our movement resorted to direct action, Periyar, during his meeting with Chief Minister Omandurar, had promised to stop all the actions relating to Hindi, whatever be the stage of the agitation, if the Central government went ahead with its plan of launching a war against the Nizam of Hyderabad. We share the opinion of the Central government on the question of Hyderabad's accession to the Indian Union. So, our central committee, with a view to helping the Centre win its war against Hyderabad decided to suspend all the direct-action programmes temporarily.'

The Indian Army won the war against Hyderabad, leading to its accession to the Union. But the State government refused to accept Periyar's demand on the language issue as a gesture of gratitude to the Dravidar Kazhagam for suspending hostilities and extending its cooperation to the Centre like a brother. It sang the old song in a new tune. Realising that the government would not budge unless it was taught a lesson through another protest, the Kazhagam gave a battle cry. Periyar made this appeal to students: 'The anti-Hindi agitation will resume by this month-end. I don't know how the government will try to suppress it. I don't know whether they will rely on lathis, guns, explosives or jail. My student comrades! Be ready to get out of schools and colleges as soon as we give a call. You can take care of your education later. We can even run a school in jail. Bring your teachers along with you!'

On October 23-24, 1948, the Dravidar Kazhagam convened a special conference at Erode to identify new arenas of battle. The town wore an unusually festive look. Black-shirt volunteers thronged the streets. It was a gathering of over 50,000 people. Arignar Anna presided over the conference. His speech, which was like a cascading waterfall, was a call to the participants to get ready for battle. He said: 'This is what this conference wants to convey to the lords ruling us: We will not be mute spectators to the attempt to destroy our rights. Your attitude has taken away our fear for our lives. Come to the battlefield again now that the Hyderabad trouble is over. We've come forward to sacrifice our lives to save our language. You who live with the reputation of being "paragons of virtue" are willing to kill your siblings for the sake of an alien language. This conference says to the rulers: Our party's popularity is at its peak. Other parties will entice people with assurances of winning the next election and a place in the Assembly. We do not lure people to our party with enticements. We invite the brave, not the vain. We invite the courageous who can brave oppression, not the political gamblers. We invite the warriors who accept home and jail as one, not the decorative dolls of the Assembly. We need one child from each family who can save our poetic language. We need people of integrity who are strong enough to withstand the attacks of authoritarianism for the sake of their land and language.'

Then, Alagirisamy stood up to speak. The emaciated, tuberculosis-ravaged appearance of this brave fighter shocked the audience. His legs and hands trembled as he said in a tremulous voice: 'Comrades! We may have to go to jail after this conference. I read newspaper reports that said this will be the last conference. As far as I am concerned, considering my health condition, I am afraid this may truly be my last conference. I came here only to say my final goodbye to my leader.'

The audience was in tears.

Unveiling the map of Dravida Nadu, Thiru Vi Ka declared: 'Arise! Arise! Save Tamil. Brave every opposition. Rescue our Mother Earth.'

Condemning the State government for tyrannising its own people, Periyar said: 'The struggle will continue even if all our people do not come together. I will not be bothered in the least, even if there is no support. I will do my duty. I will resist oppression.'

The Erode conference turned out to be a training ground for the anti-Hindi warriors. The conference passed resolutions calling for a prolonged struggle. It resolved to 'resume the picketing programme, which had been suspended', from November 1, 1948 onwards.

The other important resolutions were: 'In order to show our hatred for the Omandur Ministry's insistence on imposing Hindi despite the fact that we have very respectfully pointed out that it will not only ruin the arts, culture and civilisation of this land but also imperil the educational development of little children, we appeal to the people to show black flags to the Chief Minister and Education Minister and boycott them whenever they go on tour in the State. It calls upon our comrades to defy any ban on our picketing programme and campaigns; not to legally counter any case filed against the agitators; not to seek bail even if they are arrested and not to pay any fine imposed on them consequent to their arrest. They can issue statements explaining the reasons for their arrest and any legal action.'

Thus, the Erode conference gave a battle cry. The agitators prepared for battle after a period of rest. The youth among them impatiently awaited the day, wondering, 'Why can't it come tomorrow itself?'

On November 1, a huge public meeting presided by Thiru Vi Ka was held in Chennai's Gymkhana grounds. When Arignar

Anna sounded the drums of war, it was as if the agitation was being led by legendary Chera Minister Villavan-Kothai or the Pallava king Karunakara Thondaiman, who had led the invasion of Kalinga. Thiru Vi Ka thundered: 'Oh, Rulers, don't be the victims of your arrogance. As one who knows the mind of the people, I say this: don't stand on your pride in this matter. Give up the policy of making Hindi compulsory. Don't be adamant. Don't be deceptive and proud. Don't antagonise Periyar. Assess the situation and come to a conclusion by tonight. Issue an order giving up the policy of compulsory Hindi before the satyagraha starts tomorrow. Seek the path of dharma. Seek the path of love.'

There was an eclipse on November 1, so the picketing began the next day. Thousands of people gathered in front of Muthialpet school, waiting for Anna, hailing him as 'the ambassador of the intellectual world, the lion that comes roaring to the struggle to save the mother tongue, the general of our army and the son who would sacrifice himself to save Mother Tamil.' Volunteers like Mrs Alamelu Appadurai[41], Kalaichelvan, Saalai Kabir, OC Pandian, and CS Dravidamani were among the picketers. Anna oversaw the agitation. Five volunteers picketed outside the school every day. TM Parthasarathy and Kanchi Manimozhiyar[42] visited the agitation venue daily, encouraging and helping the volunteers.

Since the Chief Minister had permitted Periyar to lead a peaceful agitation, none of the agitators was arrested. However, it created a buzz across the city. The ruling class became worried that the situation would escalate if it remained a mute spectator. Tamil Nadu Congress Committee president, K Kamaraj, said at a public meeting: 'The Madras Ministry does not take into account the people's opinion while implementing important schemes. The education minister has issued a statement oblivious to the fact that 1,800 people went to jail in protest against the government's decision to make Hindi compulsory; this has created an unwarranted crisis. My personal opinion is that Hindi should not be made compulsory.'

The momentum of the agitation created fissures in the ruling party. In the meantime, it intensified across towns. Realising this, the government issued prohibitory orders under Section 144 of the Criminal Procedure Code in Kumbakonam, Thoothukudi, Madurai, Kovilpatti, Tiruvarur, Thirukovilur, Nannilam, Kodavasal, Peralam, Kallakurichi, Villupuram and Vellore. It banned public meetings.

The Kazhagam decided to defy the order of the government that denied them a democratic right, much like the British government. Kazhagam volunteers in Kumbakonam took out a procession every day defying the ban. The police lathi-charged them, attacked them with the butts of their rifles, kicked them, arrested some of them and left them in forests. NV Natarajan was bleeding as a result of the lathi blows. He was handcuffed and paraded through the streets. Periyar and other leaders like KK Neelamegam, Ponnusamy, advocate Muthu Dhanapal and Mrs Maniyammai were arrested. The police charged them with violating prohibitory orders. They were sentenced to two months' rigorous imprisonment. Other volunteers were handed prison sentences of three or four months. Under the pretext of doing his duty, a police sub-inspector named Adithan unleashed a reign of terror.

The Kumbakonam agitation was called off on December 30, 1948. But it had become the prime example of the rulers' cruelty. The Kazhagam gave a call to its members to observe January 1, 1949, as a day of protest against the government's oppression. On that day, processions and public meetings were held all over the State. The prohibitory order was shattered in many places. Comrade Singaram was sentenced to six months' rigorous imprisonment for violating the ban in Tiruvarur. In Kurinjipadi, 13 comrades, including KVP Palaniappan and Kalaamani, were sentenced to rigorous imprisonment. In Panruti, seven comrades, including N Nadarasan and N Rajavel, were sentenced to six months imprisonment.

After the anti-oppression day, Arignar Anna intensified the picketing programme. Forty-eight leading comrades, including Kanchi Manimozhiyar, TM Parthasarathy, CTT Arasu, K Govindasamy and N Jeevarathinam[43], joined the agitation on a single day. Twelve women, including Sathiyavani Muthu[44] and Alamelu Appadurai, participated in the picketing programme. The women's agitation was led by KA Maniammai and NV Natarajan. The agitation continued for over 100 days in the face of the government's oppression, the arrogant speeches of the ministers, the condemnation of the ruling party's agents and the abuses of musclemen who thrive in serving the interests of the Northerners. The agitation was suspended when schools closed for summer vacation.

Meanwhile, Periyar's decision to marry[45] Maniyammai created a storm in the Dravidar Kazhagam. Many leaders became unwilling to lead the agitation. The cadre members were also not interested. The agitation was given up.

The anti-Hindi sentiment created by the agitation of 1948 eventually succeeded in 1950. Education Minister Avinashilingam Chettiar resigned in 1949. The government's order on the compulsory study of Hindi was scrapped. Hindi was made an elective subject.

Chapter 5
The Constitution and the Official Language

'The members of the Constituent Assembly wanted an Indian language to be the official language of the country. They said that Hindi has the qualification to be the national language. However, Hindi cannot be made the official language in practice. Only English is used at the all-India level. Members from non-Hindi regions fear that Hindi is being imposed on them. They are all proud of their own languages. Hence, the Constitution clarifies what the national objective should be and how conciliatory the approach should be until that objective is achieved.'

—Granville Austin

The 17th chapter of the Indian Constitution consists of provisions relating to official languages. Articles 343 to 351 refer to the languages to be used by the Central and State governments, the courts, the Parliament and the State assemblies, and that Hindi should be imposed in the Central government's administration 15 years after the Constitution comes into force. Article 343 says unequivocally that the Hindi language in Devanagari script should be the Centre's official language. And it also says that the Centre should use the internationally accepted numerals.

Under the Constitution, the President of India can order that Hindi should be used in the Central government departments, although English would be the official language in all these departments for the first 15 years of the Constitution. Article 343(3) says that Parliament can enact a law on the continuation of English as the official language and the use of Devanagari numerals after 15 years.

India has about 1,652 languages. Of these, only 18 find a place in the Eighth Schedule of the Constitution. However, the Schedule does not identify either the national or official language among them. It just refers to them as languages.

The Constitution came into effect on January 26, 1950. According to Article 343, Hindi would be the official language of the Central government from January 1965 onwards. Article 344 of the Constitution also mentions an official language commission. This commission was to make recommendations to the President on ways to speed up the use of Hindi as the Central government's official language and limit the use of English, the language to be used in the courts, the numerals to be used in government departments, and on languages to be used in Centre-State communications. This commission was also to make recommendations on the development of science, industrial growth, cultural development, and the demands of non-Hindi speakers, their welfare and their place in government jobs. The commission was to be formed in the fifth year of the Constitution. A parliamentary committee consisting of 20 Lok Sabha members and 10 Rajya Sabha members was to study the Official Language Commission's report and forward its recommendations to the President. The President, that is, the Central government, would issue an order on the basis of the parliamentary committee's recommendations.

The Official Language Commission and the Parliamentary Committee were formed with a view to making Hindi the official language of India.

According to Article 345 of the Constitution, a state government can make one, or more than one, language the official language of the State. English will continue to be the official language until the State government concerned legislates on the official language. The present language (English) will continue to be the language of communication between the Centre and the states. The state governments can communicate with the Centre in Hindi if they wish to.

Article 347 says that if a considerable number of people want their state language to be recognised as the official language of the State and if the Centre considers their demand to be just, that language should also be accepted as the official language.

The Constitution, which firmly lays down that Hindi alone should be the official language of the Central government, allows the states to make more than one language their official language. This fact illustrates the extent of the Central government's Hindi chauvinism.

Article 348(1) of the Constitution says that the proceedings in the Supreme Court and every High Court, the government's Bills and amendments in Parliament and the State Assemblies, all the laws passed by the Centre and the State governments, the ordinance promulgated by the President or the Governors, the orders, rules and regulations of the Central and State governments should be in English. However, the Governor, with the approval of the President, can permit the use of Hindi or any State language in the high courts. If a State Assembly enacts a law in a state language other than English, it should provide its authoritative English translation. The Centre should not allow the use of languages other than English in the Supreme Court or the High Courts unless there is a recommendation to that effect from the Parliamentary Committee on the basis of the Official Language Commission's recommendation.

Every citizen has the right to submit an application to the Centre or State government in his / her mother tongue. In elementary schools, lessons should be taught only in the children's mother tongue.

Article 350A and Article 350B confer on minorities the right to get elementary education in their languages. They provide for the appointment of a special officer to give a report on the minorities' languages.

Article 351 urges the Central government to undertake propagation of Hindi as a duty. The Constitution orders the Central government to propagate Hindi all over the country by borrowing necessary words from Sanskrit and without interfering in the use of the languages listed in the Eighth Schedule.

If we analyse all the constitutional provisions relating to the official language, we can easily recognise the following injustices:

1. Despite the Eighth Schedule recognising 18 languages, Hindi is allowed to be used by the Centre as the official language without any justification.
2. Although the Constitution says that Hindi will be enthroned as the official language only after 1965, the President has been empowered to use that language in the central administration even before 1965.
3. The Official Language Commission is supposed to recommend how quickly Hindi can be made to function as the official language. It has not been empowered to make recommendations on the development of other national languages, including Tamil.
4. The Constitution urges the Centre to take up propagation of Hindi from Kashmir to Kanyakumari as its primary duty.

How did these atrocious provisions that seek to make non-Hindi speakers, who constitute a majority in the Indian subcontinent, find a place in the Constitution? Did no one protest against this injustice? Did no one oppose it? What is the reason for this domination by Hindi fanatics? Why did political leaders not realise that accepting undeveloped Hindi as the official language in a country that has languages known for their antiquity and excellence is an injustice that would reduce non-Hindi speakers to the status of second-class citizens? Why have the Hindi fanatics not accepted that replacing English, which had been the administrative language for more than 150 years, with Hindi would harm national unity? Why do they think that the dominance of Hindi is more important than the unity of the country? Why was Hindi given a place in the Constitution in 1950 itself, when it was clear that it was to become the official language only in 1965?

Here, we will answer these questions.

The Congress, which had been under the influence of Hindus from the beginning, always intended to make the study and propagation of Hindi compulsory by removing English and enthroning Hindi. As far back as 1918, Gandhiji said: 'I state humbly and boldly that there is no use of talking of freedom unless we give the official language status to Hindi and accord the State languages their due place.' However, the Congress gave up its insistence on Hindi as the official language and started talking of Hindustani, hoping that would get the cooperation of Muslims in the freedom movement. It changed the organisational rules accordingly and passed a resolution in support of Hindustani.

A committee formed under the leadership of Pandit Nehru stated that Hindustani, which is spoken by people in at least half of India, should be developed as the common language of the country. The Nehru Committee report that recommended recognition of Hindustani as the national language and encouragement of regional languages was written in English, not Hindustani. Although Congress leaders spoke in support of Hindustani, in practice, they used English. Pandit Nehru explained that English was an indispensable language for us because of our association with it in the past and its importance at the international level.

Initially, the Congress did not face any internal conflict or contradictions over the issue of the national language. Winning national freedom was its primary objective, and all other issues were pushed to the background. However, it became a burning issue after the formation of the Constituent Assembly and created strong differences among the leaders.

National language became an important issue when the rules for the formation of the Constituent Assembly were to be drawn up, and Babu Rajendra Prasad, who was elected as its leader, announced that all proceedings of the Assembly would be recorded in Hindustani or English and that the members could speak in their respective mother tongues with the permission of the Chair. Many members, including Pandit Nehru, opposed this decision. This was part of an informal discussion. Seth Govind Das, a Hindi fanatic, spoke in favour of the decision of the Assembly's sub-committee in charge of drafting its rules. He said: 'The record of the Assembly's proceedings should be in Hindustani. It is painful that the Constituent Assembly proposes to make English the official language in free India.' Mr KM Munshi interjected, saying, 'Hindustani is the national language, indeed. However, English is in use in the Assembly. So, English should not be given up.' Consequently, the Assembly rules were not changed. English continued to be used in the Assembly.

Fanatics tried to add Hindi as the official language in the Constitution claiming that that was the official language of the country. The sub-committee on fundamental rights decided to add the provision on the official language to the fundamental rights section and remarked in its report that Hindustani written in Devanagari or Persian script should be the first official language and that English will be the second official language. However, when the Constitutional Law Advisory Committee met in April 1947, it gave up on the idea of incorporating the official language in the section on fundamental rights. Vallabhbhai Patel announced in the Constituent Assembly that the committee formed to formulate the Central government's powers will decide the section in which the provision on the official language will be incorporated. In the meantime, the State Constitution Committee that was formed to go into the question of a state's powers discussed the language issue and recommended that the regional language of a State, and English or Hindustani, will be its official language.

The fourth session of the Constituent Assembly began on July 14, 1947. As Pakistan's secession was confirmed without an agreement between the Congress and the Muslim League, communalism and religious hatred were at their peak. Taking advantage of this volatile situation, Hindi fanatics moved many amendments to the effect that Hindi should be the official language of India, not Hindustani, and that State Assemblies should use either the regional language or Hindi and not English. The language issue triggered a turmoil in the Constituent Assembly.

In order to reach a consensus within the Congress on the question of the states' official language, a meeting of its Central Parliamentary Board was convened. Of the 63 participants, 32 voted for Hindi. On the issue of numerals, eight more votes went in favour of Devanagari. Thereafter, Vallabhbhai Patel announced in the Assembly that a decision had been taken on the language issue. Within a week of these developments, the Union Constitution Committee discussed the issue of the Central government's official language. Amendments were moved in the committee to the effect that Hindi alone should be the official language, Devanagari script should be accepted, and English could be used for ten years if Parliament wished to. But within the Congress, its Central Parliamentary Board did not discuss these issues. It postponed a discussion on the official language on the grounds that the issue had created conflicts and contradictions within, leading to the stalling of important works and that it could arrive at a decision in the final stage.

Gandhiji was disappointed by the Congress' decision to give up Hindustani. He said: 'The Congress has always worked for broader objectives. But now there are bad signs of the party going against this approach. The Congress should stand like a mountain in times of crisis. It should not lose its courage in the language issue.'

Constituent Assembly member K Santhanam[46] said: 'Hindustani would have been accepted as India's national language had the secession of Pakistan not happened. The general anger against Muslims turned against the Urdu language.'

At no point in time did the Constituent Assembly officially discuss the issue of replacing Hindustani with Hindi[47]. When the final draft of the Indian Constitution was submitted to the President of the Constituent Assembly in February 1948, it did not have a separate provision on the official language. However, it stated that Hindi or English would be the language of Parliament and that these two would be alternative languages in the states.

The crisis and contradictions witnessed in the Constituent Assembly found their reflection in the Congress too, when it sought to amend its organisational rules. PT Tandon was the leader of the group that insisted that the party's affairs should be conducted in Hindi and not in Hindustani. The language issue came to the fore again in 1948 during the election of the Congress president. Tandon, who was fanatic about establishing the dominance of Hindi, was a contestant. Pattabhi Sitaramayya, from a non-Hindi-speaking state, contested against him. To the surprise of many, Rajendra Prasad, a pro-Hindi leader, did not support Tandon. In fact, he asked Tandon to withdraw from the contest. But Tandon refused to do so. Eventually, Sitaramayya won the election with the support of Rajendra Prasad.

Rajendra Prasad's stand remained a mystery for a long time. But it became clear later that it was his tactical move with a long-term objective. The language to be used in the Congress was not important. What was important was which language would be accepted as the official language in the Central government. Rajendra Prasad supported Sitaramayya with the objective of securing the support of non-Hindi-speaking states to enthrone Hindi as the official language of the Central government.

This fact came to light from the way Sitaramayya behaved in a meeting of the Congress' Central Parliamentary Board, which was held in the following year.

When the Constituent Assembly met on November 4, 1948, the Hindi fanatics tried to establish the dominance of that language. LK Maitra[48] responded angrily to the Hindi fanatics' claims that if we don't speak in Hindi and conduct the House proceedings in Hindi, freedom will become meaningless. Later, Giani Gurmukh Singh Musafir, the future Chief Minister of Punjab, cast the deciding vote in the Constituent Assembly in favour of Hindi.

Enraged by their speeches, TT Krishnamachari said: 'I would, Sir, convey a warning on behalf of the people of the South for the reason that there are already elements in South India who want separation and it is up to us to tax the maximum strength we have to keeping those elements down, and my honourable friends from Uttar Pradesh do not help us in any way by flogging their idea, "Hindi imperialism"...'

There was no consensus among the Congress members on the language issue. Supporters of Hindi and English started strengthening their ranks. Hindi supporters wanted an immediate decision on the language issue. Supporters of English opposed this. The situation was not conducive to reaching an agreement. Realising that this situation would go against Hindi, the Assembly President, Rajendra Prasad, said, 'It will be better to discuss important constitutional issues in a peaceful manner.' and suggested that the House could discuss the language issue later. Pandit Nehru supported this suggestion. Advising Hindi fanatics to be patient, he said: 'We can't achieve our objective if we are in a hurry. If we try to impose something unpalatable to the minority using our majority in the House, the House or the country at large will not be able to achieve what they want to achieve.'

At least half of the members of the Constituent Assembly were against the Hindi fanatics. However, the latter were unfazed by this. They did not think that reaching an agreement on the language issue was essential nor did they respect the rights of non-Hindi speakers. They believed that eventually, they would be able to make Hindi acceptable as the party's (Congress') decision and that Rajendra Prasad would do this successfully.

Rajendra Prasad and Pandit Nehru had differences of opinion over the language issue and they openly aired their views. Rajendra Prasad said: 'The Constitution should be adopted in Hindi. So, a Hindi translation of the text should be accepted constitutionally.'

Nehru refused to accept this proposition. He said: 'The Assembly cannot do the translation. It should be done only by experts. Moreover, the Constitution should be adopted in English. If we accept its Hindi translation as official, the House will see heated debates on the translation of each word. And the lack of consensus will delay things. Hence, we cannot accept a Hindi translation officially.'

In his capacity as Chairman of the Constituent Assembly, Rajendra Prasad wrote many letters to Nehru suggesting that the Hindi translation of the Constitution should be accepted. But Nehru said firmly that the Constitution written in English should be the official version.

The discussion on the language issue, which had been postponed, found a place in the agenda of the Constituent Assembly when it met on August 8, 1949. Many amendments were moved on behalf of Hindi fanatics. One of the amendments proposed that Hindi or English could be used as the official language of the Central government in the first 10 years of the Constitution. The problem was that if the decision was about using Hindi or English, there would be no compulsion to use English. There was the danger of English being removed from the Constitution. Opposing this amendment strongly, English language supporters said that in the first 15 years of the Constitution, English alone should be the official language, that Hindi should not be imposed and that both English and Hindi could be used if two-thirds of the members wanted to. Hindi fanatics did not accept this suggestion. They were adamant that English should not be the official language of the Central government after 15 years and that a law should be enacted to ensure that.

Meanwhile, despite intense deliberations on the language issue, the Central Parliamentary Board of the Congress could not reach a consensus. Hence, a committee was formed to evolve a consensus. The committee consisted of Messrs N Gopalaswamy Ayyangar[49], TT Krishnamachari, Alladi Krishnasami Iyer, KM Munshi, Dr BR Ambedkar, Muhammed Saadulah[50], MN Roy, Abul Kalam Azad, Pandit Govind Ballabh Pant, PT Tandon, Balakrishna Sharma, SP Mukherjee and K Santhanam. This committee's opinion, known as the Munshi-Ayyangar Formula, was conveyed to the Central Parliamentary Board of the Congress.

Yet there was no agreement on whether to use the Devanagari numerals or the internationally used Arabic numerals. The Hindi fanatics were adamant that the Nagari numerals should be used and insisted on taking a decision in the party by division voting in the Parliamentary Board. Both sides polled an equal number of votes. Party president Sitaramayya, who presided over the meeting, did not vote. Nehru cautioned against the use of the Nagari numerals when the Board was vertically divided. As a result, that idea was given up. However, Tandon and his supporters did not want to abide by the party's decision. They insisted that after 15 years of the Constitution, English should not be used as the official language at the Centre and that the Devanagari numerals had to be accepted.

Under the Munshi-Ayyangar formula, Hindi would be the Union government's official language and universally accepted numerals should be used; English would also continue to be the official language for 15 years; Parliament could enact a law for its continuation after that period; in the meantime, the President could pass an order allowing Hindi to be used in the administration; the judgements of the Supreme Court and the high courts, the laws and Draft Bills would have to be in English; the states could accept the State's language or Hindi as the official language; until such time, English would be the official language in the states.

It was on the basis of the Munshi-Ayyangar formula that the Eighth Schedule recognising State languages was incorporated into the Constitution. However, the Eighth Schedule referred to them as just 'languages' and not as national languages or official languages or even as Indian languages. The Schedule was added only to show that Hindi supporters should not be seen as disrespecting the non-Hindi State languages. Otherwise, the State languages did not get any rights just because they were mentioned in the Schedule.

The Congress' Central Parliamentary Board met on September 2, 1949, under the presidency of Sitaramayya to discuss the Munshi-Ayyangar formula. Heated discussions commenced between supporters of Hindi and English. The meeting arrived at a decision and the leaders wanted to move official amendments in the Constituent Assembly on the basis of the decision. The Hindi fanatics insisted that the decision should be based on division. In the voting, both sides got 77 votes each. Sitaramayya, who presided over the meeting, did not vote, maintaining neutrality, although he belonged to a non-Hindi-speaking state. In the end, the meeting ended without a decision on the Munshi-Ayyangar formula. The mystery of Rajendra Prasad's support to Sitaramayya in the party president's election was thus solved in this meeting.

Although both sides agreed on the use of English as the official language in the first 15 years of the Constitution and encouraging the use of Hindi along with it, their disagreement over which numerals to use continued. The Hindi fanatics in the party insisted on the use of Devanagari numerals. As the party could not decide on this issue, the decision was left to the Constituent Assembly.

The Constituent Assembly discussed the official language issue in its meeting on September 12, 13 and 14, 1949. Like soldiers waiting for war, the two sides sat daggers drawn, sharpening their arguments. Rajendra Prasad presided over the meeting. Among the participants were Prime Minister Jawaharlal Nehru and North Indian leaders such as PT Tandon, Abul Kalam Azad, Mahavir Tyagi[51] and Seth Govind Das, and South Indian leaders–Dr P Subbarayan, Quaid-e-Millat Ismail[52] Sahib, TT Krishnamachari, TA Ramalingam Chettiar[53] and PT Chacko[54]. Realising that the situation in the Assembly was unusually tense when the language issue was coming up for discussion, its President, Babu Rajendra Prasad, said: 'Members should place their arguments without hurting the feelings of others. The Assembly should take a decision that is acceptable to the entire nation.'

On behalf of the government, Gopalaswamy Ayyangar introduced and explained the provisions of the draft Constitution. He said: 'This is not my opinion alone. Nor is it of my friends. It is an agreement reached amid irreconcilable differences among the members. There are two aspects to it. One of them is the acceptance of one of the Indian languages as the common language of the country. We cannot decide on that immediately. English should continue as the common language, because Hindi has not developed sufficiently in the industrial and scientific sectors. It needs time to develop. The second aspect is about numerals to be followed all over the country. To reach an agreement among ourselves, we present here two concessions: One, the President can issue an order saying Devanagari numerals could be used along with universal numerals. Two, he can make a recommendation on the script to use for the official language.'

Although Jawaharlal Nehru supported enthroning Hindi as the official language, he underscored the importance of English and the need to respect the sentiments of non-Hindi speakers. He said:

'It is true that English has given us many benefits. We've come to know of many things through English. We have also progressed a great deal. However, no country can become great through an alien language.... No language can be imposed on those opposing Hindi. Such imposition will not succeed either. The foreigners who dominated us could have achieved it through political power. But history shows that they failed in this effort. We can achieve victory in the language issue only by earning the goodwill of the non-Hindi speakers in various states.'

In his speech, the Hindi fanatic PT Tandon shamelessly uttered a lie that most people in the Madras Presidency like Hindi. Many members interjected, saying, 'No, no.' At this point, Maulana Hasrat Mohani[55] from Uttar Pradesh [United Provinces] interrupted and said: 'There should be a referendum to decide whether Uttar Pradesh is a Hindi-speaking State or a Hindustani-speaking State.' He refuted the Hindi fanatic Tandon, saying, 'Not a single person in UP speaks Sanskrit-mixed Hindi.' President Rajendra Prasad, who was a Hindi supporter, intervened, saying, 'This House has been empowered to formulate a constitution for the country. Its rules do not permit holding a referendum. So, a referendum cannot be held on a big issue, or on a particular problem.'

Maulana Abul Kalam Azad said: 'As far as the language issue is concerned, I have expressed my view. I regret that the issue of Hindi has not been resolved in the manner that it should have been resolved.'

Quaid-e-Millat Ismail Sahib said: 'Some friends of ours want an ancient language to be the official language of the Union. If it were granted, then I can boldly say that Tamil, or to put it generally, the Dravidian languages are the earliest among the languages that are spoken on the soil of this country. No historian or archaeologist will contradict me when I say that it is the Dravidian language that was spoken first here on the soil of this country, and that is the earliest language. Tamil has a rich literature of a high order. It is the most ancient language. It is, I may say, my mother tongue. I love it and I am proud of it. However, I am, and so are the other Tamilians, sensible enough not to insist that this undoubtedly most ancient language of the country should become the official language, because we know it is not spoken by as large a number of people as other languages. If we look at the past, as I said, it is this language that must become the official language of the country, but the speakers of this language do not put forward such a claim.' When he said this, the Hindi fanatics were livid that a senior Muslim leader was speaking in support of Tamil.

Dr P Subbarayan reminded the Assembly of how strong the anti-Hindi agitation was in Tamil Nadu. He said: 'It is very important that you should understand the South Indian position. If I tell you what exactly happened for three months when I held charge of the portfolio of education in Madras, and Hindi was introduced as a compulsory subject in the first three forms of the high schools, you will understand why I am anxious to go back from here with something done, something accomplished. For three whole months, every morning when I got out of my house, I heard nothing but cries of 'Let Hindi die and let Tamil live', 'Let Subbarayan die and Rajagopalachari die.' That was the cry that went up for three months and, what is more, we were constrained to use even the Criminal Law Amendment Act against which we have railed previously.'

Despite Subbarayan's speech, the Hindi fanatics did not change their stance. It was as if they had barred their hearts with iron gates.

Ramalingam Chettiar said: 'Mr President, this is a very difficult question for us from the South to solve. It probably means life and death for the South....I appeal to the North Indian people not to take such an attitude, instead to acknowledge that we are all living together in a common country. It is only then that India can proceed and be successful and form a united nation.

'Unless you weld the nation and you make everybody feel that they have a share in the country and it is their country, unless you do that, if you go on keeping alive the spirit of domination of one part over the other, I am sure the result is not going to be the progress or the safety of the country. Sir, with these words I appeal again to the Hindi speaking people to give up their attitude of domination and to adjust themselves.'

PT Chacko from Kerala said: 'A national language can be decided upon only by mutual agreement. It cannot be done by taking votes; that is what I believe. No language can be imposed upon an unwilling people. No Nation has ever succeeded in imposing the language of the majority upon the minority.'

Even after these intense debates, the Assembly did not reach a consensus. A majority of the members did not want to take a decision based on voting, either.

As a last-ditch effort, a meeting of the Congress Parliamentary Board under the presidentship of Pattabhi Sitaramayya was convened on the afternoon of September 14, 1949, to find a compromise on the language issue. Fearing that any decision imposed through the majority would create a big divide in the party, the supporters of English decided to accept some amendments that were sought to be moved in the Munshi-Ayyangar formula. These amendments were: Parliament can enact a law on using English and Nagari numerals after 15 years of the Constitution; Hindi can be used in the high courts with the approval of the President of India; draft bills, laws, and government orders can be brought out in State languages; Sanskrit will be added to the Eighth Schedule.

The Hindi fanatics thought that they had won, because the use of Hindi as the official language after 15 years had been accepted; assurance had been given on the use of Hindi numerals; Sanskrit (which was considered a dead language) had found a place in the Eighth Schedule.

The supporters of English were content that English would continue to be an official language for the first 15 years of the Constitution; that international numerals alone would be used officially; that they could enact a law providing for the use of English after 15 years; and that Hindi alone was not the official language and English also would be one. They believed that non-Hindi speakers would not allow Hindi to be accepted as the only official language after 15 years.

Over 400 amendments moved by both sides were withdrawn. The Congress members were ordered to speak and vote in the Assembly based on decisions taken at the Parliamentary Board.

Based on the amended Munshi-Ayyangar formula, the Constituent Assembly adopted the provisions relating to the official language. These provisions are now in Part XVII of the Constitution.

Chapter 6

The August Agitation

> *'The August agitation has proved the people are ready for a struggle. The beginning of this anti-Hindi sentiment is the precursor to a big, long-drawn battle. The people have woken up. Their emotional upsurge will grow and destroy their oppressors.'*
>
> —P Jeevanandam

Hindi fanatics used the issue of the official language policy in their conspiracy to appropriate the benefits of India's freedom for which non-Hindi speakers also shed blood, faced torture in jails and sacrificed their lives. The Southern Congressmen, who lacked the courage to openly condemn their chauvinism and conspiracy and were supporters of English, described the administrative disruption and other problems that would be caused by the imposition of Hindi and the harm that would befall non-Hindi speakers, who would require time to learn Hindi. They pontificated that five years would be sufficient for non-Hindi speakers to learn that language. Hindi fanatics did not accept even this idea. Others said that five years would not be sufficient for this purpose and sought 30 years' time. At a Hindi Sahitya Sammelan (literary conference) held in Delhi, Hindi fanatics decided to give 10 years. But the Southern Congressmen and English supporters did not accept this decision.

Finally, Congress leaders decided to give 15 years as a compromise. This decision was incorporated in the Constitution.

Belying the trust of non-Hindi speakers, Hindi fanatics started working on their idea of the language policy from 1950 onwards. They illegally imposed Hindi in every section of the administration. Hindi letters alone were imprinted on coins. It was imposed in the Armed Forces. People with knowledge of Hindi were given special preference in Union government jobs. They campaigned that speaking and writing in Hindi was a matter of national pride and prestige. Ministers openly stated on public platforms that learning Hindi was essential for jobs in the future.

The hopes of non-Hindi speakers, especially Dravidians, that things would be different after 15 years, were shattered. Things came to such a pass that it became imperative to nip in the bud their attempts to enthrone Hindi.

Periyar, the great Tamil leader who had been opposing Hindi tooth and nail since the beginning of his political career, strongly condemned the Union government's effort to impose Hindi in every department under its control. The Dravidar Kazhagam conference in Salem in June 1952 resolved to black out with tar the names of railways stations written in Hindi. This was the third phase of the anti-Hindi struggle. Periyar went on a whirlwind tour of the State to intensify the agitation. He appealed to the cadre of Dravida Munnetra Kazhagam [DMK, which had been formed in 1949 by a section of leaders who broke away from the Dravidar Kazhagam, DK] to participate in the agitation. The DMK, which shared Periyar's views on language, convened a meeting of its executive committee members and district secretaries to discuss the issue. Since the party had already decided at its Tirunelveli conference held under the presidentship of Karunanidhi to fight against the imposition of Hindi, they agreed to participate in the August agitation. Addressing a public meeting in Salem, Anna said: 'Many people wonder whether the DMK would participate in the August agitation or not. Although the Dravidar Kazhagam and the Dravida Munnetra Kazhagam are two divided entities, when they are faced with such an issue, they can act as a double-barrelled gun. I have accepted responsibility of blacking out the Hindi words on the name board of the Erode junction. This is the politics Periyar has taught me. As soon as Periyar announced that even those who broke away from the DK could join the agitation, I convened an emergency meeting of the DMK's executive committee and deliberated on joining the August agitation. As we remain separate politically, we are conducting the agitation separately. The agitation on August 1 will be massive.'

Both the Kazhagams officially announced the names of the agitators and the venues of their agitations. This created a sensation across the country. Aware of the pervasive anti-Hindi mood in the State, the Rajaji government knew that any move to suppress the agitation would escalate into a bigger struggle, and adopted a tactical approach. When an opposition member, SP Adithan, asked the government how it was planning to handle the agitation, Chief Minister Rajaji said, 'The government will not unleash the police force against the Dravidar Kazhagam agitators.'

In a statement, Anna explained the significance of the August agitation thus: 'It was in August that the DMK conference at Kovilpatti issued a warning. It is also in August that our satyagraha is going to start. It was in August that the earlier agitation began, when Avinashilingam Chettiar was Education Minister. Our struggle will begin with determination. Periyar has announced August 1 as the date of the agitation aimed at quelling the enemy's bigotry. We issued a warning in August 1950. Periyar has also chosen August for the agitation. The double-barrelled gun is going to attack the North Indian imperialism. We'll do whatever is possible in the fight to fell the common enemy. We'll work against the dominance of Hindi. August is about to begin. We'll win! We'll win!' This statement was issued a day before the agitation.

On August 1, leaders and cadres of the DK and the DMK marched to railway stations carrying pots of tar and brushes and blacked out the Hindi names on the board. In Trichy, about 5,000 DK volunteers led by Periyar took out a huge procession to the station shouting slogans like, 'Long Live Periyar', 'Let Hindi Die! Let Tamil Live'. As soon as the procession reached the station, Periyar and a few volunteers blacked out Hindi names.

When Anna went to the Erode railway station, nearly 10,000 volunteers followed him. When he blacked out the Hindi letters on the name boards, they shouted, 'Long Live Arignar Anna!' 'Long Live the Bernard Shaw of the South!' 'Let Hindi Die!' In Madurai, Navalar Nedunchezhiyan, Madurai Muthu and M Ayyasamy were among the agitators. Kalaignar Karunanidhi, singer Nagore Hanifa, MS Mani, and S Nedumaran blacked out the Hindi letters at the Trichy post office. In Coimbatore, the agitation was led by EVK Sampath, actor KR Ramasamy[56] and SA Rajamanickam. In Chennai's Egmore station, NV Natarajan, CV Rajagopal, Ramamirtham Ammaiyar and Sathiyavani Muthu participated. In Cuddalore, it was KA Mathiazhagan. Among other major agitators were Kuthusi Gurusamy, TP Vedachalam, AP Janarthanam, KM Subramanian and Maniyammai.

Hindi names in about 600 railway stations were blacked out.

The fact that this took place in over 600 places without any tension, confusion or violence was a sign of the August agitation's massive victory.

The DK and the DMK celebrated the victory in Chennai. Addressing a meeting on the Marina in Chennai, Periyar said: 'Rajaji not sending the police force to suppress my movement is said to be an act of generosity. It is wrong. It is not an act of his generosity. It is human nature to escape and act tactically. The Acharya has rich experience of anti-Hindi agitations. He has well understood the nature of an agitation like this. We do not harbour the illusion that Hindi is destroyed just because we have blacked out Hindi names in railway stations. It will be a victory if Hindi is completely removed in Tamil Nadu. That the agitation went off without violence or any untoward incident in over 600 stations is a massive victory in itself.'

The August agitation of 1952 was a warning to Hindi imperialists. Periyar, who wanted to rouse people to fight and ensure that Hindi fanatics do not gain the upper hand, thought that August 1 every year should be observed as the day of blacking out Hindi letters.

A farmers' conference organised by the Dravidar Kazhagam in Mannargudi on July 12, 1953 adopted the following resolution: 'We are pained to note that names are written in Hindi—an act akin to piercing our hearts with spears—even after the people of Tamil Nadu blacked out Hindi on the name boards of railway stations. This conference calls upon the Tamil people to black out Hindi again on August 1 this year. It also calls upon the people, including women, to participate in the agitation, unmindful of any prohibitory order issued by the government.'

The DMK did not participate in this agitation. Some Congressmen, who were unhappy that the government had first permitted Periyar to conduct the agitation and then remained a mute spectator, and some members of the Tamizharasu Kazhagam who wanted to be in the good books of the Union government, started campaigning against the agitation. They appealed to their volunteers: 'If the members of the Dravidar Kazhagam black out Hindi with tar, you wipe it out with kerosene. If they come with tar pots, we should go there with kerosene bottles. We should block them by lying down in their paths.' It was as if the ghost of Ettappan, the man who had betrayed Veerapandiya Kattabomman and turned him in to the British, had possessed many of the living.

As announced by Periyar, in every place in the State, Dravidar Kazhagam volunteers marched in batches towards the railway stations and blacked out Hindi names. About 2,000 volunteers led by Periyar took out a procession to the Salem railway station. Ten Congress goondas lay down on the platform preventing Periyar from reaching the Hindi name board. The policemen asked Periyar to go back. He told them that he would consult his volunteers and came out of the station. The volunteers shouted slogans asking Periyar to go back and black out the Hindi name board. When an aged Periyar tottered towards the name board, the Congress volunteers, sensing that the mood of the people was changing from enthusiasm to anger, themselves blacked out the Hindi name of the station and fled the scene! Among the agitators in other places were Kuthusi Gurusamy in Chennai, TP Vedachalam[57] in Trichy and AP Janarthanam in Tambaram (Chennai).

Like the August agitation of 1952, the one in 1953 also passed off peacefully without any untoward incident. The agitation lost its vigour and momentum because the government decided to keep away. An editorial in *Viduthalai* said: 'Now, a message to the Dravidar Kazhagam volunteers. We have already announced that the agitation to black out Hindi was only a campaign. It was carried out this year just as it was last year. That is, the government showed its face and you smeared it with tar patiently. Just as we appreciate your courage, we have to appreciate their patience also.'

Periyar conducted the Hindi black-out agitation for the third time, on August 1, 1954. But this time, the campaign was very mild, lacking the earlier fire. He hailed Kamaraj as a true-blue Tamil (Pachai Thamizhan) for having trumped Rajaji in the race for chief ministership and in order to show support to the Kamaraj Ministry, he made the August agitation a mere formality. He was afraid that intensifying the anti-Hindi agitation would not be good for the Kamaraj government, and thus he sheathed the sword.

In sum, the August agitation was not against a particular order of the government. It was carried on as a protest against the Union government for imposing Hindi in every department without respecting the justice of the series of agitations conducted by the DK and the DMK. The railway stations and the Central government departments had name boards bearing names in

English and Hindi alone. People welcomed the blacking out of only the Hindi names on them. As a result of the agitation, State languages finally found a place on the name boards. In Tamil Nadu, it was Tamil.

Chapter 7

The Imposition of Hindi

'We cannot ignore the fact that Hindi fanatics are creating conditions that are conducive for an explosive situation in the country by imposing Hindi on non-Hindi speakers. I think this will ruin the country's progress and security.'

—General KM Cariappa

An objective analysis of the reasons given for Hindi to be accepted as the national language will show how chauvinistic and domineering the Union government's language policy is. The following are the reasons it has cited:

1. Among Indian languages, Hindi is known to and spoken by a majority of people.
2. When English is removed from the status of being the official language of India, Hindi alone will be eligible to replace it.
3. Only Hindi will help strengthen India's unity.
4. The Indian Constitution has recognised only Hindi as the official language at the Centre.

These are the reasons cited outwardly. Understanding their real meaning is the responsibility of those who wish to find a just solution to the language issue.

In a republic, it is usual for people to put forward a scheme or express an ideology to claim majority support for it. In support of their argument, they may even give false information and statistics. Hindi fanatics have been adopting this narrow, skewed tactic from the beginning. Addressing a meeting in Allahabad in 1936, Purushottam Das Tandon, a staunch supporter of Hindi, said the country had 22 crore Hindi speakers. When Urdu supporters condemned him for giving wrong statistics, Tandon's supporters gave the vague reply that Tandon did not refer to Hindi speakers and that he meant all speakers of North Indian languages living above the Vindhyas, including Urdu, which is similar. Hindi fanatics sustain their campaign citing Tandon's false statistics.

Addressing the Kamban festival in 1955, President Rajendra Prasad said: 'We have accepted one language in the interest of the nation. If any other language was known to over a half of the population, I am sure we would have chosen that as the national language.' This statement of the President does not mean he wanted to make a language other than Hindi the official language of the government. What he really meant was that since Hindi was spoken by over half of the Indian population, they had chosen it as the official language in a democratic way and the other Indian languages were not eligible for that status. It was just a reiteration of his stance.

When the Census was taken in 1951, the number of speakers of every Indian language was enumerated. However, in order to show a higher number of Hindi speakers, the number of speakers of languages like Rajasthani, Punjabi and Urdu were added to it. Even if assessed by misleading statistics, Hindi speakers constituted only 42 per cent of the population, and not half of it[58].

After maintaining that 22 crore people spoke Hindi, the stance was softened by saying Hindi speakers constitute over half of the population; now, eventually, they are tottering towards the view that Hindi speakers form the single largest linguistic group. They have not yet arrived at the truth.

In an effort to show a higher number for Hindi speakers, they have now floated a new lie that more people know Hindi as the second language compared to English. In a book titled *The English Language Question*, MP Desai gives the following statistics:

The number of people who know Hindi as the second language:

State	Population (in lakhs)	% of people who know Hindi
Andhra	203.2	8.02
Telangana	80	1.35
Tamil Nadu	277.7	8.98
Chennai City	14.2	1.75
Kerala	140.1	14.22
Karnataka	228.4	9.87

Desai mentions these statistics were based on the 1951 Census. The argument that so many people (the figures given in the table) in Andhra, Tamil Nadu, Kerala and Karnataka know Hindi is unacceptable. It is doubtful whether even Joseph Goebbels, who was in charge of propaganda during the Nazi regime, would have uttered such a lie to the people of Germany.

In 1956, JP Naik, Member-Secretary of the University Grants Commission, presented a report which shattered these arguments about Hindi speakers. The statistics given by JP Naik are as follows:

Table: The proportion of speakers of Indian languages:

Language	% of speakers
Hindi	30.4
Telugu	8.6
Bengali	7.7
Marathi	7.6
Tamil	7.0
Urdu	4.6
Kannada	4.0
Malayalam	3.9
Oriya	3.6
Punjabi	2.5
Assamese	1.6
Kashmiri	0.4
Other languages	12.8

Table: The proportion of people who know Hindi in non-Hindi-speaking states:

State	% people who know Hindi
West Bengal	6.67
Assam	6.62
Gujarat	3.48
Karnataka	1.28
Andhra	1.21
Kerala	0.21
Tamil Nadu	0.20
Orissa	1.78

If you compare these statistics with the figures given by MP Desai, you can understand the systematic false propaganda of Hindi fanatics.

JP Naik himself has stated that the status of Hindi in non-Hindi-speaking states shows that Hindi is not spoken widely.

According to the 1961 Census, the population of the Indian subcontinent is 44 crores. Of this, the proportion of Hindi speakers is 13.3 crores. And they do not speak the same type of Hindi. It has over 96 variants with major differences and contradictions. The Hindi spoken by one section of people is not understood by another section of Hindi speakers. They are different in meaning, syntax, grammar, pronunciation and so on. Bihari, Maithili, Awadhi, Magahi, Chhattisgarhi, Bhojpuri, Western Hindi, Eastern Hindi and Khadi Boli are some of the important variants of Hindi. The Sahitya Akademi recognises Awadhi as a separate language and has been awarding books written in that language. Hence, the fact that Hindi has many variations cannot be hidden for a long time.

Hindi is the mother tongue of Sri Prakasa, freedom fighter and former Governor of Madras. He said: 'Hindi is spoken by different sections of people in different ways. Even in a region known as a Hindi-speaking area, the language spoken by one section of people is not understood by another section. Hindi has hundreds of dialects. Attempts are on to make them separate languages. If we add the variants which non-Hindi speakers have to speak, we will see a confused language. Each person will claim that he/she speaks Hindi. But it will not be understood by anyone else.'

The speakers of Rajasthani, Maithili, Bhojpuri, Magahi, Chhattisgarhi and Awadhi have protested against the move to link their languages with Khadi Boli. Among those who fought to keep the separate identity of these branches of Hindi were Rahul Sankrityayan[59] and Banaras Sitaram Chaturvedi[60]. It is improper to treat different branch languages as Hindi and display them as the strength of Hindi speakers. There is an attempt to enthrone

Khadi Boli, which is mainly spoken by people in the Hindi region. The number of Khadi Boli speakers is just 1.5 crore.

The claim that 22 crore people, which constitutes one half of the Indian population, speak Hindi has been exposed as a lie and people have now realised that it is Khadi Boli Hindi which has become the official language. Dr Lakshmanaswami Mudaliar, Vice Chancellor of the University of Madras, was right when he said: 'We've been told that Hindi is spoken by a majority of Indians. I've not heard a statement that is farther from the truth.'

If we analyse the issue on the basis of merit, Hindi has never been eligible to claim the status of an official language. On the origins of Hindi, Dr Suniti Kumar Chatterji, a renowned linguist and litterateur, writes that Hindi is one of the youngest languages of India. Khadi Boli Hindi, he says, is recognised by the Constitution as the official language and may become the national language. But, according to him, there is no evidence of a language called Khadi Boli Hindi before 1850. His view shows that Hindi emerged as a language much later in history. Supporting his observation, other experts say that modern Hindi, which evolved from 14 language groups, is in a primary stage of growth and is not even a hundred years old. No language can grow in just a hundred years: it can only be in the primary stage of development.

That Hindi does not have sufficient number of literary and scientific books is a universally accepted fact. Many people, including Nehru, have admitted that Hindi does not have the kind of rich vocabulary and literary, artistic and scientific work that languages like Tamil, Telugu and Bengali have. Basheer Ahmed Sayeed, former judge and legislator, has said: 'Hindi, which is hailed and developed as the national language by Hindi fanatics, does not have any strong historical background. Nor does it have any traditional strength. This new language does not have a rich culture and history. It does not have a place in the literary world.' A language without a rich tradition, antiquity, literary wealth, the treasures of knowledge or historical greatness seeking to replace English is like a tiny tot wanting to run a family.

Hindi supporters have created the impression that India has disintegrated into small states, that all the attempts to integrate it as one nation have failed and that Hindi is the only tool that can bring about its unity. Though the nationalists claim this every day, India has not disintegrated. Language cannot be a tool to unite a nation. If it is an instrument of unity, the ancient Tamil country would not have existed as Chera, Chola and Pandya kingdoms. Americans would not have revolted against the domination of Britain. Arabic speakers live as different nations. Northern and Southern Rhodesia would not be two countries. North and South Korea would not have come into existence. When history shows that one language cannot unite all those who speak it, it is foolish to say that Hindi will unite people speaking different languages.

Hindi will not help unite India in any way. If attempts are made again and again to impose it, the threads that keep India united will keep snapping. Hindi did not create unity in Punjab. On the contrary, it has cut off whatever ties it had. In Uttar Pradesh, it did not integrate Urdu speakers. On the contrary, it has isolated them. Stating that Hindi is the only means to create unity, Hindi fanatics want it to be imposed on others. At a meeting in Dehradun, Union Minister C Subramaniam said: 'The DMK is not disrupting India's unity. It is done by the linguistic chauvinism of Hindi speakers. Any improper and hurried action will create a fear among South Indians and disrupt in a big way the attempts to create national unity.' His statement makes it clear that Hindi fanatics are the dangerous forces that could destroy India's unity. There is a fear among intellectuals and politicians that the very language that is projected as a tool of unity will drag India's unity to the graveyard. To say that Hindi will foster unity is akin to prescribing castor oil as a remedy for dysentery.

Arguing that the Constitution is God's commandment and

it should be respected, the Hindi fanatics say: 'The Constitution has recognised Hindi as the Union government's official language. Hence, Hindi has to be accepted.' When the rules of the official language were introduced in the Constituent Assembly for discussion, no intellectual in the House hailed them as just and honest rules. Like valiant soldiers, they passionately argued against them and suggested alternatives. Speaking against Hindi, they put forth various proposals from different angles—'Make Bengali the official language,' 'Make Hindustani with Roman letters the official language', 'Let English continue as the official language,' 'If you want to choose a rich and ancient language, make Tamil the official language' and so on. They moved more than 300 amendments. They highlighted the atrocities committed by the government against non-Hindi speakers and the country at large. However, since the Assembly was dominated by one party, the Congress, Hindi alone was made the official language.

If Hindi alone is allowed to become the official language, those with Hindi as their mother tongue will become the privileged elite in the political, social and economic life of the nation. Others will become second-class citizens. Hindi supporters cannot hide this fact under any pretext. Ivor Jennings, a constitutional law expert, said that if Hindi was made the official language, Hindi speakers in the North will become dominant, just like the English speakers of today. According to him, English at least was a neutral language that could be studied by everyone equally, but Hindi will accord a privilege to some and impede others. A similar view has been expressed by the DMK leaders and many learned people who are aware of the dangers of the dominance of a particular language. It has been said often by experts on linguistic and political matters that if the language spoken by the people of one State is made the official language of the Union government, the languages and literature of the other states will never develop. That those who have Hindi as their mother tongue will get unjust advantages, and, in fact, would rule the country.

During the British rule, a few Indians who had learnt English could not compete with even mediocre Englishmen for higher official positions. All the high positions were occupied by Englishmen. A similar situation will arise if Hindi is made the official language. Non-Hindi speakers with a sharp intellect cannot compete with even a mediocre person whose mother tongue is Hindi. Hindi speakers will occupy the high positions. They will occupy not only Union government posts, but also key jobs in the states in the long run. Nehru himself has admitted that the fear of non-Hindi speakers that they would face discrimination because of Hindi's status is the fundamental reason for opposition to that language. 'Without doubt, discrimination will be there for a considerable period of time,' he said. Nehru thought that discrimination would continue only for a considerable period of time. But in reality, the discrimination will be permanent. Hindi, which is the mother tongue for a section of people, is an alien language for others.

The Official Language Commission has suggested that in the all-India competitive exams for high government posts, Hindi question papers could be translated into the languages of students in the non-Hindi-speaking regions without causing much disturbance. Such translated question papers in a simple language, it said, could be considered just 'eligibility papers.' Moreover, it said, students speaking South Indian languages need not answer one or two tough questions found in the Hindi paper. These concessions were given in view of the opposition to Hindi. But the committee says unequivocally that these are not permanent concessions and will continue only in the period of the country's transition to the official language. In course of time, when Hindi enters every department, they may say that all officials should have sufficient knowledge of Hindi to ensure efficient functioning of the departments. When this happens, non-Hindi speakers would be made to stand outside government offices waiting for the mercy of Hindi speakers—as depicted in a popular folk tale in Tamil, in which the protagonist Nandan, who, as a saint belonging to an untouchable caste, had to worship Lord Shiva from the outer precincts of the Chidambaram temple.

So, these concessions are ruses to make people accept Hindi as the official language. In a situation where Hindi is used in Indian government offices, Parliament, courts, the Union government's communications with the State and intra-State communications, Hindi speakers will become the privileged elite of the country. This will make non-Hindi speakers envious, angry and disappointed. How else would they feel after accepting a life of slavery?

For a human being, a language other than his mother tongue, and its allied languages, would be alien. Tamil is the mother tongue of Tamils. Languages like Kannada, poetic Telugu and poetic Malayalam, which branched out from Tamil, are fraternal languages. But Hindi is an alien language. Hindi is born out of a language that evolved in a culture which is completely different from the Dravidian culture. Hindi and the Dravidian languages have nothing in common in terms of script, vocabulary and literature. Just because Hindi speakers, Dravidians and Bengalis live under the same political structure, Hindi cannot become their fraternal language. Linguists do not define a fraternal language on the basis of the political unity of a country. They decide it only on the basis of the linguistic family to which a language belongs.

Will Sinhala become a fraternal language of a Sri Lankan Tamil just because Tamil and Sinhalese live under the same government? Will Malay become the fraternal language of a Malaysian Tamil? For Hindi speakers living in South Africa, Afrikaans will not become their fraternal language. Will Hindi speakers who have been granted citizenship in Britain accept English as their fraternal language? Will Arabic spoken in Arabia not be a fraternal language of Urdu speakers in India? Will a Hindustani living in England say that Hindi is not his fraternal language?

Hindi, viewed in any manner, is not a fraternal language of Dravidians and Bengalis. Hindi is more alien to Dravidians than English. In the last 200 years, English has become familiar to people from Kanyakumari to Kashmir. It has become the unremovable link language among the educated. But the status of Hindi is completely different. As far as South India is concerned, if one goes to a village and speaks or writes Hindi, people will not even know what language it is. So alien is Hindi to South Indians.

It is remarked that people who have learnt the English language of the British can also learn Hindi. This is tantamount to accepting linguistic slavery. The way people approach a language, tolerate an injustice and accept a language's dominance is completely different from the way we must deal with this issue in an independent country. People do not expect rights, linguistic security, welfare measures and privileges to be automatically granted by a government run by foreigners. They have to fight for these things. But in a free country, they expect rights and welfare measures from the government. They have the right to demand an equal share in every sector. Saying that non-Hindi speakers should remain passive in the matter of linguistic rights as they were under the British rule is tantamount to depriving them of freedom. It is an atrocity which confers all the benefits of freedom only on Hindi speakers.

The entry of English did affect the growth and distinct identity of Indian languages. But even after Independence, the despicable situation continues because of the imposition of Hindi. The first step in establishing linguistic dominance is to say Hindi will capture only the place of English, that it will not snatch away the rights of regional languages and that Hindi is opposed to English alone. Once this objective is achieved, the next step will be to suppress regional languages. This will happen 25 years later.

Unlike bodies such as the United Nations, the Commonwealth, the Southeast Asia Treaty Organisation (SEATO) and the North Atlantic Treaty Organisation (NATO), the Indian government is a sovereign institution. It has much more power, strength and revenue than the State governments. If Hindi is imposed on all its departments and offices, Hindi will become dominant in more than half of the government institutions in India.

In every State, Central government offices are more in number than State government offices. The language used in Parliament, the Supreme Court, the Central Secretariat will become the medium of instruction in colleges. It is said that the high courts' proceedings will be in regional languages. If Hindi is accepted as the national language, the State or regional language will certainly not be the medium of instruction in colleges. Hindi will encroach into these institutions too. Hindi will be made a compulsory subject in colleges initially. After a period of time, colleges with Hindi as the medium of instruction will be opened. Or, it will become the medium of instruction in some colleges.

In this situation, students aspiring for political prestige, higher social status, higher salaries and higher positions of power will ignore the provincial language and choose Hindi as the medium of instruction. This is the reason why students interested in Tamil do not wish to take up Tamil as the medium of instruction.

Those supporting Hindi will raise the following questions and force people to accept Hindi as the medium of instruction and as the language in courts in the name of national integration:

1. If all High Court proceedings are conducted in the respective provincial language—Tamil in the Madras High Court, Telugu in the Andhra Pradesh High Court and Malayalam in the Kerala High Court, for instance, what will be the language of the Supreme Court?
2. If the universities in each State choose the respective provincial language as the medium of instruction, how will it create proper relationship among academics?
3. As far as graduates are concerned, they develop their knowledge in the language they have chosen as the

> medium of instruction. If they develop their knowledge in their respective provincial languages, how can the Union government make use of their knowledge?

The government's policy is that all laws should be in Hindi. This will make Hindi pervasive in the legal and judicial institutions in every State. If the laws are enacted in Hindi, knowledge of Hindi will be essential for Assembly members to debate on these laws effectively. Those who do not know Hindi will be forced to become third class citizens even in State politics.

If Hindi is used as the medium of communication between Central and State governments, knowledge of Hindi will be compulsory for the staff working in the Secretariat of each State. This is evident from the view of the Official Language Commission which says: 'If there is a need for State government employees to communicate with their counterparts in the other states and the Union government, it will be correct to compel them to learn a new link language (Hindi).' When Hindi is used in State administrations to this extent, it is political chicanery to say the growth of provincial languages will not be impeded and that linguistic rights of the states will not be snatched away. In that situation, the provincial languages will be confined to primary schools, lower-level State government offices, shopping centres, the bhajans of the devout, kitchens and so on, as they were during the British rule.

Hindi fanatics have worked systematically to destroy provincial languages. This is evident from the fact that in the so-called Hindi-speaking states of Uttar Pradesh, Bihar, and Madhya Pradesh, the governments have been suppressing other languages. When an Assembly member sought permission to speak in Urdu, Chief Minister Govind Ballabh Pant angrily retorted, 'If you want to speak in your Urdu, go to Pakistan.' Recently, 53 Assembly members submitted a signed application seeking permission to speak in Urdu. The government refused permission and ordered them to speak in Hindi. In response to this, Parliament member AR Wadia said: 'I want to ask you openly–Urdu is the mother tongue of lakhs of Hindus in UP Yet Hindi fanatics are keen on killing Urdu. If they are ready to kill Urdu in their own State, which Indian language will they accept as the national language?'

This makes clear the Hindi supporters' attempt to kill other languages.

In the Hindi-speaking State of Bihar, the State government is suppressing Oriya and Bengali. It refuses to give grants to schools teaching these languages. It has even closed down some such schools. Even in areas where Bengali and Oriya speakers live in considerable numbers, it does not allow use of these languages even at the lowest levels of administration. The Singhbhum district has 21 per cent Oriya speakers, 18.15 per cent Bengali speakers and 14 per cent Hindi speakers. The Khortha language is spoken by 28 per cent of the State's population. But the Bihar government has ordered that people should communicate only in Hindi. Thus, Bihar proclaims that it is second only to Uttar Pradesh in driving out the other languages. It was because Hindi fanatics refused to accept Punjabi as the official language of Punjab that the State was divided into Punjab and Haryana.

With the help of the government, Hindi fanatics are trying to destroy the other languages, deny the rights of people who speak them, and refuse to respect them because of fear that the growth of the provincial languages will reduce the value of Hindi, accepting them politically will expose the weakness of Hindi and that if they are allowed to exist, Hindi's dominance will come to an end. The Central government too, has become the servant of Hindi fanatics. Refusing to help the provincial languages grow, the Centre is concentrating on developing only Hindi. Even a fool will understand the Centre's Hindi fanaticism if he looks at the number of books brought out by the Union government and the grants for the development of Hindi.

Table: Money spent by the Central government for the development of Indian languages (in lakh Rs).

Year	Fund allocated for Hindi	Money spent for Hindi	Fund allocated for other languages	Money spent for other languages
1963-64	51,91,000	50,31,000	11,30,000	6,12,000
1964-65	81,86,000	2,44,95,000	16,00,000	5,67,000
1965-66	2,07,42,000	1,70,00,000	1,20,00,000	10,00,00
Total	**3,41,19,000**	**4,65,26,000**	**1,47,30,000**	**21,79,000**

The above data confirms the Central government's step-motherly treatment of the State languages. It has spent crores of rupees for Hindi, but a meagre sum for other languages. Even that meagre amount has not been spent properly. The government has spent Rs 4,65,26,000 for Hindi which is spoken by 13 crore people. At the same time, it has spent just Rs 21,79,000 for the development of 13 provincial languages spoken by 30 crore people. If the government were to treat all the languages equally and spend money in a fair manner to develop them, it would have spent Rs 4,50,00,000 for Hindi and Rs 10,75,00,000 for other languages.

It is not only that the Centre did not help in the development of non-Hindi languages. In fact, it worked vigorously to push them down. The provisions in the 17th part of the Constitution are against the wishes of non-Hindi speakers.

In order to make Russian the common language of Russia, the Tsar suppressed other languages. His government took care to ensure those languages did not enter even the lowest levels of government departments. It banned writing or speaking in Lithuanian and sentenced the violators to death. SG Barve, member-secretary of the Official Language Commission, has said: 'I was told that the Tsar government had a policy for suppressing languages other than Russian... whatever be the adverse effects of using Russian in government, the legal institutions and higher education, there was one big benefit, which was enjoyed by the Soviet government also. The benefit was that it created a situation in which entire Russia got used to the Russian language.'

It appears that the Indian government is also working systematically to destroy provincial languages in order to create a common language.

Any self-respecting man will be outraged when he thinks of the adverse impact of compulsory Hindi on the culture and flawless traditions of the people of Dravidam and Bengal. As a result of the imposition of Hindi, interest in the mother tongue will die down and knowledge of Hindi will be considered a mark of scholarship.

A Tamil who dreamt of his language infusing every street with its fragrance will be distraught to realise that it has disappeared from his own street. Only a person who has learnt Hindi will be considered an intellectual. Only Hindi books will be on sale. All the name boards will carry Hindi words. Most of the cinemas will screen only Hindi movies. Hindi literature alone will be respected. People will also read only Hindi newspapers. Unwanted Hindi culture and the habits of Hindi speakers will get blended with the Dravidian culture and destroy it eventually. Just as the British became our lords during the British rule, turbaned Hindi speakers will become our masters. Dravidians and Bengalis will lead a life of slavery, losing their language, culture and their distinct identity. CP Ramaswami Iyer has said: 'Trying to impose Hindi in every walk of life will be an act of injustice against other sections of people. If that effort is intensified, the progress of non-Hindi speakers in the fields of literature, media and politics will be hampered.' Dravidians, who have been the guides of the world from generation to generation and are on the pinnacle of a great civilisation, would never, and should never, accept a life in which they will be like dead men alive, whose progress is halted, whose culture has degenerated and whose civilisation is ruined.

The Union government is unable to refute the reasons given by non-Hindi speakers for rejecting Hindi. Evading a direct answer to the questions raised by opponents of Hindi, it equivocates. Faced with a groundswell of opposition against Hindi imposition, the rulers have been giving promise after promise that Hindi will not be imposed on anyone. Govind Ballabh Pant, former Home Minister, has said the government is not going to impose Hindi on non-Hindi speakers. Speaking in Parliament in 1959, Prime Minister Nehru said the talk of Hindi imposition should stop: 'I will go a step further and tell non-Hindi speakers that if they do not wish to learn Hindi, they need not learn Hindi.' Addressing a meeting in Chennai's Marina on August 15, 1960, President Dr Rajendra Prasad said: 'You expect us to respect your feelings. We do respect them. We do not want to impose a single Indian language on you… We have decided not to impose Hindi on you.'

If these statements, 'Hindi is not going to be imposed', '… there is no question of imposing Hindi', '… if people do not like to learn Hindi, they need not learn it', '… we have decided not to impose Hindi on you' are true, why should they allow Hindi to continue as the official language? On whom are they going to impose Hindi? There is no need for them to impose Hindi on Hindi speakers. If they say that they are not going to impose Hindi, are they going to impose it on Americans, Germans and Russians? After inscribing Hindi as the official language in the Constitution, talking about not imposing it on anyone is political deception.

They are intensifying their efforts to establish Hindi imperialism. Hindi is embossed on coins. Hindi is printed on currency notes. The name boards of government departments are written only in Hindi. Statements, orders and notes are written in Hindi. The government has recognised Hindi Prachar Sabhas and funds them. The President and the Union Minister sign in Hindi. Laws and the government's communications are translated into Hindi. Ministers mostly speak in Hindi in Parliament. In news photographs, only Hindi is used. Hindi numerals are used on milestones and on car number plates. Hindi propagation happens relentlessly on All India Radio in the name of 'Vividh Bharati.'

The government has made Hindi a compulsory subject in high schools all over the country. Though Hindi was said to be an elective language in Tamil Nadu, the government compelled students to study it. After the DMK came to power in 1967, it implemented the two-language policy, putting an end to the teaching of Hindi in schools. Hindi has been imposed in the armed forces and the National Cadet Corps in schools. Military commands are given in Hindi. Knowledge of Hindi is made compulsory in the armed forces. It has been made compulsory for Central government employees also. Employees who have passed the Hindi exam have been given special concessions and salary hikes. Those who skip Hindi classes are punished and fined. Disciplinary action is initiated against them. Hindi has been made compulsory for some jobs. Employees are under pressure to learn Hindi because they get promotions and higher salaries if they do so. Knowledge of Hindi is compulsory for Central government recruitments.

The government's assurances on the language issue are aimed at softening anti-Hindi sentiments. There is no point trusting the rulers. Non-Hindi speakers have no option but to fight against the imposition of Hindi.

No imperial power has succeeded in establishing the dominance of one language in a multilingual country. Nor has it survived. People have succeeded in bringing down such governments. As soon as Pakistan was created, its government declared Urdu as the official language in East Pakistan. Bengali speakers in that region rose in revolt against this decision. Accusing the Hindus of East Pakistan of instigating this struggle, the Pakistan government unleased oppressive measures on the people. At a public meeting in Dhaka, Muhammad Ali Jinnah appealed to the people to accept Urdu. People in the crowd said No. Jinnah continued to urge them to accept Urdu. They refused again and shouted slogans against him. He left the meeting in a huff. But, after a week, an order from the capital Karachi said that Bengali would continue to be the official language in East Pakistan.

Estonia and Lithuania, which are smaller than Indian districts in size, were under the rule of Germans. The rulers tried their best to destroy their languages. The people of these regions held huge demonstrations against the Germans' linguistic chauvinism, braving the government's oppression. After the Second World War, these regions demanded freedom from Germany because of the latter's destruction of their language.

No community with self-respect will tolerate the destruction of its mother tongue and culture. To protect these, people will be prepared to make any sacrifice. Political unity and party discipline and oppression will not be able to put them down for long. Once their passion for language and culture intensifies, they will break party discipline, snap political links and blunt any form of oppression. They will either succeed in subduing the oppressors or sacrifice themselves in the fight for freedom.

Chapter 8

The Devanagari Script

'There is undoubtedly a Devanagari movement with which I have allied myself whole-heartedly and that is to have it as the common script for all the languages spoken in the different provinces.'[61]

—Mahatma Gandhi

Hindi fanatics are not content with enthroning their language and thus enslaving us. They have also planned to destroy the ethnicity, literature, culture, civilisation and customs of non-Hindi speakers, which are based on their respective mother tongues. Just as a disease sets in as soon as germs enter a human body, all these destructive attempts will follow once Hindi is enthroned. When that happens, any action against them will be passé, protests will not result in victory and all our reasons for opposing Hindi may not appeal to the people.

One of their plans to root out non-Hindi speakers in the subcontinent is to impose the Nagari script. They are not political greenhorns, so they will not insist on the Nagari script nor impose it with the help of the law in the present situation. They know well that if they go ahead with their plan now, even pro-Hindi states like Orissa, Bihar, Rajasthan, Maharashtra, and Gujarat will join the anti-Hindi states and reject Hindi altogether. That is why they insist on Hindi being made the official language and maintain a calculated silence on the Nagari script. They strongly believe that once they establish their official language, they will ultimately succeed in imposing the script as well.

Hindi fanatics and Congressmen do plan to replace all the scripts of other provincial languages with the Nagari script and make it compulsory to learn and teach in that script. The Congress has not said that it has given up this plan, nor has it failed to draw people's attention to it. Like the Tamil language, Hindi does not have a script of its own. It has appropriated the Sanskrit script, which is known as the Devanagari script. They call Sanskrit the language of Gods. That is why they call it Devanagari.

Gandhiji said: 'A majority of people are still illiterate. We have to keep this in mind.' In his view, imposing the scripts of different languages on people who are too lazy to think for themselves and who have wrong feelings in their hearts will be suicidal. To impose many languages on an illiterate people, you have to first impose a common script, which should be Nagari; all Indian languages should be written in that script; if you ask people to learn different scripts, it will be a waste of time and will spoil their thinking; people should accept the Nagari script as if they have no love for their own mother tongue, no regional sentiment, no interest in traditions. This is not Gandhiji's dream; this is Gandhiji's order to Congressmen[62].

So, Tamil speakers should give up the Tamil script, Telugu speakers the Telugu script, Kannadigas the Kannada script, Malayalis the Malayalam script and all of them should use the Nagari script—Hindi letters—to write in their respective mother tongues. If they give up the scripts of their mother tongue and adopt the Nagari script, what will be the fate of the mother tongue? What will happen to the literature in those languages? What will happen to the art and culture? The very thought is like a thousand spears piercing our hearts.

The various scripts with their distinct identities are like forts defending the languages. If the script of one language encroaches on the script of other languages, the latter will be destroyed first. If people learn their mother tongue through the Nagari script, their interest and ability to study their literature will be reduced. In the long run, their ability to read their own literature will disappear. It will be alien to them.

When speakers of a language lose their ability to study and develop literature, arts, history, philosophy and poetry in their mother tongue, time will wash away their language, culture and civilisation, while the literature written in the Devanagari script and the traditions associated with that literature will enslave them.

Pandit Nehru was not against the view that provincial language scripts should be replaced by a common script. Anticipating the extent of opposition to that view, he suggested that three scripts should be used to reduce the resentment:

1. 'We should try to evolve a new script by integrating the scripts of Devanagari, Bengali, Gujarati and Marathi in such a way as to be used in typewriters and other modern gadgets.'
2. 'Hindi and Urdu scripts could be integrated to create a new script which could be used in typewriters and modern gadgets.'
3. 'We should try to integrate the Devanagari script with the scripts of Southern languages. If this is not possible, we should try to find a common script for the southern languages of Tamil, Telugu, Kannada and Malayalam.'

Gandhiji did not agree because integrating the scripts of many languages would lead to turmoil. It would not be easy to learn other languages using three different scripts, as proposed by Nehru. He insisted on accepting Devanagari as the common script of all Indian languages.

When other languages are sought to be learnt through the Devanagari script alone, the literature, epics, and poetry belonging to only that script will be honoured. Only they will become popular. In short, while other languages die, Hindi will live. Gandhiji did not deny this truth and openly admitted that non-Hindi scripts will be ruined. His golden words were: 'There is no doubt that the scripts of various languages will disappear if every language is written in the script of just one language. We are making this arrangement only to enable people from different states to read and write the languages of other states. To realise this objective, we should first make Devanagari script compulsory.'

Some people may wonder whether it was Gandhiji who said this. If anyone other than Gandhiji had said this, the anti-Hindi sentiment would have snowballed into a war. Congressmen were hesitant to point out the dark spots in the divine light radiating from Gandhiji. They nodded their heads even when he said something wrong.

Those who want to impose the Devanagari script justify it by saying that it will help people to learn other languages easily and communicate with other states. The reasoning behind this is insincere. This is part of the attempt to boost Hindi religious culture and establish the idea that 'Hindi is India, and India is Hindi'. If they really believe that a common script is necessary to be able to learn other languages, they should have thought of adopting the Roman script. The Roman script with 26 letters prevails all over the world. Many developed European languages are written in this script. Modern machines like typewriters and teleprinters, which are designed to use Roman letters, are available all over the world at low cost. If Devanagari is accepted as the common script of Indian languages, people can learn only Hindi and related languages. But with the Roman script, they can learn many European languages and strengthen their relationship with the world. Supporters of Devanagari script cannot deny this fact. They evade this suggestion by arguing that only Indian scripts should be adopted, and according to them, Devanagari is the ideal choice.

Asking non-Hindi speakers to choose between Devanagari script and Roman script is tantamount to asking them whether they would like to die by drowning or by hanging. Accepting the scripts of other languages in place of the language they have known for many generations would be a suicidal move. When we look at the numbers: who all are learning other provincial languages, and which states they are communicating with using those languages, the justification proffered by Hindi supporters will be exposed as lies.

Tamil Nadu has three and a half crore people. Do all the 40-crore people of India living in other states communicate with them? Probably a few lakh people communicate with Tamils for the purpose of business, education, religion, administration and so on. Some of them may visit Tamil Nadu just for a day. They may have no reason to visit the State often. If you exclude the one-time visitors who have no reason to come to the State ever again and those who need not have a permanent relationship with Tamils, the number of Tamils who need to learn Hindi will not be even five lakhs. Will any intelligent Tamil agree to give up the script that 3.5 crore Tamils have been using for thousands of years just for the sake of these five lakh people?

The country has not had a common script so far. Have business relations not developed despite this? Have religious relationships broken down? Whoever wants to communicate with or relate to some other State will learn the language of that State. Saurashtrians living in Chennai know Tamil. Tamils living in Mumbai know Hindi and Marathi. These languages have not been imposed on anyone. They did not establish relationships with the speakers of other languages through a common script. It is wrong to say that only after learning a state's language can one communicate with and relate with that State.

Gandhi was in touch with the people of the entire subcontinent, but he did not learn the 14 important languages of the subcontinent for this purpose. He was able to relate to them through English. Kamaraj, who cannot speak or write proper English, functioned as the president of the All India Congress Committee. Not knowing a language other than the mother tongue was never an impediment in carrying out administrative functions, communicating and solving problems.

To say that learning other languages through a common script would lead to the development of new literature in all languages is to mislead the people. All language learners do not study literature. A common script is not needed to create literature. Foreign missionary scholars like Robert Caldwell and Veeramamunivar (Constantine Giuseppe Beschi) did not learn Tamil through a common script or the script of their mother tongues. They learnt Tamil through the Tamil script and adorned Mother Tamil with immortal literary works. One can understand the elegance and distinction of a language's literature only by learning it through the script of its language.

Those who study the literature of their mother tongue systematically for years together do not necessarily create literary works. Two thousand years ago, Thiruvalluvar and Ilango Adigal created immortal literary works. Geniuses like Kambar, Sekkizhar and Seyankondar adorned the Tamil literary world a thousand years ago. So far, no one with similar talent has appeared in Tamil Nadu. There has been no great poet in Sanskrit after Valmiki. No Awadhi poet of eminence has appeared after Tulsidas. In Bengali, there has been no greater poet than Rabindranath Tagore.

Similarly, Marathi has not seen a writer like Dnyaneshwar so far. There has not been another literary genius like Surdas in Braj, Guru Nanak in Punjabi, Vidyapati in Maithili, Sankardeva in Assamese, Sarala Das in Oriya, and Narsinh Mehta in Gujarati. They are the emperors of the literary world. But they did not create immortal literary works just because they knew their language. They had extraordinary talent, deep knowledge, imagination and creativity, which they expressed through their language. Will a common script be enough to produce such geniuses?

President S Radhakrishnan said: 'The Devanagari script is used in Sanskrit, Hindi, Marathi and Nepali languages. The Nagari script as it exists today does not have the vowels 'e' and 'o'. The sound 'va' used in Marathi, Tamil and Telugu is not found in the Devanagari script. The Tamil letter sounding 'zha' is in the name Dravidar Kazhagam. The heavy consonant 'R' is not in use in Devanagari.' The Central government created the facility for writing telegrams in the Devanagari script in some states. But people did not come forward to make use of it. It is this defective Devanagari that Hindi supporters are eager to impose on the population.

We oppose the Nagari script not because it is defective. Even if it was perfect, we would oppose unto our last breath the proposal to make it the common script.'

Hindi fanatics and the Congress are waiting for an opportune moment to impose the Devanagari script. Leaders like Gandhiji were eager to bring the change during the freedom movement itself. Gandhiji had said that they should make use of the national awakening to create a common script for the entire country. Why did Gandhiji make such an appeal at a time when the people of India had risen up in revolt against the British, whom they denounced as 'whites', 'aliens' and 'firangis'? It is because he thought that people would not pay much attention to the issue in such politically turbulent times. But the strong resentment of the Muslims, communal riots and religious turmoil put the brakes on the common language issue. Hindi supporters did not find the right opportunity to prioritise the common script issue. However, it is wrong to assume that they have given up the plan just because they could not implement it fully then. The day we accept a common script, we will be in danger of accepting a common language.

The speeches of nationalist leaders on the language issue make it clear that the desire still lies dormant in their hearts. Addressing a literary meeting in Hyderabad on August 7, 1957, Dr Rajendra Prasad, former President of India, said: 'We know that other languages could be learnt through the Devanagari script. If we write the provincial languages in Devanagari script, we can learn the language well. When this comes into practice, that will be a great day.'

In his view, the day we put an end to famine, scarcity, and poverty is not a great day; it will be a great day only when people accept a common script. No other proof is needed to prove Prasad's eagerness to impose the Devanagari script. As if to prove he is not inferior to Prasad on the language issue, Dr Radhakrishnan said: 'When the Nagari script is accepted in non-Hindi-speaking regions, those letters will be introduced to people living in those regions. They can adopt this script for their languages. There should not be any compulsion in this matter. The choice should be voluntary.'

Hindi supporters think that Hindi and its script will spread among the educated sections of the country if it is made the official language. It will be made compulsory in colleges and schools and government exams and will become necessary for departmental promotions. This will increase incomes, which will enrich Indians. A section of such beneficiaries will move to non-Hindi-speaking regions. Once Hindi is perceived as the source of college degrees and a good life, the voice of those who oppose the Nagari script will be weakened.

Therefore, we cannot be complacent and assume that the Indian government will never order that all provincial languages should be written in Devanagari.

Chapter 9
Three Language Formula

> *'Mother tongue education and English should be made compulsory. Where necessary, any other language mentioned in the Eighth Schedule could be made an elective subject.'*
>
> —Sir CV Raman

Though the teaching of Hindi across the country was part of a long-standing system, it was crystallised into a policy in an official document only in 1968 with the National Policy on Education. This document said that regional languages were already in use as the media of education in the primary and secondary stages of schooling. In addition, it said, 'At the secondary stage, state governments should adopt and vigorously implement the three-language formula, which includes the study of a modern Indian language, preferably one of the Southern languages, apart from Hindi and English in the Hindi-speaking states.' This encapsulated the National Education Policy's critical prescription of three languages to be taught at the secondary level: Hindi, English and the language of the respective states. Accordingly, in the non-Hindi-speaking states, the 1968 policy prescribed that Hindi should be studied along with the State language and English. It added: 'Suitable courses in Hindi and/or English should also be available in universities and colleges with a view to improving the proficiency of students in these languages up to the prescribed university standards.' This document said that the establishment, in non-Hindi states, of colleges and other institutions of higher education that use Hindi as the medium of education should be encouraged. It said every effort should be made to promote the Hindi language and that 'in developing Hindi as the link language, due care should be taken to ensure that it will serve, as provided for in Article 351 of the Constitution, as a medium of expression for all the elements of the composite culture of India.

The three-language formula is part of a conspiracy to sweet-talk Dravidians and Bengalis into accepting Hindi. The Centre's Official Language Commission created this formula and ordered the State governments to follow it. Students whose mother tongue is Hindi acquired education through only two languages—their mother tongue and English. But students with other languages as their mother tongue were ordered by this policy to learn Hindi compulsorily, projecting it as the national or official language. Non-Hindi-speaking states did not accept this wholeheartedly.

If one section of people is compelled to learn three languages while another section learns only two languages, it puts the former at a disadvantage. If one part of their study time is devoted to learning Hindi, their concentration on other subjects will decrease. It will bring down their educational standards, decrease their opportunities to develop knowledge and lead to other problems. The Union government formulated the three-language formula without considering these issues.

Under the three-language formula, those with Hindi as their mother tongue will have to learn Hindi, English and a language other than their mother tongue listed in the Eighth Schedule of the Constitution. Students whose mother tongue is not Hindi will have to learn their mother tongue, English and Hindi. To take a stand on the issue, the Madras government convened a meeting of all political parties represented in the State Assembly. Arignar Anna participated in the meeting on behalf of the DMK.

The meeting altered the three-language formula for students of non-Hindi-speaking states, suggesting that they should learn their mother tongue, English and any language that is not their mother tongue. As far as the Tamil Nadu government was concerned, this was the three-language formula. Under this scheme, learning Hindi is not compulsory. A student can learn it only if he/she wishes to. A student who does not want to learn Hindi can learn Telugu or Malayalam or any other Indian language.

In a note sent to the Official Language Commission, the Tamil Nadu government explained its position thus: 'The Language Commission wishes to make Hindi a compulsory language in the three-language formula. The Tamil Nadu government does not accept this proposal. As per the decision of the Tamil Nadu Assembly, a student has the option not to learn Hindi. If he/she wants, he can learn a North Indian language or Urdu or any other Indian language.'

Although Hindi is an elective subject in the non-Hindi-speaking states under the three-language formula, it was made compulsory in practice. Hindi teachers have been appointed in all schools. Students are compelled to learn Hindi from the 9th standard onwards. Under the formula, a student has the right to learn a language other than Hindi. But no student is allowed to learn a non-Hindi language. How many schools teach Telugu instead of Hindi? How many schools teach Malayalam, and how many students learn it? All the students are compelled to learn Hindi.

The members of the DMK often spoke against this injustice perpetrated in the name of the three-language formula. In response, the Chief Minister's refrain is: 'There is no question of imposing Hindi. Students learn Hindi of their own volition.'

There cannot be a greater lie in the world. And none other than the Chief Minister would dare to utter it.

Students of Tamil organised demonstrations and picketing

programmes against Hindi, burnt Hindi books, committed self-immolation and fell to the police force's bullets in their fight against the imposition of Hindi. This being the truth, stating that students are learning Hindi voluntarily is an unconscionable lie.

In deference to the wishes of the Union government and Hindi fanatics, the governments of Tamil Nadu and other non-Hindi-speaking states have imposed Hindi on students in the name of the three-language formula. But they do not follow even the basics of this formula in the Hindi-speaking states. They teach only Hindi and English. To deceive the non-Hindi-speaking states, they tepidly teach a North Indian language as the third language.

Sanskrit is the mother of Hindi. Both have the same script and grammar. If you remove Sanskrit words from Hindi, it loses its life and limbs. This being the situation, teaching this hybrid language as the third language is incorrect. One cannot understand the Dravidian culture and its rich language through Sanskrit. Nor will it help strengthen the ties among the people of the South. Hence, the basic objective of national integration will be defeated. Non-Hindi speakers are unconcerned about this problem.

The keenness they show in making Hindi compulsory in the non-Hindi-speaking states is absent when making a Southern language compulsory for North Indians. The Official Language Commission, which suggests that Hindi should be learnt at least for three or four years before the age of 14, does not compel Hindi-speaking students to learn any South Indian language.

The statement of the Official Language Commission says: 'When a Hindi-speaking student will not benefit much by learning another Indian language, it seems unfair to compel him to learn that language. In this situation, this problem can be solved amicably by making arrangements in Hindi-speaking areas to teach other languages and persuading people in those areas to benefit from these arrangements.'

The Commission, which emphatically says there is no need

for Hindi speakers to learn South Indian languages, and it is neither compulsory nor essential, is equally emphatic that it is not sufficient to just facilitate the learning of Hindi and that it should be compulsory. This stance exposes the extent of Hindi chauvinism.

In a country whose literacy rate is a pathetic 20 per cent, compelling students to learn three languages is like shifting the burden carried by an elephant onto the back of a cow's calf. Many illiterate parents can't even identify the letters of their own mother tongue. We should realise that 95 per cent of our students do not have proper knowledge of our own literature. In such a grim situation, it is difficult for them to learn three languages. And it will not yield any benefit in practice.

It is true that European students learn three languages. But their situation is completely different from that of Indian students. Most of the European languages belong to the same linguistic family. Their scripts, too, are similar, and grammar does not differ much. It is clear that such a situation does not exist in India.

One should understand the difficulties a student in Tamil Nadu faces learning Tamil, English, and Hindi. These languages belong to three different linguistic groups. Their scripts and grammar are completely different. Their etymology, history, and cultural background are different. In such a situation, to compel a student whose mother tongue is Tamil to learn another alien language is to ruin his knowledge and stunt his development.

Helen Smith Cairns, a renowned psycholinguist, says that if a two-language formula is to be implemented in a country, those languages should be from the same linguistic family and that the country should have the same cultural background. If this is true of a two-language formula, we need not explain how useless and unnecessary our three-language formula is, with completely different scripts, grammar and cultural settings.

It is not only that the three-language formula is troublesome and ruins the knowledge of our students; there is no benefit whatsoever in learning Hindi. If the time and effort wasted on learning Hindi is spent on studying the mother tongue and English, it will be more beneficial.

An alien language can never give the kind of satisfaction that the mother tongue gives an individual. In the Indian sub-continent, the knowledge and benefits a non-Hindi speaker derives from English cannot be gained by learning Hindi. If English is milk, Hindi is buttermilk. Buttermilk can be made from milk. But milk cannot be made from buttermilk. Learning English can give you the kind of benefits Hindi may give. But in India, Hindi cannot provide the kind of knowledge and benefits English can. It was for these reasons that many educationists opposed the three-language formula and suggested that it was sufficient for a student to learn the mother tongue and English under the two-language formula.

P Kodanda Rao, a socio-political activist from Karnataka, explained this clearly when he said: 'The Indian government and State Chief Ministers support the three-language formula. English, Hindi and the regional languages have three different scripts. They think these should be learnt. It is difficult to do this. The two-language formula, consisting of English and a provincial language, is easier to implement. Moreover, the two-language formula can achieve what the three-language formula can, without much difficulty.'

The three-language formula as it exists today does not make Hindi compulsory in non-Hindi-speaking states. This fact troubles Hindi chauvinists. Under that formula, people of Hindi-speaking states need not learn a South Indian language. This troubles some people in the Southern states. Under the pretext of satisfying these two sections, the Congress Working Committee decided at its meeting in June 1966 to intensify the implementation of the three-language formula. According to this decision, Hindi will be compulsory in non-Hindi-speaking states, and people in these states should learn their provincial language, English and Hindi. And, in the Congress' view, people of Hindi-speaking states should learn Hindi, English and any other modern Indian language.

This was not a decision aimed at making the people of Hindi-speaking states learn South Indian languages. The objective of this new language policy is to make Hindi compulsory across India. In doing this, the Congress has openly declared and strengthened Hindi's implicit dominance in the old three-language formula.

What is implied in this decision is: 31 crore non-Hindi speakers should learn Hindi, but 12 crore Hindi speakers will learn any one of the remaining 13 national languages; people of Uttar Pradesh can learn Bengali; one can study Marathi in Rajasthan; people of Madhya Pradesh may learn Gujarati; so Hindi speakers will learn our languages in parts; but all of us should learn their language fully.

Thus, the new language policy formulated by the Congress was nothing but a new stamp of approval for Hindi's dominance. Anna strongly condemned the injustice being meted out to non-Hindi speakers in the name of the three-language formula. A conference held on behalf of the Official Language Commission in Calcutta to condemn the three-language formula passed the following resolution: 'We oppose the three-language formula implemented in schools and colleges. Only the mother tongue and English should be compulsory. Wherever possible, any one language mentioned in the Eighth Schedule can be taught.' Among the participants who expressed their opposition to this formula were Suniti Kumar Chatterji, an outstanding educationist; Roy Harendranath Choudhury, former Education Minister of West Bengal; Prof Nirmal Chandra Bhattacharya, a member of the Bengal Legislative Assembly; Jayapal Kumar Gupta, retired Indian Civil Service officer; Dr BC Chakravarti, principal of the Jadavpur Medical College; Jadavpur University's Prof KN Mazumdar; and educationists Kiren Kumar Sanyal and KK Sinha.

However, Home Minister GL Nanda introduced in Parliament the three-language formula approved by the Congress even after the condemnations voiced by the leaders of the DMK, the sole representative of Dravidians in the language issue, and the scholars of Bengal. This move served to strengthen the position of Hindi chauvinists. The parliamentary resolution on this issue clearly says that the imposition of Hindi is the sole objective of the three-language formula. Although it says that Hindi speakers can learn any one of the modern languages, it is only a ruse to make non-Hindi speakers the victims of the three-language formula. We don't want to compel them to learn our language. Similarly, we don't want to be forced to learn their language. Saying 'You learn my language, and I'll learn your language' is a political deception. In practice, Hindi speakers will never learn any other Indian language. And no situation will arise that will make them learn those languages compulsorily.

As decided by the DMK and the Official Language Commission, it is enough to learn the mother tongue and English compulsorily. Learning a third language should not be made mandatory. If a student wishes to learn an Indian language as the third language, we can facilitate that. This will be useful to students who live in the border areas and in cities.

In every State, some areas contiguous to another State have two dialects. In such places, another dialect can be taught as an elective third language. Since students in those areas have opportunities to speak, write and learn another language, it will be easy to teach that language. For instance, in Kanyakumari district, which is contiguous to Kerala, it will be useful to teach Malayalam as the third elective language. Similarly, Kannada and Telugu may be taught in the North Arcot district, which borders the states of Karnataka and Andhra Pradesh.

A third language will be of use to students in cities. For instance, Telugu will be useful for Tamil students and Tamil for

Telugu students; in Bombay, Gujarati will be useful for Marathi students and vice versa; in Bangalore, Kannada students will find Tamil useful and vice versa.

Instead of formulating the three-language issue in this way, it was a sin for the Congress to formulate a policy that makes Hindi compulsory and for Parliament to accept it, dismissing the opposition of students and the public and rejecting their fair arguments. It was not only a green signal for Hindi imperialism but also a dangerous move to turn India into a bloody battlefield.

Chapter 10

The Importance of English

'Removing English and imposing Hindi is tantamount to axing the roots of our progress and unity.'

—Rajaji

Rajaji is a prominent figure among those who want English to continue as the official language of the Indian subcontinent. The explanation he gives, the evidence he cites and the truth he expresses based on his experiences appeal even to Hindi fanatics. Unable to reply to the questions he poses, the government fumbles. Hindi supporters are stunned. He has been fighting the ideological war with unrelenting determination.

It is wrong to think that English struck root in the Indian subcontinent only because of the British rule that lasted about 150 years. Social reformers who wanted to transform India's social structure realised the importance of English and demanded that Indians be taught English. Raja Ram Mohan Roy, an outstanding social reformer, requested Lord William Amherst, the governor-general of India, to make it compulsory for Indians to learn English.

As imperialism expanded, the British government was forced to introduce English, a language that entered India on the request of some Indians, in its administration. During the rule of Lord William Bentick, English was given the status of the government's administrative language. The British, who wanted to rule India permanently, introduced English in all sections of the administration. It was Lord Macaulay who made English an integral part of Indian life by introducing English as the only medium of instruction.

We cannot find a solution to the language issue by ignoring the reasons proffered by those who want English to be the official language permanently. Although their reasons appear to stray a bit from the truth, we cannot forget that they are based on experience.

These are the reasons they cite:

1. As English has been used in every department of the government and in communications with foreign countries since the advent of the British government, imposing an Indian language or Indian languages in the administration will disrupt and distort its uniformity, unity, and clarity, which were brought about by the use of English. Will a new language in the administration give the same benefits in a short time that using one language for over a hundred years has given us? Dethroning English is like searching for ghee after selling the butter in one's hand.
2. Our thinking will not be enriched unless we study and understand English, which is among the most developed languages in the world. If we remove English, the best gateway to knowledge, the source of innovations and the stepping stone to progress, no Indian language that replaces it can bring the rare benefits that English has yielded.
3. English remains a factor in India's unity and the lifeblood of its integration. Its removal will shake the foundations of the country. If the unity created by English is disrupted by its removal, it will not be a loss for English; it will be India's loss.

4. Accepting one Indian language as the official language will trigger linguistic conflicts in an India which is home to many languages that are spoken by a considerable number of people. When one section of people, who were living as equal citizens with other sections, tries to become rulers and enslave others, speakers of other language will not be mute spectators. The country will be beset with increasing chauvinism and linguistic wars. To save the country from such dangerous consequences, English, which exists as a neutral language, should be allowed to be the sole official language.
5. English is not the mother tongue of the people of India, except for a few lakh Anglo-Indians. The difficulty in learning English is common to all. But it will benefit everyone without discrimination. It is true to say that only English will keep the scales even between all languages of India.

Those who demand that English must be the official language do not share one common objective. They can be classified into three groups. 1. Those who support English for its potential and uses 2. Those who support English only as an equal or secondary official language 3. Those who support English lest Hindi is imposed.

The first group does not discriminate between their own language and an alien language. They wholeheartedly believe in the importance and use of English. They also strongly believe that no Indian language can produce treasures of knowledge and bring about progress the way English has done. They also believe that the removal of English will forever close the doors of the world of knowledge and push India into an age of darkness. They hold that India's internal unity, administrative coherence, excellence, industrial progress and scientific development are the results of how the country has been using English.

The second group argues that it is prestigious to have one Indian language, especially Hindi, as the official language of the country. However, as Hindi has not developed enough to be the official language, they want English as the second official language. They don't support the idea of English being retained as the official language forever. They consider it a stopgap arrangement. They think by accepting both Hindi and English as official languages, the country's prestige will be retained, and it will not lose the benefit of English. In the context of increasing language agitations, adopting this two-language formula is the only solution.

Most of the people in the third group oppose Hindi's dominance. When the problem of removing English and installing an Indian language as the official language arose, the Congress promoted the idea that Hindi alone qualifies for that status. If any Indian language is to be the official language, Tamil or Telugu or Malayalam will not be allowed to take that place. This group knows it very well. So, to prevent Hindi from being imposed as the official language, they project English instead of demanding that Tamil or Telugu be made the official language. This, they believe, will help protect the interest of the 30 crore non-Hindi speakers. They have no love for English. Nor do they accept that an Indian language cannot give the benefits that English can. They love their mother tongue and demand a due place for their language in the administration. Most anti-Hindi agitators belong to this group.

It is essential to understand the reasons given by people who oppose Hindi and who are determined to dethrone English from the official language status, as they see it as a matter of shame for independent India to continue using the language of their colonisers.

The Congress, which succeeded in instigating people in every field to rebel against the British, together with Hindi fanatics, have added some strength to their argument that English is the alien language of those who enslaved us for nearly 150 years. Many people hated English not because it was defective, but because they hated the British. N Madhava Rao, who was a member of the Drafting Committee of the Constitution, said: 'The objection to English because it is an alien language was the result of the hostility created towards anything British before Independence.'

Hindi fanatics believe that if their hate campaign against English succeeds, it will be advantageous for Hindi.

It is true that English was not born on Indian soil. But Hindi fanatics do not realise that if they brand English as an alien language because it was not born in India, even some recognised Indian languages might be pushed to the status of foreign languages. Urdu came from Persia. We have recognised it by including it in the Eighth Schedule of the Constitution. The original language of Aryans is Sanskrit. They migrated from Central Asia and settled in the plains of the Indus and the Ganges. It was from Central Asia that Sanskrit came to India. Hence, Sanskrit may also be branded as an alien language. Sanskrit entered India 4,000 years ago. It is 1,000 years since Urdu came to India. It is 200 years in the case of English. Though they came at different times, there is no denying that they came from outside the country. According to the view of Hindi fanatics, all these are foreign languages. But learned people with a clear mind would not accept this. A language is defined as alien, not based on its origins; it depends on the extent of its spread and links among the people. Sanskrit has mixed with many Indian languages. It is the basis of the culture in North India. It remains the guardian of the Northern culture, contributing many immortal literary works to it. Owing to the long rule of the Mughal kings, Urdu took root in India. A lot of Urdu words are found in Hindi, Hindustani, Punjabi and Rajasthani. Urdu is the mother tongue of about five crore Muslims living in India. After proudly accepting Sanskrit and Urdu as Indian languages, branding English alone as a foreign language is odd.

English is the mother tongue of Anglo-Indians living in India. After conferring on them civic rights without discrimination, it is meaningless to call their mother tongue an alien language. In 1956, Nehru said in Parliament that English should have been incorporated into the Eighth Schedule of the Constitution because many people spoke that language and it is the mother tongue of Anglo-Indians. KM Munshi said English was an Indian language because it had been adopted by Indians. Defence Minister YB Chavan said that English was an Indian language, not a foreign language. Hindi fanatics do not have the kind of positive view that even the ruling party's great leaders had.

It is irrelevant and meaningless to argue that allowing English to be the official language is a matter of shame. We have adopted the political norms of the English, accepted their legal processes and used their inventions. We have even become the servants of their fake culture. We are part of the Commonwealth headed by them. We go to them with a begging bowl, asking for loans. It is not clear why people who do not consider all these as matters of shame believe that accepting English as the official language is shameful.

It is a vicious campaign to say that the English-educated live as a separate class at the top of the social structure. All those who are atop the social structure are not English-educated. English is not the only tool that catapulted them to higher positions. Are the lakhs of English-educated people in Kerala in high positions? Are there not people who are at the lower stratum of society even after getting an English education? In the current situation of increasing unemployment, how can they live as a separate class? Among the educated sections, English has removed social conflicts and caste atrocities to a large extent and made them relate to each other like brothers and sisters. Even the Tamil Nadu government has said that English has entered the domains of the speakers of each national language and broken down the caste barriers and sentiments among the intelligentsia. In short, English has helped the educated sections to become cultured and civilised. Their caste and religious relations and cultural ties have not snapped. Their social relationships have become strong. However, it is wrong to say they live as a separate class that is above other sections of society.

It is foolish to say that allowing English to be the official language is shameful or to say that learning English is an act of betrayal. It is meaningless to call English an alien language. The allegation that the English-educated live as a separate class is baseless. Yet, democrats, custodians of culture and those who love their mother tongue do not want the continuation of English as the official language. Let us analyse why: In the Indian subcontinent with 44 crore people, only 1,10,00,000 (one crore and ten lakhs) know English. For most of them, English is a second language. Allowing a language spoken by a minority to be the official language is like erecting a wall between the administration and the people. Since legislative and judicial proceedings and foreign relations are conducted in English, they are very clear and nuanced. But the common people do not approach these institutions easily and, where required, seek the help of the English-educated. If the administration is conducted in the language known to the people, it will benefit them. An applicant does not know what action has been taken by an official on their application. Voters do not know what the legislator elected by them spoke in the legislature. Taxpayers do not know what the government's plans for them are. The plaintiff and the defendant do not understand what their respective lawyers argue in courts.

There is a huge gap between the administration and the common people. English can never fill this gap. Is it possible for 43 crore people to learn English so that they can understand the functioning of the administration run by a few lakh people? An administration does not exist for its own sake. If the administration functions as a mysterious entity beyond the comprehension of the people, it cannot be called the people's administration. Allowing a language spoken by a very small minority to be the official language in a democracy guided by the principle that 'everything is for the people' will not benefit either the people or the cause of democracy.

The cultures of the Indian subcontinent are distorted by the dominance of English. People's love for English should be curbed to save these cultures. There is truth in the question raised by some people whether India has a distinct culture and whether the country has the same cultural basis from Kashmir to Kanyakumari. Basically, India does not have a uniform culture, a civilisation, a language or similar customs and practices. But various distinct cultures shine bright across the country. It is an undeniable fact that these have been harmed by English.

The common people do not know much about the great heroes, emperors, literary geniuses, reformers of Mother India. But they know such details about England. Divorces, ostentatious lifestyles and unethical behaviour are imports of English culture. If we analyse how these factors have disrupted our culture, we can easily understand the dangers of English dominance. If we don't blunt the language which is the source of cultural invasion, we cannot protect our culture.

A majority of people are unwilling to accept English as the permanent official language. We cannot create a love for English among people who have lived for 150 years cursing the British. There is no sign whatsoever that people who oppose English will have a change of heart and accept that language. Their growing love for the mother tongue has reduced their passion for other languages. There is a growing sentiment that only their language should rule the country. In this situation, English can never be the permanent official language of the subcontinent. Its continuation as the official language is unnecessary and madness. A time will surely come when it must be brought down from that status. But it is foolish to dethrone it in a hurry.

It is one thing to accept English as the official language, but understanding its benefits and giving importance to it is a different matter altogether. It is essential to protect it on Indian soil, but not as the official language. Gandhi said: 'I don't hate English. I myself have benefited from the literary treasures of English. We should acquire the treasures of knowledge, such as science, through English. Hence, English is essential for us.'

English alone will help us to acquire knowledge of the rare principles of science, industry, physics, chemistry, astronomy, nuclear power and space travel. As far as Indians are concerned, they cannot climb the stairs of the world of knowledge without the help of English. We can access the literary treasures of different languages in the world through English. The London Museum has a collection of 45 lakh books. The Library of Congress in Washington has a collection of 50 lakh books. The Biblical National Library of Paris has a collection of 40 lakh books. Over half of these books are in English. No other language in the world has such literary treasures.

Many countries in the world have realised the importance of English. Even the worst enemies of Britain have not refrained from teaching English. SN Moos, Representative of the Government of Mumbai, said that no country in the world has ever banned the teaching of English.

English is being taught in France since 1918. After the Second World War, it is taught in Scandinavian countries, Turkey, and Greece. Countries like Italy, Spain and Portugal have shifted from French to English. In all the West Asian countries, English is taught. In Russia, 40 per cent of students learn English. Many students in Poland and Czechoslovakia learn English. In Japan, English is the second language. In Egypt, English is a compulsory subject. In Sweden and Germany, English is a compulsory subject in middle schools. But none of these countries have accepted English as the official language. They have accepted only their mother tongue as the official language.

The government should use English without losing its benefits. Let English be the key to treasures of knowledge. Let it not become the dictatorial ruler of the country.

Chapter 11

The Official Language Commission and the Parliamentary Committee

> *'I think the entire report has nothing to show that any effort has been taken to know, understand and sympathise with non-Hindi-speaking people. The fact that India is a polyglot country where people are passionately proud of their own language is ignored.'*
>
> —Dr P Subbarayan[63]

Dr P Subbarayan's view truly reflected the limited extent to which the Official Language Commission understood and respected the sentiments of non-Hindi-speaking people. The commission neither understood their sentiments nor tried to ascertain their views. It refused to acknowledge their limitless love and affection for their mother tongue. It ignored the immortality of literature and the unparalleled glory of epics. Its attitude was based on the idea that only Hindi speakers love their language.

The commission prepared its report in the belief that expressing views against Hindi, exposing the weaknesses of the language, and trying to understand the real nature of Hindi were acts of sedition. It betrayed non-Hindi-speaking people by ascertaining and reporting their views according to its own wishes. If the commission's report is analysed, it becomes clear that Dr Subbarayan was polite in condemning it and that the commission acted as an errand boy of Hindi imperialism.

The Official Language Commission was constituted by the President of India on June 7, 1955, under the chairmanship of BG Kher. It had 21 members, including the chairman and eminent personalities, such as Dr SK Chatterji and Dr P Subbarayan. The President did not constitute the commission to understand the sentiments of non-Hindi-speaking people and make recommendations accordingly. The real idea was to drive away English and find ways to establish the dominance of Hindi at the earliest.

The Commission's terms of reference were:

2) (a) the progressive use of Hindi language for official purposes of the Union; (b) restrictions on use of English language for all or any of the official purposes of the Union; (c) the language to be used for all or any of the purposes mentioned in Article 348 of the Constitution; (d) the form of numerals to be used for any one or more specified purposes of the Union; (e) the preparation of a time schedule according to which, and the manner in which, Hindi may gradually replace English as the official language of the Union and as a language for communication between the Union and State governments and between one State government and another.

These were the areas for which the commission was mandated to suggest recommendations. It did not have the power to recommend that English should not be removed in phases and that Hindi should not be imposed.

Article 344 (3) of the Constitution mandates the commission to focus on two important issues while making its recommendations:

1. It should pay special attention to the interests and just demands of non-Hindi-speaking people.
2. It should consider the industrial, cultural and scientific developments in the Indian subcontinent.

However, the commission showed no interest in these areas. It was keen on finding out in which departments Hindi could be imposed and did not show the same level of interest in protecting the interests and fair demands of non-Hindi-speaking people. In its frenzy to remove English as the official language, it paid no attention to discovering how developments in science and industry could be accessed without English. Its enthusiasm dried up when it came to the development of languages such as Tamil, Telugu, Malayalam, Kannada, and Bengali.

The methods adopted by the commission (dominated by Hindi fanatics and puppets of the ruling party) to ascertain popular opinion exposed its irresponsible attitude and linguistic chauvinism. It prepared a questionnaire and sent it to officials of State governments, judges and some public institutions. It received only 1,094 written responses and 930 oral submissions. It was an act of arrogance to decide on an issue affecting the lives of 40 crore people based on the opinions of such a small sample. The States Reorganisation Commission led by S Fazl Ali collected the views of 1,52,250 people. It also received 2,000 petitions. But the Official Language Commission prepared its report based on the opinions of just 2,024 people.

When the Congress supported Hindi, it was senseless to expect the State governments led by it to go against Hindi. How could one expect officials drawing salaries from these governments to express an opinion that goes against the government's view? Similarly, the principals of educational institutions dependent on State government grants were not ideologically committed enough to express their views in a frank manner.

Had the Official Language Commission really wished to ascertain the views of the people, it should have sought opinions from movements and groups that had raised the banner of revolt against Hindi imposition. Did it seek the opinion of the DMK, which had been fighting against Hindi imposition since 1938? Did it contact the Dravidar Kazhagam, which had also been against Hindi imposition? It was not that it simply did not seek their opinions; the commission completely ignored these movements.

It sought the opinions of supporters of English, who philosophised from their armchairs without launching any agitation in support of their stand on the language issue. It did not seek the views of anyone other than the supporters of Hindi and English but based its report only on the views of Hindi supporters. 'All the views contained in this report are the views of Hindi speakers alone. Only the Hindi-speaking population will benefit from the report. In the entire report, there is no hint of even a small effort to ascertain the opinions of non-Hindi-speaking people,' said Dr Suniti Kumar Chatterji[64].

Since the Congress party wished to enforce discipline within the party on the language issue, its State governments, lacking the courage to raise their voice against Hindi imperialism, were content with supporting the continuation of English as the official language even after 1965. The commission refused to accept even this beggarly demand.

Dr Subbarayan, himself a member of the commission, said: 'The respondents from West Bengal, including government representatives, had strongly voiced their opinion against the imposition of Hindi. Similarly, the respondents in Chennai, including the Chief Minister, expressed their opposition. After saying initially that English could continue even after 1965, the government, in a subsequent letter, said that it would welcome an amendment to the Constitution in this regard.'

The recommendations of the Official Language Commission served to enslave non-Hindi-speaking people. Although Hindi fanatics such as PT Tandon, Seth Govind Das and Dr Raghu Vira[65] were not part of the Commission, their spectres seem to have participated in it fully. The norms set by the commission were heart-rending; its explanations made us shed tears of blood, and its recommendations were like death blows to us.

One of the recommendations that would ruin the independent lives of non-Hindi-speaking people was that a method should be evolved to achieve uniformity between the Union's language and the states' languages in the use of scientific and technological terms. The implication here was that Hindi technical terms should be adopted by the state languages also.

Here is a summary of some of the important recommendations of the commission:

- The entire statute book of the country should be in one language, which cannot, of course, be other than Hindi. Therefore, the language of legislation of the states as well as of Parliament and consequently the language of all statutory orders, rules etc. issued under any law should be the Hindi language.
- The machines (such as typewriters) needed for communicating in Hindi should be produced soon.
- If the policy of making Hindi optional for government servants does not yield necessary results, a deadline could be set for them to learn Hindi.
- Penalties could be imposed on government servants if they fail to attain or learn the prescribed standard of Hindi by the deadline.
- While recruitment is done for public services, it is not wrong to expect the applicants to be as proficient in Hindi as they are in English.
- Since most of the work at the Central Secretariat of the Union government is carried out in Hindi, the staff should be well versed in Hindi.
- Learning Hindi can be made compulsory for those State government employees who are required to communicate with either the Union government or other State governments.

- As far as the Union government is concerned, Devanagari numerals should be used, and where necessary, international numerals should also be used.
- Since the laws enacted by the Union government and the State governments must be in the same language, standard orders and rules should be in Hindi.
- When the time is conducive for linguistic transitions, the Supreme Court should conduct its proceedings only in Hindi.
- When the time is conducive for linguistic transition, High Court judgments and orders should be in Hindi; facilities should be established for transition and translations.
- The Union government should immediately publish in Hindi the law books of the Union and the states.
- Considering the language requirements of aspirants for all-India services and central institutions, we deem it fit to prepare public service commission exam questions in Hindi.
- We also recommend that as part of its effort to propagate Hindi, the Union government should give liberal financial assistance to institutions teaching Hindi so that they can expand their operations.

When the consequences of these recommendations are understood, our hearts break. Guns, bombs and cannons are not needed to destroy the lives of non-Hindi-speaking people. Such recommendations did the job. At a time when people prepared to enjoy the fruits of their freedom from British imperialism, the Official Language Commission conspired to make them slaves to another imperialism. It created a terrible situation in which freedom was only for Hindi-speaking people.

The commission submitted its report to the President on July 31, 1956. Article 344 (4) of the Constitution laid down that a Parliamentary Committee should be formed to review and give its opinion on the report of the Official Language Commission. Accordingly, a Parliamentary Committee comprising 20 Lok Sabha members and 10 Rajya Sabha members was constituted five years after the formation of the Official Language Commission. GB Pant was its chairman. Although this committee was constituted democratically, the methods it adopted to study the language issue reflected a dictatorial attitude.

The Parliamentary Committee did not come forward to honestly assess the new situation in which anti-Hindi sentiments were growing by the day in non-Hindi-speaking states, and new demands were being raised. It refused to seek the opinion of even the State governments, officials, linguists, educationists, and judges. It only reviewed the report of the Official Language Commission. In its meetings, the Congress party's discipline was enforced. All the meetings were held in secret, keeping out journalists and people interested in the language issue. It functioned behind closed doors in the manner of conspirators planning to topple a government. The committee appeared to be scared that their plan to create a new imperialism would be defeated if people came to know of it.

In his dissent note in the Constituent Assembly, Frank Anthony, a representative of the Anglo-Indian community, said that the biggest shortcoming of the Parliamentary Committee was its refusal to find new evidence, keeping in mind the major changes that had taken place in the country. It refused to acknowledge the growing opposition to the imposition of Hindi. Also, he said, it ignored the resolution by the West Bengal Assembly demanding status quo on the language issue and its refusal to accept Hindi as the official language.

It is important to understand that Hindi fanatics have been working systematically from the outset. It was not a Parliamentary Committee but a Committee of Parliament. Had it been a Parliamentary Committee, it would have sent its report to the Speaker of the Lok Sabha. And he would have presented it before the Parliament. The House would have had the right to accept or reject or change or amend the report. However, even at the time of the drafting of the Constitution, they strategically worked for the formation of a Committee of Parliament instead of a Parliamentary Committee. Constituent Assembly members from the non-Hindi-speaking states, intoxicated as they were by the sense of freedom, failed to see the big difference between the two types of committees. Hindi fanatics also added the provision that the committee's report should be sent to the President of India. As a result, Parliament lost its rights, except the one to discuss the report. It was in the pathetic situation of being powerless to amend the report's shortcomings, remove its atrocious recommendations, or iron out its contradictions. Thus, this 30-member committee became the group that gave the final verdict. The right to legally challenge the report was also denied. We need not explain the consequences, considering the fact that Hindi fanatics like PT Tandon and Seth Govind Das were members of the committee. How could truth survive in a place invaded by Satan?

The Parliamentary Committee did not make any noteworthy changes in the Official Language Commission's report. It accepted the report without any amendment. Although the wordings of its recommendations look new, the impact was the same.

The Parliamentary Committee submitted its report to the President on February 8, 1959. The President passed it on to Parliament. Members from non-Hindi-speaking states were disappointed and said their just demands had been rejected by the committee. The committee's biased report, prepared without any inclination to find a just solution to the language issue, provoked even those Southerners who had been supporting Hindi to raise their voice against it. Some of them wanted to move amendments. But the Home Minister argued that Parliament did not have the right to amend the report. And the Speaker accepted his argument. Many observers hung their heads in shame at the powerlessness of Parliament, which is supposed to be an all-powerful body in a democracy. Thirumalai Rao, a Lok Sabha member from Andhra Pradesh, said: 'Parliament seems to be in a weak situation. The report has been placed before the House for discussion. But the right to move any amendment has been denied. Does this House only have the right to give a general opinion?'

What was the use of anyone asking questions? The members were denied the right to move amendments. Parliament discussed the issue like a mock Parliament conducted in schools. Members from the non-Hindi-speaking states strongly condemned the atrocities perpetrated against them in the House. They warned that the attitude of Hindi fanatics was creating a dangerous situation, pointing out that their frenzy to force Hindi was growing so much that it was an insult to others. Renuka Ray, a Lok Sabha member from West Bengal, said: 'They (Hindi supporters) say, "You should speak in Hindi if you are patriots; you should plan to speak in Hindi as we do, and if you don't speak in Hindi as we do, it shows that you are not interested in learning Hindi." I was learning Hindi. But I stopped. I stopped learning Hindi because they provoked me. I wonder why it (Hindi) should be imposed on us.'

The Parliamentary Committee's report was not so reasonable that it did not require any amendment. It had many aspects that needed to be changed, and new aspects had to be added. Nehru himself said that he did not want to create the wrong impression that he accepted every sentence written by the committee's members. 'Nor do I demand that every member present here should accept every sentence in it,' he said.

Hindi imperialists might be overjoyed that Parliament accepted the report without any amendment. But Dravidians will ensure their joy is nothing but a water bubble.

Chapter 12

Black Flag

The Parliamentary Committee condensed the Official Language Commission's report, divided it into paragraphs, organised the content into separate sections with headlines and submitted it to the President without making any significant changes. Just like the Official Language Commission, the Parliamentary Committee also betrayed the non-Hindi-speaking people. Ignoring this injustice, the President issued an order based on the Parliamentary Committee's report, forcing the imposition of Hindi and making it the sole official language from 1965 onwards.

The Presidential Order was released on April 27, 1960. It distressed the people who had trusted the assurances of Pandit Nehru in Parliament that Hindi would not be imposed and the Centre would not ignore the demands of non-Hindi-speaking people.

Although the government refused to find a just solution to the language issue, the Ministers were equivocal about it, and the nationalists forgot that it was a problem at all. Crores of Dravidians had hoped that the DMK led by Annadurai would surely put an end to Hindi's dominance and protect the interests of non-Hindi-speaking people. The DMK, which had earned their trust and goodwill, sprang up like an injured tiger upon seeing the Presidential Order. It resolved to put an end to this appalling attitude of the North and fight once more to protect Tamil.

Its general council met at Kumarapalayam on June 19 and 20 to discuss the order and prepare for battle. This meeting was another milestone in the DMK's history. The general council members from every district participated in it and they all expressed their determination to protect Mother Tamil, trounce Hindi and launch an offensive on not only the order of the President but also on his attack on non-Hindi-speaking people. The two-day meeting passed the following resolution: 'Despite the fact that the Dravidar Kazhagam and the Dravida Munnetra Kazhagam, as the guardians of the Dravidian race, struggled, made sacrifices, and went through imprisonment to stall each and every effort made to impose Hindi in the Dravidian land with the objective of destroying the goal of establishing a separate country and installing Northern imperialism, despite the warning of the DMK on behalf of the people of the South against the Official Language Commission's report and its effort to establish Hindi's dominance, despite the assurances of Pandit Nehru in Parliament twice (after he understood how resentful the people of the South felt) that a decision on Hindi would not be taken without consulting and obtaining the consent of non-Hindi-speaking people, the President has, violating and disrespecting those assurances, issued an order stating that Hindi would be the official language and that arrangements should be initiated to ensure that it becomes the official language. The people of the South not only strongly condemn the order but also urge the President to withdraw it.'

It further said that the President's order is a challenge thrown at the people of the South and the DMK. It urged the President to withdraw the order by August 30 and announce that a decision on Hindi would not be taken without consulting the people of the South. If the President failed to do so, the council said, the DMK would launch a movement to free the South from Hindi imperialism. It would set up an action committee to guide the movement. The resolution further said: 'If the President does not agree to change his attitude, the general council will mobilise people to conduct protest meetings and rallies across the State; it will go ahead with the protests in defiance of any ban.'

Anna addressed a huge public meeting at Kumarapalayam to explain the resolutions to the people. When he listed the North's deceits one by one, the crowd became agitated. When he spelled out the impending dangers to their mother tongue, the party cadre became angrier. When he explained the implications of the President's order, the crowd turned into an ocean of resentment. 'Pandit Nehru gives sweet-sounding assurance. The President issues an order in violation of that assurance. If Nehru had humanity, should he not have resigned by now? Babu Rajendra Prasad should withdraw his order. Otherwise, the Kazhagam has decided to launch an agitation.'

After the general council meeting at Kumarapalayam, the DMK stages reverberated with war cries. Every word spoken by the leaders landed in the enemy camp like an arrow. Anna's speeches, which used to run like a gurgling stream, turned ferocious like a river in spate and the Congress bobbed like a ship. Anna said: 'The arrogant say that Hindi should take the place of Tamil. We oppose only that. We are not Tamil fanatics. We are Tamil's guardians. We are not so wretched as to insist on imposing Tamil in the land of Hindi. The native Tamil speaker who has become the advocate of Hindi imposition is a wretched, shameless person. He is just a body that lives only to eat. It is the presence of such debased characters that has emboldened the Hindi fanatic to proclaim arrogantly that he will impose Hindi.'

The agents of imperialism hung their heads in shame on hearing this.

DMK general secretary VR Nedunchezhiyan, known for his oratory, said: 'The fanatic northern imperialists who are ruling the country think that everyone in Tamil Nadu is a Kamaraj or a Kakkan. The time has come to show that this land has people living with honour, too. We have been struggling since 1938 to prevent the entry of Hindi into this land. Yet, Hindi tries to dominate the land of Tamils. Northerners want this land to be their slave forever. It is to defeat this attitude that we have raised a banner of revolt now.'

Kalaignar M Karunanidhi, who was sentenced to rigorous imprisonment in the Kallakudi agitation, said: 'Realising that great Tamil epics like *Silappadhikaram, Kundalakesi* and *Manimekalai,* and great literary works such as the Padhinenkeezhkanakku poems (the 18 Sangam Age poetry anthologies), *Thirukkural, Agananuru, Purananuru, Kalingathu Parani*[66], *Tholkappiyam* (the book of grammar), *Ettuththogai* (Eight Collections) and *Pattuppattu* awaken and enthuse us, they want to destroy Tamil and impose the Lambadis' (a nomadic people of North India) language of Hindi. Isn't he a Tamil who says, "I won't spare anyone who insults Tamil even if my mother comes in the way?" Could one with that legacy keep quiet when Mother Tamil is under attack? Are we dolls or pieces of wood devoid of emotions?'

The speech of EVK Sampath, leader of the agitation committee, was a whirlwind of emotions. He said: 'If Kamaraj has any good opinion of the people of this land and their language, he should convey to Delhi what is happening here and ask the rulers to suspend the Presidential Order. He should show Nehru the photographs of the crowds that gather at our public meetings. He should translate the speeches made here into English for Nehru. Kamaraj should tell Nehru and Rajendra Prasad that the land here is steaming hot and the people's hearts are on fire and urge them to withdraw the Presidential Order. If he does that, we will appreciate him as a visionary. But he is entering our land and trying to do something that is not possible.'

Sampath wrote a letter to the President highlighting the injustices abounding in the Presidential Order. He said, 'I am forwarding this letter on behalf of the anti-Hindi agitation committee of the Dravida Munnetra Kazhagam.

'I am sure you know very well that South India is apprehensive and worried by your order dated April 27, 1960, imposing Hindi on the people of the South and other non-Hindi-speaking people in India. We hope that good sense will prevail at the highest level of the government and they respect the sentiments of other sections of people and that, ultimately, an acceptable assurance will be given by August 30, 1960. In the event of our expectation not being met by then, we will have to start a struggle against the imposition of Hindi.

'In the meantime, it is learnt that you will be visiting Tamil Nadu around Independence Day. We regret that your visit has been planned at this juncture. The Dravidian society not only opposes your intimidating, ill-advised order of April 27, 1960 but also eagerly expects you to withdraw it.

'There can be no two opinions on the political significance and implications of your visit. So, we request you to seriously think about your proposed visit. We hope that you will decide to visit the State after taking a decision acceptable to the people of the South based on the assurance of the Prime Minister and avoid the unnecessary confusion that your proposed visit is causing among our people. We expect your reply by the end of this month.'

The President did not reply to his letter.

The Kamaraj government was rattled by the speeches of the DMK leaders who were preparing to launch an agitation with new vigour. It refused to permit meetings and withdrew the permissions it had given earlier. On July 12, 1960, it issued an order banning meetings in places like Perambur and Kuyapettai, for which it had already given permission. When DMK general secretary Nedunchezhiyan and agitation committee leader Sampath telephoned Anna, who was then in Trichy, and told him about the ban order, Anna told them to defy the ban and hold the meetings. At 6 pm that day, the two leaders addressed the meetings at Kuyapettai and Perambur despite the ban. Addressing a meeting at Thaduthatkondur on July 13, 1960, in defiance of the ban, Perasiriyar K Anbazhagan said that the government's prohibitory order was not confined to Thaduthatkondur and that it was done at the instance of Congressmen who wanted to quell the growth of the Kazhagam all over the State.

After the DMK swung into action to prepare people for battle, the Tamil Nadu Congress Committee met in Madurai on July 14 and passed a resolution praising the Presidential order as flawless. It appeared to tell Northerners, 'Don't be scared; we, the slaves, will torture the DMK men in a way that'll please you.' This statement made people realise that brokers who want to destroy Tamil are not confined to Delhi, and their henchmen live in Tamil Nadu, too, in the guise of Congressmen.

State Education Minister C Subramaniam issued a new justification: 'The State government has informed the Union government that English should be considered the official language along with Hindi even after 1965. Prime Minister Nehru also supported this view in Parliament. The recent order of the President has confirmed the State government's view on this. In this context, the DMK's demand for scrapping the Presidential Order would lead to a situation in which Hindi will be the official language constitutionally.'

The agitation committee's leader strongly condemned the Education Minister's motivated statement intended to divert people's attention from the stamp of Hindi chauvinism on the President's order: 'Minister Subramaniam fudges the issue. He wants to hear "cheers" from someone. He wants to show his gratitude to his bosses. After imposing Hindi in all the schools, he says there is no Hindi imposition. He utters a lie openly. In front of us, he holds forth that there is no imposition of Hindi. It is this frightened and dishonest way of speaking that we call political cowardice and political fraud,' he said.

The agitation committee met at the DMK headquarters on

July 15, 1960, to find ways to implement the decision taken at the general council meeting at Kumarapalayam. The meeting attended by, among others, the agitation committee leader, Sampath, party general secretary, Navalar Nedunchezhiyan, deputy general secretary, NV Natarajan, KA Mathiazhagan, K Anbazhagan, Madurai Muthu, Anbil Dharmalingam, Kovai Rasamanikkam and poet Kannadasan, took the following decisions:

1. To conduct an anti-Hindi conference in Chennai under the leadership of Anna which would be inaugurated by Nedunchezhiyan; to form a reception committee with Sampath as the president and Mathiazhagan as the secretary.
2. (a) The branch committee secretaries are to list the names of volunteers who want to participate in the agitation and send the lists to the agitation committee leaders; (b) To exempt from the agitation students, doctors and lawyers who are supporters of the DMK or its members.
3. The DMK's branches and associated organisations should collect funds for the agitation from every household and from shops through 'hundis' from July 20 to 27 and send the collections to the party headquarters.

The agitation committee worked efficiently to conduct the conference at Kodambakkam, Chennai. As decided earlier, Anna presided over the conference, which attracted about two lakh people. Enthusiastic DMK cadres from every district reached the venue by private buses. Nedunchezhiyan inaugurated the conference. The welcome address by Sampath turned into a battle cry against Hindi imperialism. He said: 'In a way, this conference is historic. I propose to invite Anna to preside over it and other leaders will second the proposal. Anna's concluding speech will be the last appeal to Hindi brokers. His speech will be the resolution of this conference. It will decide the future of this country. So, we'll all listen to it and work unitedly to implement the decision.'

Anna's presidential address dared the traitors of the North to come to the battlefield and served as the final warning to the slaves sitting inside the fort.

'There is no option but to launch a struggle. We have decided to plunge into battle because if we don't, even after all the doors have been closed on us, it would mean we have no dignity and self-respect left. Repressive measures will be let loose on us. We may lose our limbs. Some may even lose their lives. This is not mere rhetoric. You should prepare yourself to make any kind of sacrifice.'

When Anna asked the crowd whether it would welcome the President who had issued an order violating the assurance given by Pandit Nehru, the sea of humanity roared back, 'We won't, we won't.' When he announced that black flag demonstrations would be held all over the State from August 6 to 16 (except August 15) the gathering of two lakh people shouted in unison, 'We will show black flags, we will show black flags.' Anna handed black flags to the Chennai Mayor, Abdul Khader, Sampath, Nedunchezhiyan, Karunanidhi, NV Natarajan, CP Sittrarasu and Sathiyavani Muthu, saying, 'I give you a black flag, make it red.' The crowd roared again, 'Hindi down down, Hindi down down.'

The Congress government knew well that if the DMK showed black flags, the entire country would look like a moon drowned in black clouds. It had not forgotten the lessons of January 6, 1958, when black flags were shown to Nehru. The DMK's decision disturbed the government so much that Chief Minister Kamaraj said in a suppliant tone, 'Why are you holding a black flag protest against the President? Why don't you hold it against me?' The President, too, seemed rattled by the DMK's planned protest, realising that unless, in deference to the sentiments of non-Hindi-speaking people, he gave some assurance, they would shout deafening slogans against Hindi and ask him why he was visiting the State having imposed Hindi and insulted the Tamil language. His apprehension became evident from his speech at the Hindi Prachar Sabha in Hyderabad on March 3, 1960, a few days before his scheduled visit to Chennai. He said: 'I strongly believe that the sentiments and problems of non-Hindi-speaking brothers will not be ignored when the language issue is taken up for review or discussion in the future. As has been said often by Nehru in public and in Parliament, Hindi will not be imposed on anyone.'

The President's assurance reinvigorated the Dravidians.

The agitation committee leader wrote to Prime Minister Nehru on behalf of the DMK, explaining the compelling reasons behind the party's decision to hold a black flag protest against the President.

In this detailed letter, he wrote:

'Dear Mr Nehru, I take the liberty to write this letter to bring to your immediate attention certain developments which have caused great anguish to us. You may be aware that the protests being held in non-Hindi-speaking states, especially West Bengal and Tamil Nadu, came to an end after your assurance in Parliament that Hindi will never be imposed on people who refuse to accept it. The situation became fully clear because of your assurance. However, there was an apprehension that when it is implemented, the power centres responsible for it might dilute the assurance.

'Unfortunately, the order issued by the President this April has proved that apprehension to be true. This order tries to enforce the procedure that gave rise to agitations in non-Hindi-speaking states. I don't want to explain that in this letter. I believe it is enough to state that the order does not follow the letter and spirit of your assurance—that Hindi will not be imposed on people who don't want to accept it and that the voice of non-Hindi-speaking people will be decisive in this issue. For many reasons, this agitation was the one directed at the President, who is the voice of the government in principle.

'So, I request you to intervene in this issue and reassure the people of non-Hindi-speaking regions that at least you will abide by your assurance. Whatever be the case, if you give such an assurance, that will serve as a guarantee that the government will act reasonably. I believe that the assurance you give will mitigate the crisis at this juncture.

'I write this letter in the hope that you once again deal with this issue with your characteristic discretion and give the Tamils the assurance they expect. Your reply will strengthen the hands of our party and help to end our agitation.

'I am planning to travel to Chennai tonight. There, my comrades and others who are greatly concerned about this issue are waiting eagerly to know your thoughts. This is because it was your earlier assurance that made them happy and gave them the hope that the government in Delhi will act reasonably and honestly in this matter that affects the lives of Tamils. I will be grateful to you if you reply at the earliest.'

The agitation committee leader's letter must have rekindled old memories in Nehru, reminding him how the people of Tamil Nadu had insulted him in 1958. Fearing a similar situation that would pave the way for the end of his government, he sent a written reply to Sampath through an intermediary, reiterating his earlier assurance. The letter read:

'Dear Sri Sampath,

I have received your letter of August 3 this morning. I must say that I am greatly surprised at what you have written. There has been no occasion at any time for our government to go back in any way on the assurances I gave in the Lok Sabha regarding the language question. Indeed, in the President's order, a reference is made to my assurances. The Home Minister confirmed this in the Lok Sabha a day or two ago. I see that the Finance Minister of the Madras Government has also made this point quite clear. I cannot, therefore, understand why any misunderstanding should arise on this issue. We stand by the assurances given.'

The agitation committee examined Nehru's letter. It felt that the doors of success had been opened without any confusion or protests, that an assurance had been given to protect the interests of Tamils without beatings and bloodshed and that the North had retreated on hearing the war cry of the South.

The DMK dropped all plans to launch protests as a written assurance was given by none other than Nehru, the world-renowned scion of a noble family, and they felt that the government would not act contrary to its earlier assurance. The DMK general secretary, Nedunchezhiyan, issued the following statement: 'We hereby inform our party comrades, supporters and people at large that the general council's decision to hold a black flag protest has been dropped in view of the success we expected.'

Addressing a meeting celebrating the victory, Anna said: 'I believe with certainty that this letter and its assurances are not to be laughed at in political circles. It is a document that needs to be written in golden letters in the history of Dravidam.'

Until then, the successful anti-Hindi movement had only been against the Madras government. But the DMK spearheading and winning the latest round of the agitation challenging the Indian government marked the beginning of a new phase in the Dravidians' struggle for their rights.

The DMK's decision to drop its plan of holding a black flag protest in view of the assurances of our world-renowned Prime Minister and allowing the President's visit to Tamil Nadu to go unhindered is an instance of its high culture. But the ruling party's move to kill the very same assurances later is a testimony to its political indecency.

Chapter 13

The Official Languages Act

'I oppose this Bill in four statements—because it is contrary to the assurance Nehru gave to non-Hindi-speaking people; because it is a planned move to impose Hindi through the back door; a planned move to divert the attention of the Assemblies of the non-Hindi-speaking states; and, lastly, because it is an act of deception against non-Hindi-speaking people.'

—Frank Anthony

Home Minister Lal Bahadur Shastri introduced the Official Languages Bill in the Lok Sabha on April 13, 1963. The Bill was tossed around like a ship caught in a storm. The Hindi fanatics had come to the House to enact the climax of their ghostly dance. In solidarity with them, more than 3,000 people held a demonstration outside the Parliament building. A Hindi chauvinist named Swami Rameshwaranand[67] burnt a copy of the Bill in front of Parliament. When the Home Minister introduced the Bill in Parliament, Rameshwaranand, Mani Ram Bagri[68] and Hukam Chand Kachwai[69] stood up and shouted slogans, leading to massive commotion. It became clear that the House could not discuss the Bill with such disruptors around. The three members were suspended for the rest of the session. Nehru said that the House had witnessed loathsome and shameful scenes, which were unprecedented at that time. This, he said, was a bad beginning.

It is foolish to think that the Bill was against Hindi and in favour of non-Hindi-speaking people just because the Hindi fanatics disrupted the proceedings at the time of its introduction. The fact is the Bill was a hundred per cent pro-Hindi and harmful to non-Hindi-speaking people. It paved the way for enthroning Hindi and strengthening the hands of Hindi chauvinists. These truths will become clear if we examine the Bill.

According to the Bill, Hindi alone would become the official language on January 26, 1965, and English could be used as a second official language[70]. The Hindi translations of the laws, orders, directives, norms, and bylaws to be issued by the government with the President's assent would be considered official. If the laws enacted and orders issued by the State governments were translated into Hindi and published in the State Gazette, these would be considered official.

Under the third rule of the Bill, Hindi would occupy the place of English. There would be no compulsion to use English. It could be used if one wished to. But there would be no legal right to demand the use of English. The Congress had deliberately imposed Hindi on the administration and ignored English even when there was no legal sanction to use Hindi. How could it be expected to continue to use English after Hindi had officially taken its place?

Anglo-Indian member Frank Anthony and DMK member Nanjil K Manoharan condemned the Bill's failure to remove the injustices meted out to non-Hindi-speaking people and the burial of Nehru's assurances.

Introducing the Bill in the House, Home Minister Lal Bahadur Shastri said: 'I would like to tell the House that the main purpose of this Bill is to fulfil the general wishes of the Members of this House, because, the Members of this House had considered the report of the Parliamentary Committee. As far as I know, the House had given its general approval to the recommendations made by the Parliamentary Committee.'

Frank Anthony said: 'No. We did not give approval. It was not put to vote. We were not allowed to move amendments.'

Lal Bahadur Shastri replied: 'Perhaps voting did not take place.'

Frank Anthony said: 'We were not allowed to move amendments. He must not make wrong statements.'

Lal Bahadur Shastri replied: 'Anyhow, it shows there was a considerable majority in this House which agreed with the recommendation of the Parliamentary Committee. I have no doubt about that.'

The Minister who began by saying that Parliament had approved the Committee's recommendations shifted his position to say that voting alone did not take place and concluded that those who supported the imposition of Hindi were in a majority. This was an example of the intransigence of Hindi chauvinism, not the Minister's smartness.

On August 7, 1959, Nehru had assured non-Hindi-speaking people that English would remain the alternative official language and a decision on this issue would be left to non-Hindi-speaking people, not Hindi-speakers. Although this assurance did not offer a complete solution to the issue, some observers believed it brought solace to non-Hindi-speaking people. Nehru reiterated this assurance time and again. Addressing a conference of university vice-chancellors in August 1962, he said: 'You know that political circles have been discussing the question of continuing to use English as the second official language. The government has also decided to use it as the second official language. We have said this two years ago. But we had not fixed a time frame for that. We said a time frame will be decided later. Even that decision will be left to the non-Hindi-speaking states. There have been strong objections to the continuation of English as the official language. But going back on the government's assurance will be highly improper.'

Every newspaper carried the news of Nehru's assurance to

non-Hindi-speaking people, which was aimed at winning the support of Dravidians to the government during the crisis caused by the Chinese aggression of 1962. They gave huge publicity to his assurance that English would continue as the second official language and that he would not remove that status until they want it to be removed.

In 1959, it was assured that English would be the alternative official language. Later, it was said that it would be an associate language. Though these two formulations look similar, the learned know the difference between them. 'Alternative language' means those who do not know Hindi can use English. However, 'second language' means that Hindi and English would coexist, but English would not be an alternative to Hindi. Material in Hindi would be translated into English. In the case of 'alternative language,' Hindi and English would have the same place. In the case of 'second language,' Hindi would have the higher position and English would be inferior to it. Changing the status of English as an alternative language to that of a second language showed how Nehru moved closer to the Hindi camp.

Nehru's assurance had two important aspects: (a) English would continue as the official language. (b) non-Hindi-speaking people alone would have the right to remove that status. However, these aspects did not find a place in the Official Languages Bill. When the government lacked the courage to incorporate these two aspects in the Bill, it was surprising that the rulers, including Nehru, were still trying to make people believe that the assurance was being protected by the Bill and that it would be protected in the future, too.

It is with the objective of driving English out that the rulers used the word 'may' in the Bill, which means that there is no compulsion to use English. At the same time, they have deliberately used the word 'shall' to ensure that Hindi should be used as the official language after January 26, 1965. The Lok Sabha seriously debated this. Hindi fanatics and some Congress members argued without any qualms that the use of the word 'may' was correct.

The argument continued like this:

Nehru: It is quite absurd to say that the word 'may' also means 'may not.'

Frank Anthony: Why absurd? That is the natural meaning.

Nehru: Maybe, but I disagree with the Honourable Member.

Frank Anthony: If you disagree with the natural meaning, what can I do?

Nehru: I disagree with the Honourable Member in this context. I say it is not the natural meaning in this context. The dictionary meaning of 'may' or 'may not' be so, but, in this context, it simply means that the barrier is removed. I defy, I challenge anybody to prove that this Bill does not remove that limitation and barrier. That is the main purpose of this Bill.

It is not as if Nehru did not know that 'may' also means 'may not.' But he refused to accept it. Hindi fanatics had forced him to hide his knowledge and speak like an illiterate. Even some Congress members referred to the resentment caused by the word 'may'. Yashodha Reddy, a Congress member from Andhra, pleaded with Lal Bahadur Shastri: 'With a humble appeal, I would request him with folded hands that he should consider our request and replace "may" with "shall".'

Hindi imperialists were in no mood to relent. The rulers refused to incorporate the second aspect of Nehru's assurance that it would be left to non-Hindi-speaking people to decide how long English will also continue as the second language. Nehru gave a long explanation in the House to prove his assurance.

When he said the objective of the Bill was to keep his assurance, Frank Anthony interrupted him, saying, 'May I know—I am not questioning the motives of the Prime Minister—how the Bill reflects his assurance? How are the non-Hindi-speaking people going to be consulted? How will "may" be prevented from being interpreted as "may not"?'

Nehru replied: I shall deal with those points. I do not see how this Bill will say anything about consultation with non-Hindi-speaking people.

Frank Anthony: Why not?

Nehru: I will say, according to my thinking, it is quite absurd and unconstitutional.

Frank Anthony: Why is it unconstitutional? Give us some reasons. I am a lawyer, and so is the Prime Minister. Why is it unconstitutional?

Nehru: The assurance has nothing to do with the Bill or the Act being passed in this Parliament. The whole thing seems to be absurd on the face of it, limiting the power of Parliament, limiting the power of the Assemblies.

How did this 'reasoning' occur to Nehru suddenly? Why did it not occur to him when he gave his assurance and reiterated it time and again? What would be the harm if that privilege was given to non-Hindi-speaking people? Does the government not give exemptions and concessions to Jammu & Kashmir in its laws after proclaiming that Jammu & Kashmir is part and parcel of India? The Ninth Schedule of the Constitution says that the sixth and seventh sections of the Official Languages Act shall not apply to Jammu & Kashmir. Why this exemption? When Jammu & Kashmir is granted exemptions and concessions on every issue, how is it wrong to give a special privilege to non-Hindi-speaking people in the matter of continuation of English as the official language?

The government did not wish to incorporate Nehru's assurance into the Bill. Nor did it have the courage to say this openly. Had his assurance been ignored by his successors, we would have felt sorry about the situation. But how can we tolerate the atrocity of his assurance being ignored in his lifetime, and worse, by himself? DMK Member Manoharan aptly said that he would like to recall Machiavelli's quote that one should give as many promises as possible, but one should not keep them. If the Prime Minister was following this dictum, I would call him the Machiavelli of the 20th century, he said.

During a discussion on the Bill, Home Minister Lal Bahadur Shastri and other Congress members referred to the committee mentioned in the fourth rule of the Bill as Parliamentary Committee. But members like Frank Anthony argued that it was, in fact, a Committee of Parliament. If it were a Parliamentary Committee, they argued, should its report not have been sent to the Speaker instead of the President? A heated argument ensued between the Home Minister and Frank Anthony. Finally, the Minister had to accept Frank Anthony's explanation. He could not divert the House's attention from it. Eventually, he admitted that the committee that was formed after a gap of 10 years was not a Parliamentary Committee but a Committee of Parliament.

Frank Anthony said that the truth had come out then. Shastri hit back, saying that he would not accept Anthony's accusations, which he had been making throughout the debate. Anthony said that he stood by his accusation and that it was a case of open deception. The Minister refuted the charge. Anthony said this was a deception. The Minister responded by saying that he would not get emotional like Anthony. Anthony angrily reiterated his charge, to which Shastri said: 'As I mentioned earlier, I will not get emotional like Anthony.'

Anthony did not relent. He said: 'What prevented the formation of a Parliamentary Committee? I know for a fact that the present committee ignored Parliament.'

The charges levelled by Frank Anthony against the committee

to be formed in 1965 were true. There was no use whatsoever in forming a Committee of Parliament instead of a Parliamentary Committee. In the case of the former, Parliament would have no right to move amendments to its report. It could just conduct a debate. The committee was purposely formed in such a manner as to ensure that Parliament did not make any amendments in its report. So, the fourth rule of the Bill was a blatant betrayal, a systematic deception.

Participating in the debate in the Rajya Sabha, Anna strongly condemned the Bill. He said: 'I am dissatisfied with the present Bill because it does not satisfy the sentimental objection raised to Hindi being made the official language, and that sentimental objection comes not from a small part of India, but from the southern side of India as a whole.'

The Congress government ensured the passage of the Bill, ignoring the warnings of political leaders, the strong resentment of intellectuals and the condemnatory voice of non-Hindi-speaking people of India.

The Chief Minister of Tamil Nadu, M Bhaktavatsalam, gave a strange explanation, saying that while the Official Languages Act was just, the assurance of Nehru was greater and holier than that. During the January 25, 1965 protest when the State Assembly discussed the official language issue, the same Chief Minister said: 'Even now I say that the Prime Minister's assurance should be given legal sanction. This is the policy of this government. If all the members of the House unanimously support this policy, I am ready to move an amendment right now.'

The blood shed by Dravidians and the lives they sacrificed during the January agitation led to a change of heart in the slaves of Hindi imperialism. Congressmen themselves openly admitted and condemned the wrongs of the Official Languages Act. They also openly spoke about the need to amend it. They wanted to amend the Act's third rule, replacing the word 'may' with 'shall' and making it mandatory to get the approval of three-fourths of the states to remove English as the official language. The Chief Minister of Tamil Nadu had been saying that English should continue even if one State wanted it. Would such amendments solve the language issue? Would non-Hindi-speaking people achieve equality in the administration? No. They would only divert people's attention from the real issue. It would not satisfy them.

Such amendments would make English and Hindi the official languages of non-Hindi-speaking people and Hindi-speaking people, respectively. But they would not prevent the unfair and dishonest advantages that Hindi speakers would get. A just solution to the language issue did not lie in amending the Act alone. It lay in amending the Constitution immediately in such a way as to give official status to all the 14 national languages of India.

Chapter 14

Setting Aflame the Constitution

'There is a bloodthirsty hound in the heart of the rulers. The DMK is prepared to give any amount of blood to satisfy its thirst. The DMK agitation will be conducted in such a way as to check whether the hound's frenzy will subside after tasting our blood'.

—Arignar Anna

The Official Languages Act enacted by the Union government in 1963 was a verdict against non-Hindi-speaking people. Hindi imperialism refused to deviate from its fascist path even after its detractors made friendly pleas and fiery speeches highlighting the law's harmful effects. It went ahead firmly and anointed Hindi as the official language. Realising that Hindi imperialism could be felled only through a prolonged struggle, the DMK started beating the drums of war.

Addressing a rally on the Marina in Chennai on April 29, 1963, Anna said: 'We should plan a prolonged agitation, taking as much time as they took to plan their methods to impose Hindi, and every one of us should go to every nook and corner of Tamil Nadu to explain to people that the imposition of Hindi will be like a thunderbolt striking the heads of Tamils and Dravidians; we will lose our treasure of knowledge if Hindi is made the official language, we will lose our ability to rule, the Hindi-speaking people of the North will be our ruthless rulers. Only if this idea is entrenched in the hearts of knowledgeable people will Tamil Nadu stand up and voice its opposition when we launch the agitation. I realise that the time for such a battle has come.'

To find ways and means to debilitate Hindi imperialism, which had deceived us by going back on its promises, the DMK's general council met in Chennai on June 8, 9 and 10 in1963 and passed resolutions strongly condemning the atrocity perpetrated by the rulers through the Official Languages Act, making Hindi the official language and removing English. It urged the government to not only recognise Tamil, the foremost Dravidian language and official language of the State, as an official language of the Union government, but also to ensure the continuation of English as the official language until all the national languages are given the official language status. It announced the formation of an agitation committee comprising the party's district secretaries and State-level organisers with M Karunanidhi as the president and NV Natarajan as the secretary to 'protect our linguistic rights, to prevent the atrocities of Hindi chauvinism, to defeat the conspiracy to reduce us to the status of second-class citizens, and to establish the rights of the people of the South.'

The Kazhagam's decision gladdened the hearts of the people who were worried about the dangers of the Official Languages Act. It strengthened their belief that even if everyone else abandoned them, the DMK would not. Tamil society was proud and happy that the general council had given the task of leading the struggle to Karunanidhi, the most eligible person to do that, a brave soldier unafraid of being jailed.

A massive public meeting was held in Chennai to explain to the people these important decisions. Addressing the meeting, Kalaignar Karunanidhi said: 'I am ready to carry out the order given by Arignar Anna and the general council members. I get goosebumps when I say this. It fills my heart with great joy. Although my mother is not alive to feel happy when I tell her that

I've been chosen to lead the contingent marching to the battlefield; the presence of Anna—my elder brother forever—gives me the courage to fulfil the task he has assigned to me. I am ready to sacrifice my life.'

The crowd's cheers ripped through the skies.

Anna said: 'The Dravida Munnetra Kazhagam has decided to get into direct action against the imposition of Hindi and has formed a committee to carry it forward. This committee will visit various places to ascertain the views of our comrades and the situation prevailing in those places and convey its opinion to me by August. After that, I will lead the agitation from the front. This is not a rhetorical agitation. This is an agitation to protect the Tamil language and the Tamil culture. This is an agitation to protect our rights in various realms, ranging from politics to the arts. You can choose the field you like and join the agitation. I request you to take up this task as a matter of pride and as the least one can do as the son of Mother Tamil.'

With its four lakh members, 4,500 branches, 3,000 associate units, 50 MLAs, seven Members of the Legislative Council, nine Members of Parliament, and 11 municipalities, including the Chennai Corporation under its control, the DMK had sounded the drums of war. Hearing the war-cries of the Kazhagam, which had fought and won whenever any harm came the way of Tamil, made the Union government tremble with fear. It was petrified at the prospect of a massive domestic struggle just when the country was facing foreign [Chinese] aggression.

Speaking at the District Congress Committee meeting in Nainital, Home Minister Lal Bahadur Shastri appealed to the DMK to drop its plan of agitating. 'If the opposition parties think about holding agitations at this juncture, they will realise that their plan is not right,' he pontificated.

Condemning the indirect threat from the Home Minister with an imperialist mindset, Arignar Anna issued a statement:

'Mr Shastri has appealed to the DMK to give up its anti-Hindi agitation. Although his appeal is couched in polite terms, threats and intimidation are inherent in it. He is intimidating us, citing the law and the Constitution. Shastri's speech has made one truth clear. That is, those at the helm do not sympathise with the demands of non-Hindi-speaking people. Not only that; they are keen to implement their Hindi policy aggressively. The policy of imposing Hindi is absurd. The DMK's objective is to touch the hearts of those who are adamant on adhering to that policy.'

The DMK firmly rejected the Home Minister's appeal. It swung into action and started preparing for the agitation, brushing aside threats, intimidation, and the hue and cry and mischief of the imperialists.

The agitation committee met in Arivagam on July 16, 1963 under the leadership of Kalaignar Karunanidhi and decided to intensify the agitation and set up camps to prepare lists of agitators. It took the following decisions:

1. The members of the agitation committee should travel in the districts with the help of the respective office-bearers and prepare lists of volunteers who will participate in the agitation.
2. The agitation committee is making arrangements to intensify and make widespread the campaign against the imposition of Hindi in August and September.
3. The committee will make serious efforts to conduct public meetings, one-act plays and cultural programmes, and explain the ill effects of the imposition of Hindi through posters, pamphlets and the media.
4. Four conferences will be held on August 5, August 25, September 22 and October 6. On the eve of these conferences (August 4, August 24, September 22 and October 5) internal meetings will be held involving office-bearers, general council members, and the taluk and

branch secretaries of the districts contiguous to the four conference venues.

5. The committee requests all the units of the Kazhagam to observe an anti-Hindi week from September 15, the birthday of Arignar Anna.

In accordance with these decisions, the anti-Hindi agitation was intensified. Party campaigners addressed meetings comparing Hindi to a demoness, a ghost, a poisonous snake and a mad dog. The campaign was fiery. Pamphlets and cartoons were brought out. Cultural programmes and one-act plays were conducted. In Salem, Thanjavur and Tirunelveli districts, regional-level anti-Hindi conferences were held. At the camps organised on the eve of each conference, the agitation leader Kalaignar Karunanidhi discussed the plans with the party cadre and prepared lists of volunteers for the protests.

The agitation committee reviewed the ideas put forward by the cadres at these camps. Many of the cadres suggested burning copies of Part XVII of the Constitution, which they said was aimed at enslaving non-Hindi-speaking people. To oppose the imposition of Hindi in central government offices, the cadres suggested that the party should picket these offices if the government arrogantly went ahead and implemented this policy. The agitation committee accepted both these suggestions.

The recognition accorded by the Constitution is what gives strength to Hindi's status as the official language. Realising this as early as 1960, the DMK had said: 'The Constitution must be amended to find a just solution to the language issue. The executive committee reiterates its view that this is the best solution possible.' Accepting this stand of the government wholeheartedly, several intellectuals had on various occasions requested the government to amend the Constitution accordingly. Among the major intellectuals who made this plea were Rajaji, Sir CP Ramasamy Iyer, Sir CV Raman, Field Marshal KM Cariappa, and freedom fighter

P Kothanda Rao. Voices from around the country welcomed the DMK's plan to burn copies of the Constitution.

Volunteers who were mentally strong to withstand prolonged imprisonment were enrolled for the agitation and to burn copies of the Constitution. Those who would be able to undergo only a short term in jail were enlisted for the picketing programme. The agitation committee leader consolidated these lists and handed them over to Arignar Anna at the anti-Hindi conference held in Chennai on October 13, 1963. This conference was special in many ways. The heroic speeches made by the frontline leaders of the DMK should be written in gold. In his concluding speech, Arignar Anna listed the past atrocities of Hindi imperialism and explained why the DMK had decided to burn Part XVII of the Constitution. His explanation was so persuasive that it would have convinced even his detractors.

He said: 'The rulers gave different explanations for the imposition of Hindi. Their final argument was that we should not oppose Hindi after it has been recognised as the official language in the Constitution. That is why we demand complete removal of Part XVII from the Constitution. We are not alone in demanding this. The Acharya [Rajaji] also says this. It is not only the Acharya who says this. The Tamil Nadu government itself has said in its letter to Delhi in 1956 that the section on the language issue should be amended. So, we must refute the final argument of the rulers who support the imposition of Hindi. If we have a majority in Parliament, we can amend the Constitution itself. We can't do that in the present situation. There is no option but to launch a struggle. Through our protest, we must show that we do not care for Part XVII of the Constitution. We consider it a speck of dust on our foot.

'So, as the first step in the agitation, we'll read out Part XVII of the Constitution and burn a copy of it in a public place. I will start from Arivagam at 4 o'clock on November 17, reach the

Marina and burn a copy of the Article. The anti-Hindi agitation will begin there.'

The huge gathering raised thunderous slogans of 'Long Live Anna', 'Hindi Down' and 'Let Tamil Live.' It roared like the waves of the ocean when Arignar Anna read out the first list agitators. Thus, the Chennai conference turned out to be the first challenge thrown to Hindi imperialism.

Responding to the DMK's agitation plan, Chief Minister Bhaktavatsalam said arrogantly: 'I am not scared of the agitation. I am not one to be rattled by such a bogeyman.'

To suppress the agitation scheduled for November 17, the government took oppressive action on November 12 itself. In Chennai, it arrested and jailed 18 volunteers, including CP Sittrarasu, Kanchi Kalyanasundaram[71] and district secretary C Neelanarayanan[72]. On November 13, 14, 15, it jailed 168 people in Chennai alone. At 1 pm on November 16, the police arrested organising secretary NV Natarajan and the trade union wing's secretary A Govindasamy when they were in conversation with Kalaignar Karunanidhi at Anna's residence. On November 16, Anna and his colleagues were travelling to Chennai from Kanchipuram to carry out their plan of burning a copy of Part XVII of the Constitution on the Marina and give a final warning to Hindi imperialists. When the car reached Chennai's Aminjikarai at 12.30 pm, the police arrested Arignar Anna, TM Parthasarathy, TK Ponnuvelu[73], V Ranga and KP Sundaram.

With a view to making use of the emotional upsurge created by Arignar Anna's arrest to further the cause, the DMK's propaganda secretary, Sathiyavani Muthu, asked the party cadre to hold public meetings at all the important towns and cities on November 24, 1963. A list of frontline speakers was prepared. Learning of the DMK's decision to intensify the agitation, the government issued prohibitory orders against holding public meetings and processions. The DMK leadership ordered the party cadre to hold meetings in defiance of the prohibitory orders. Sensing the DMK's preparedness to defy the orders, the government swooped down on important party leaders in every village and town. A total of 4,000 people were jailed then. Despite the government's precautionary arrests to prevent the agitation, the prohibitory orders were shattered in many towns. DMK cadre held meetings despite the orders. Those who violated or tried to violate the orders were also arrested and imprisoned.

At Sankaran Kovil, Aladi Aruna, the author of this book, was arrested and jailed when he was on his way to address a public meeting. In Madurai, once the capital of the Pandya kingdom, nine volunteers, including Anbuchezhiyan of Vathalagundu and Mrs Devaki Pandiyan were arrested and sentenced to two years of imprisonment for violating the prohibitory orders. In Tiruvarur, partymen like Chinnapillai and Balraj were sentenced to three months rigorous imprisonment. In Sendhamangalam, 22 volunteers, including VR Periyannan[74], MLA, and town secretary, A Nadarasan, were arrested and sentenced to three weeks imprisonment. In Coimbatore, KM Ilanchezhiyan, ES Shanmugam, SP Subramanian, Mrs M Rajammal, AN Rajan, K Natarajan and Gangadaran were sentenced to one-month rigorous imprisonment for violating the prohibitory orders. Cases were filed against Anna and his colleagues under Rule 5 of The Prevention of Insults to National Honour Act and Section 120B of the Indian Penal Code for conspiring and trying to burn the Constitution of India.

When the case came up for hearing, Arignar Anna did not employ an advocate; nor did he oppose the witnesses. He said that although what he tried was against the law, he acted in the interest of his country and his language and as directed by his conscience. In his affidavit, he said: 'Our view is that anyone who wishes to ensure that justice prevails and honesty triumphs is duty-bound to oppose any plan and law that paves the way for injustice. As many great people have opined, it is an act of injustice to make Hindi the official language. It is an insult to the honour of regions where non-Hindi-speaking people live. Moreover, it is a bigger insult to the honour of those living in Tamil Nadu, who have been speaking the classical language of Tamil for over 2,000 years.

'If there is no force that will remain vigilant and identify the unjust plans imposed by the rulers, democracy will be reduced to a farce and will result in a situation that is worse than dictatorship. If parliamentary methods prove to be useless, either individuals or a group can stall anti-people atrocities by awakening the public in a democratic way, by mobilising them in large numbers and using their power like a sword. Such militant individuals who can withstand atrocities perpetrated by angry rulers should come forward to take up this fight.

'There are lots of laws. And there are lots of ways to defy them. I will be ashamed and pained to defy any law if my action threatens to destroy, distort, harm, disrupt, shake or weaken the people's lives, livelihoods, rights, peace or morality. But I have the right to say that I will not be a culprit if I engage wholeheartedly in an activity with the noble intention to do great service to the people.

'None of the evidence submitted to prove the charges against us says that we intended to insult the nation's honour. Who will intend to insult the nation's honour and for what purpose? Be it my statements or the bits of our speeches cited to prove the charges against us, we have not said anywhere that insulting the nation's honour was our intention. On the contrary, on every occasion—while passing a resolution, publishing it in newspapers, or speaking about it in public meetings—we have emphasised that opposing the imposition of Hindi was the idea behind burning Part XVII of the Constitution. I would like to say categorically that we decided to burn Part XVII of the Constitution to wake up the rulers from their slumber and make them give up their unjust attitude.

'I decided to act according to my conscience. However ordinary my service may be, I acted in full belief that the creators of the plan to make Hindi the official language will realise their mistake and that their hearts will pain. I have no doubt that the people of Tamil Nadu will greet my action as one aimed at protecting their way of life.

'I am sure that if Part XVII of the Constitution is implemented, one part of the country will be pushed down and devalued. If one part of the country is devalued, it will be an insult to the nation's honour. We decided to burn Part XVII of the Constitution only to make the rulers, who are intransigent on the language issue, realise that they will insult the nation's honour by their attempt to reduce non-Hindi-speaking people to the status of second-class citizens.

'In fact, it is Part XVII of the Constitution that is an insult to the honour of the nation. We involved ourselves in the peaceful struggle and, as part of it, tried to burn Part XVII of the Constitution, because we believe, true to our conscience and true to the sense of natural justice every one of us cherishes, that resisting this dishonour to the nation was a noble act. Hence, we deny the charge that we tried to commit the crime of dishonouring the nation.'

Arignar Anna's affidavit is not just a statement of an individual. It is the manifesto of Tamil society. It will remain a guide forever for idealists in the movement as well as an indelible part of the history of India.

On December 10, Anna and his colleagues, who tried to burn Part XVII of the Constitution, were sentenced to six months of rigorous imprisonment. Anna, who had dedicated himself to Tamil society, entered jail with a smile. The agitation led by Anna was followed by similar agitations all over the State as planned earlier.

In Kanchipuram, the birthplace of Anna, the trade union wing's secretary, A Govindasamy, was sentenced to six months of rigorous imprisonment. In Madurai, one-year rigorous imprisonment was awarded to the district secretary, S Muthu, M Khader Basha, A Muniyandi[75], and Akkinirasan. In Cuddalore, the party's South Arcot district secretary, R Sambasivam, got four months of rigorous imprisonment. Ramanathapuram district secretary, SS Thennarasu, was sentenced to one-year rigorous imprisonment. Among others who were sentenced to rigorous imprisonment for various terms were Salem district leader, GP Somasundaram, Kanyakumari district secretary, PM Kannu, Navalar Nedunchezhiyan in Coimbatore, Perasiriyar K Anbazhagan and KA Mathiazhagan in Chennai, Nanjil K Manoharan in Nagercoil, Trichy district secretary, Anbil Dharmalingam, Salem district secretary, ER Kiruttinan, and Mrs Jagadambal[76], MLA, in Jayankondam. In all, 74 volunteers burnt copies of Part XVII of the Constitution. About 1,200 people were jailed for participating in picketing programmes.

Copies of Part XVII were burnt in one town each in the Chennai, Madurai and Chengalpattu districts. In Thoothukudi, the agitation continued for five days. In the Trichy, Coimbatore, Ramanathapuram and Salem districts, it was conducted in all the important towns. Initially, only five volunteers were allowed to join a squad. When many party cadres showed interest in joining the agitation, the strength of a squad was increased to 10. Many squads participated in the agitation on the same day.

Of all the participants in the agitations conducted thus far, the teams led by Madurai Muthu and SS Thennarasu were sentenced to the longest periods of punishment. Muthu's team spent five months in jail. At the end of the five months, they were sentenced to a year's rigorous imprisonment. A massive public meeting was held in Madurai when they came out of jail. Anna felicitated them. Kalaignar Karunanidhi hailed Muthu and Thennarasu as the 'Marudhu Brothers' [early freedom fighters from Sivaganga] of the Kazhagam.

While those who participated in the agitation to burn copies of Part XVII were punished under Rule 5 of The Prevention of Insults to National Honour Act and Section of 120B of the Indian Penal Code, the Sedition Act was slapped on South Arcot district secretary, R Sambasivam, Cuddalore taluk secretary, AV Dhandapani, poet Vengai Marban and Tamil teachers Muthu Thamizharasan and Pachaiyappan. The Madras government, which was servile to Hindi imperialism, thought that its tyrannical laws would make the Tamil warriors tremble with fear.

However, the volunteers continued with the agitation, unafraid of years of imprisonment, and the frustrated government went to the extent of arresting even the comrades who had gone to the agitation venues to greet the volunteers. The police arrested Chengalpattu district secretary, CVM Annamalai, MLA Nellikuppam Krishnamurthy, MR Krishnamurthy from Kattumannarkudi, Kanchipuram town secretary, Mark, and comrade Sabapathi at midnight for having garlanded the agitators. The government also filed cases against them. It also filed cases against Kalaignar Karunanidhi, NV Natarajan, lawyers PS Manian, K Thirupathi, Kaveri Manian, and party cadre Muniappan, Mutharasu, Ramachandran and AV Rasu when they went to greet and garland the agitators. The Kazhagam decided to legally challenge the arrests of partymen even for greeting, hailing, appreciating and garlanding the agitators. It appealed in the Madras High Court against the sentence of six months rigorous imprisonment of nine people, including Kalaignar Karunanidhi and NV Natarajan.

Tamil society showered the ideologically committed volunteers in all the districts with flowers. Tamils gathered in huge numbers at the agitation venues to greet them with applause and flowers.

On January 26, 1965, when Hindi was enthroned as the official language, a new battlefield emerged. The Kazhagam appealed to the people to observe January 26 as a day of mourning. After that, the January protest broke out, much to the surprise of the entire world. It created a volatile situation in the country marked by violent incidents. The idea of peaceful protests disappeared. Foreseeing that launching new struggles would have dangerous consequences, the Kazhagam decided to suspend its agitation for some time. However, the various struggles conducted by the Kazhagam made the country realise the dangers of imposing Hindi. The North's language chauvinism was unmasked. Every self-respecting Tamil realised the need to oppose Hindi's dominance. The passion, courage and sense of sacrifice generated by the Kazhagam's struggles were not in vain. These sentiments burst forth like a volcano and grew restless like the waves of the sea. Thus began the January revolution!

Chapter 15

Self-immolation

'I appreciate those who committed self-immolation in the struggle against the imposition of Hindi. This offers a ray of hope that our people are determined to ensure that democratic forces should be sustained. If the Indian government does not consider the unmatched sacrifices of political martyrs as a warning, India's unity will be disrupted.'

—Prof NG Ranga[77]

The self-immolation of Buddhist monks in protest against the military rule in South Vietnam, one of the Southeast Asian countries, was the first of its kind in the world. After them, the honour of resorting to self-immolation as a form of protest goes to the Tamils. Throughout history, nearly every country has seen martyrs who have withstood and endured various forms of violence—verbal and physical assaults, whiplashes and lathi charges, incarceration and torture, electric shocks, attacks that resulted in loss of limbs and eyes, being thrown into fire or made to lie on ice blocks, forced kidney transplantation, decapitation, poisoning, hanging, exile, etc.—during their struggle to dethrone and oppose kings and establish democracy or their attempts to propagate revolutionary ideas, introduce new norms, put an end to the atrocities committed and superstitions sustained in the name of religion and bring about renaissance. The sacrifice of Tamils takes pride of place among such do-or-die battles of the world.

Making a sacrifice when a situation demands it is one thing. Generally, this is the kind of sacrifice many great heroes and reformers make. But is there any equal to committing self-immolation, even when there is no compulsion to do it? Watching a person set himself on fire is traumatic for the faint-hearted. Self-immolation is the ultimate sacrifice. Six Tamils did it as a mark of protest against the imposition of Hindi. If the Union government refuses to realise the extent of the anti-Hindi sentiment prevailing in Tamil Nadu, even after these instances of self-immolation, the consequences will be dangerous.

Chinnasamy

The first martyr was 27-year-old Chinnasamy, a native of Keezhapazhur village in the Trichy district. He was the son of Arumugam and Thangammal and his wife's name was Kamalam and he had a daughter named Dravida Selvi. A member of the DMK, he had worked hard for its growth. He was among the crores of Tamils whose hearts sank on seeing the enthroning of Hindi and the enslavement of Mother Tamil. His agitated mind raised many questions—is my own language in peril in my free country? Why should I live if Mother Tamil herself is endangered and faces extinction? The imposition of Hindi not only disappointed him, but also forced him to take the extreme step of sacrificing himself.

When Chief Minister Bhaktavatsalam was returning to Chennai from Trichy, Chinnasamy fell at his feet at the Mambalam railway station and pleaded with him to save Tamil. Bhaktavatsalam, who used to reply brusquely to even responsible leaders from the opposition, was said to have shaken off Chinnasamy and walked away. When Chinnasamy realised that even those in power would not save Tamil from the impending danger, he was convinced that Tamil Nadu would become a slave to Hindi and it was better to die than to live in such an environment. However, he wanted Tamils to recognise his commitment to the cause. He remembered the acts of self-immolation committed by Buddhist monks in South Vietnam. On January 24, 1964, he wrote to his friends informing them of his decision to commit self-immolation. Even before those letters were opened, he had set himself on fire at 4 am on January 25, near the Trichy railway junction. He had bought 3 gallons of petrol in the wee hours of that day. He wore two sets of dhotis and shirts so that the fire would not be easily extinguished even if rescuers rolled his burning body on the ground in an attempt to save him. He created a fence of clothes around himself, set fire to it first and then set himself on fire with the ring of fire around him. The flames spread over his chest first and then singed his face. Not once did he shriek in pain. The only words that were heard from him were, 'Long Live Tamil; Down with Hindi!'

In a country of fools who wonder why there is such a battle for a language, Chinnasamy sacrificed his mortal body for the sake of immortal Tamil. Since then, Chinnasamy has been hailed as Singaththamizhan Chinnasamy (Lion-like Chinnasamy).

Sivalingam

Chinnasamy's martyrdom created an uproar among Tamils and inspired many others to sacrifice their lives. On the morning of January 26, Sivalingam immolated himself near his house in Kodambakkam. He had left letters stating that he was sacrificing his life as a protest against the imposition of Hindi. A letter was found beside a kerosene tin in which he said: 'My life is for Tamil! My body is for flames. I commit self-immolation in condemnation of the decision to make Hindi the official language.'

Mourners who saw this letter acclaimed his sacrifice with tears in their eyes.

Aranganathan

Aranganathan committed self-immolation on January 27. On the previous night, he told his wife Mallika about the hooliganism of the Congress against people observing January 26 as a day of mourning in protest against the imposition of Hindi. He explained to her the tasks before the anti-Hindi movement and the sacrifices the Tamils would have to make for the cause. Even then, Mallika had no inkling that he was going to commit self-immolation. After she and the children went to sleep, he wrote separate letters addressed to Anna, Rajaji, Nedunchezhiyan and Kamaraj informing them of his decision to set himself on fire the following morning and lamenting the consequences of Tamils losing the war against Hindi.

At 4 am on January 27, he walked up to a platform opposite his house, poured kerosene on his body and lighted a matchstick. On seeing the flames, people rushed to save him. Their efforts were in vain.

Aranganathan, who worked in a depot of the telephone department, made this ultimate sacrifice unmindful of the pain and grief it would cause his wife and children. Tamils will be ever grateful to him for his sacrifice to save Tamil and its honour.

Veerappan

On February 10, the Trichy district earned the distinction of the most volunteers committing self-immolation in the cause of their mother tongue there. That was the day on which Veerappan, a primary school teacher in Aiyyampalayam, committed self-immolation. He was known for his love and deep knowledge of Tamil. It is said that he used to discuss the fall of Tamil from glory and its enslavement by Hindi chauvinism with his friends and tell them of the need to sacrifice one's life to change the situation. He did not stop at preaching. He doused himself with petrol and committed self-immolation. When the news of his demise came,

Tamil Nadu was reverberating with the sounds of gunshots as police fired at protesters. There was none who did not praise Veerappan for his unparalleled sacrifice. Tamils are duty-bound to appreciate this virtuous man, who was not only a great teacher but sacrificed his life for the language he loved.

Muthu

The anti-Hindi sentiment had taken root in the educated sections and in the farming community. Muthu belonged to Sathyamangalam in Coimbatore. He was not content with just minding his farmland, but was interested in public affairs, too. Praising the martyrdom of Chinnasamy, Sivalingam and Aranganathan, he told a friend that Hindi would disappear in a day if 50 more people sacrificed their lives, and that Hindi would perish in fire, just as these martyrs were consumed by flames. He said this just two days before he set himself on fire. Like the other martyrs, when the flames were consuming him, he shouted, 'Long Live Tamil! Down with Hindi!'

He was taken to a hospital, but he succumbed to the burns.

Sarangapani

Sarangapani was a 20-year-old youth studying in AVC College, Mayavaram. He used to be at the forefront of anti-Hindi processions taken out by students. He was one of the students who had captured the Mayavaram railway station and operated it for six hours. He used to tell his fellow students that he was prepared to make any sacrifice in the fight against Hindi. He doused himself with kerosene and set himself on fire in his college on the morning of March 17. In an attempt to save him, his fellow students took his fully burnt body to a hospital, but he breathed his last, saying, 'I've given my life to Tamil.'

A few anti-Hindi agitators poisoned themselves to death. On January 27, Muthu from Keeranur in the Trichy district died by consuming a bed bug killer. He had studied up to 10th standard and worked in a hotel. He had gone to watch a movie in the evening and did not return home. His body was found at the Keeranur bus stand the next morning. He had written to his father, Natesa Servai, and to Anna, lamenting the imposition of Hindi and expressing his decision to dedicate his life to the cause of protecting Tamil.

Shanmugam from Viralimalai also sacrificed his life in the same manner in 1965.

The incidents of self-immolation attracted international attention. *The New York Times* covered the self-immolation of Sivalingam and Aranganathan in a big way, and the Americans were shocked. It even published an editorial on the incidents. At the United Nations, Pakistan's envoy Syed Amjad Ali spoke about it. Central leaders, including Prime Minister Lal Bahadur Shastri, were shaken by these developments.

Instead of equating self-immolation with suicide and terming it illegal, it is apt to say that the law is against the concept of sacrifice. Idealists defy bans, speak against the law, conduct picketing programmes, stop trains, go on strike and even resort to murder and arson in the pursuit of their ideals. All these are illegal acts. Don't people regard them as acts of sacrifice? At the same time, these acts of sacrifice do harm others, cause damage, and pose danger. But self-immolation harms only the one who resorts to it. It does not harm others. Even if self-immolation is illegal, it is sacrifice which does not lose its significance with time.

If Hindi imperialism refuses to bow down even after these sacrificial deaths by fire, the consequences will be dangerous.

Chapter 16

The January Revolution and a Day of Mourning

Oh, lion-like youth of Tamil Nadu,
Be more militant!
We'll serve raw blood
If the mother tongue is harmed!
Death is like sleep,
Waking up is our new birth!
We'll oppose the Hindi evil,
Unmindful of losing our sweet lives![78]

—Revolutionary poet Bharathidasan

January 26, 1965 was the day Hindi was to become the official language of India. The thought made every Tamil fulminate against it. They prepared for another battle against the government, which was ushering in Hindi with fanfare even after Tamil protests in which the protesters faced prolonged imprisonment, endless oppression and several martyrs gave up their lives for Tamil.

The DMK, which had vowed to fight and win the battle against Hindi, considered January 26 a black day that marked the attempt to disrupt the glorious life of Dravidian society. Its executive committee met on January 8, 1965 and deliberated on observing it as a day of mourning. It passed the following resolution: 'Although the DMK is aware of the significance of the

Republic Day, it has decided to observe it as a day of mourning by conducting protest meetings, wearing black badges and holding black flag demonstrations all over the State to show its resistance to the Indian State using the occasion to impose Hindi, overriding the wishes and interests of the people of the South; if the people's opposition is not expressed thus, the government will interpret it as a sign of their acceptance of Hindi as the official language.'

Although the Kazhagam's resolution was on expected lines, it created a groundswell of support among the people, especially students. Congressmen and Hindi fanatics were shocked to see the people's support for the DMK.

It was not the first time that the Republic Day was observed as a day of mourning in the Indian subcontinent. Periyar had declared August 14, 1947 itself as a day mourning. In 1961, West Bengal Chief Minister BC Roy had announced that Independence Day would not be celebrated by his government because Bengalis faced the brunt of riots in Assam. The Communist Party of India supported the decision of the Congress government.

The DMK announced that January 26 would be observed as a day of mourning, not because it was Republic Day, but because it was the day Hindi would be enthroned as the official language. Anna said: 'The sorrow or the mood of protest highlighted by the observance of January 26 as a day of mourning does not mean that we condemn the Republic Day, or we feel sad about it. Our protest and sorrow are related to making Hindi the official language. Long live the Republic. Our slogan, our objective, our policy is that Hindi should be out.'

The Constitution said that Hindi would be the official language after 15 years, but did not fix January 26 as the day on which it would enter the portals of power. Had the Congress government really wished to protect the sanctity of Republic Day, it would have fixed any other day to declare Hindi the official language. If Hindi had been enthroned on January 25 or 27, the DMK would have declared that day as a day of mourning. But Congressmen trying to sully the image of the DMK and incite riots projected the declaration by the DMK as an insult of the Republic Day.

Speaking in the Assembly on January 21, Chief Minister Bhaktavatsalam said: 'Even if the DMK observes Republic Day as a day of mourning in a peaceful way, the government will not be a mute spectator. If somebody keeps crying in a wedding hall, that person would be chucked out.' He did not stop with that comment. 'We will not allow DMK members to hoist black flags atop their houses. If there is violence, we will not offer protection,' he said.

Was anything else needed to incite Congress goondas against the DMK? The Chief Minister made this provocative statement indirectly because he happened to be speaking in the Assembly. But Congressmen speaking in public forums said: 'Punch those showing black flags. Kill them. Hack them. Fell them. Beat them. Tear them to pieces. Who will dare to stop you or question you?'

Students wholeheartedly supported the DMK's decision and were ready to voice their protest. A students' committee against the imposition of Hindi was formed. This committee called upon all students to observe January 25 as a day mourning all over the State. This message was sent to students' union leaders in every college in the State. The government posted heavy contingents of police outside colleges on the morning of January 25. Students came wearing black badges. None of them entered the classrooms. They marched on the streets holding black flags and scattering scraps of black paper on the roads. Slogans like 'Down with Hindi', 'Long Live Tamil' filled the air. Almost every street in the State reverberated with these slogans. The protest meetings and processions were peaceful and orderly.

The students of Pachaiyappa's College in Chennai burnt a 20-foot effigy of what they called the 'Hindi demoness'. As it went up in flames, they shouted 'Hindi Down Down' and the city trembled. Students of all the colleges in Chennai marched in a joint procession through the city's arterial roads shouting thunderous slogans: 'Down with Hindi, Let Tamil Live', 'We want English,' 'We'll build a platform for Tamil and a stretcher for Hindi' and so on.

The law sheds tears in the face of those who defy it, but strengthens itself again by chasing the cowards. It went down on its knees before the defiant students. They marched to Fort St George, the seat of power in the State, to meet the Chief Minister and submit a memorandum explaining the injustice meted out to them by the imposition of Hindi. The Chief Minister was not in his office, so they submitted the memorandum opposing the imposition of Hindi and pleading for the continuation of English as the official language to Industries Minister R Venkatraman. That evening, they organised a massive public meeting on the Marina. About 10,000 students attended the meeting and student leaders delivered fiery speeches against the imposition of Hindi. Their speeches reflected sentiments lying dormant in their hearts like the spring under dry riverbeds. At the end of the meeting, student leaders P Srinivasan, Naavalavan, and Raja Mohammed set fire to books written in Hindi. Even the roar of the restless waves of the ocean were drowned in the slogans raised by them.

In Madurai, thousands of college students marched through the main streets. It was like the march of the soldiers of the ancient Pandya kingdom. When they announced their plans to burn copies of Article 343 of the Constitution, which laid down that Hindi written in Devanagari script would be the official language, thousands of people lined up on both sides of the streets to watch. K Kalimuthu and N Kamaraj, students of Thiagarajar College, burnt copies of Article 343 in Rajaji Park. As the copies went up in flames, all the students roared in appreciation as if a real enemy was being burnt to death. The police arrested Kalimuthu and Kamaraj. Protesting against the arrests, the students marched from the venue through the streets of Madurai again. When they neared the District Congress Committee office, some Congressmen attacked the students with sickles and knives. A few seriously injured students fled the scene shrieking in pain. Stick-wielding Congressmen ran after them. The District Collector announced that it was the Congressmen who had attacked the procession. Cases were filed against some of the assailants and they were punished.

The Congressmen's attack on the peaceful procession led to a spate of violence across the city. Shamianas erected for celebrating Republic Day were set on fire. Khadi flags of the Congress were torn to pieces. Festoons were cut off. A Jeep parked in front of the Congress office was set on fire.

The Congress' violence disturbed the peace in Madurai and triggered student protests all over the State. In Coimbatore, Trichy, Vellore, Thanjavur, Mayavaram, Tiruppur, Erode, Nagapattinam, Tirunelveli, Chidambaram and Kumbakonam, students took out peaceful marches condemning the violence.

On January 26, the capital city of Delhi was in a festive mood. The Hindi Prachar Sabha in Delhi celebrated the enthroning of Hindi as the official language and gloated that Hindi would reign unchallenged in the country, that Hindi speakers would be the hegemons of the nation, that finally the fruits of freedom were being fully relished on that day, and that all the benefits of being the official language would accrue only to Hindi. A portrait of the Hindi fanatic PT Tandon was released. Prime Minister Lal Bahadur Shastri and Home Minister Gulzarilal Nanda were special invitees to the function. When Shastri reached the venue, the organisers presented a badge bearing the photo of Tandon to him, hailing Tandon as the 'Hindi Minister'. Shastri smiled.

Hindi speakers celebrated the day with special receptions, prayers, music and dance programmes, variety entertainment and so on. In contrast, non-Hindi speakers were anguished by the permanent misery that had befallen them. 'Now that Hindi has become the official language, Tamil will die a slow death,' was the thought in their minds.

Tamil Nadu observed January 26 as a day of mourning. Black flags and festoons fluttered across the State. Walls bore posters depicting Mother Tamil shedding bloody tears. The streets were strewn with scraps of black paper. Black balloons dotted the skyline.

Unable to tolerate the peaceful observance of January 26 as a day of mourning, Congress goondas resorted to violence in many places with the active support of policemen. In the presence of policemen, Congress goondas intruded into Arivagam, the DMK headquarters, attacked the party cadre who tried to prevent them and brought down the black flag hoisted in the premises. When their attempts to repeat this violence in Anbagam, the headquarters of the DMK's youth wing, and the office of *Murasoli,* the party news organ, failed, policemen themselves brought down the black flags.

Congress goondas broke into Anna's house when the family members were away and brought down the black flags. They broke the flower pots in the house. Shrieking Congressmen gathered in front of Kalaignar Karunanidhi's house and tried to bring down the black flag. They tried to persuade policemen to do that. But they did not succeed and had to leave the scene disappointed. When Congressmen demanded that the black flag in front of the house of actor SS Rajendran be brought down, he refused and dared them to do that. The mercenaries fled the scene. Policemen themselves brought the flag down. The government filed cases against him and his fellow actor, TV Narayanasamy. The court imposed a fine of Rs 1,000 each on them. They went in appeal to the High Court.

As a pre-emptive move, the oppressive government had arrested Anna and other frontline leaders on the midnight of

January 22 itself. It had arrested Nedunchezhiyan in Madurai and Karunanidhi at a place near Karur when he was enroute to Coimbatore. It had also arrested and imprisoned about 1,500 DMK cadres. Congressmen indulged in rioting in some places with the help of policemen. However, the day of mourning was successfully observed all over the State. The day was observed peacefully, not because of the police force's efficiency or the Congress Minister's threats, but because of Anna's appeal to the cadres to refrain from violence and maintain peace. Anna was clear that mourning for a cause should not become the cause of another mourning. Had he spoken arrogantly like the Chief Minister, the State would have turned into a killing field. After Mahatma Gandhi's death, the world felt the absence of an apostle of peace and non-violence. The manner in which Anna had ensured the peaceful observance of January 25 as a day of mourning proved there was someone to fill the vacuum created by the demise of Gandhi.

Chapter 17
Student Uprising

When the army set forth,
the weight of it broke the spine of the earth.
The hills and the trees of the forest fell,
and the rivers dried up without water.

—*Kalingathu Parani*

The police lathi charge on the inmates of the Venkateswara students' hostel on January 25, 1965; the atrocity of Congress goondas hacking six students in Madurai; the police lathi charge and teargas attack on students in Pachaiyappa's College hostel under the cover of darkness and the attack on teachers; and the police detaining 18 Law College students including P Srinivasan, Muthuraman and Muthu Ramalingam—all these oppressive measures provoked students to launch protests across the State.

They went on marches and held demonstrations condemning the oppression let loose by the government. Wherever the police force acted in a dignified way, the protests were orderly and peaceful. And wherever the police force's 'legal' actions ignited the dormant anger in the students, the results were riots, teargas attacks and firing.

Students from all the colleges in Chennai took out a massive procession. When they reached Fort St George, the students sought permission to meet the Chief Minister and tell him about their demand that English alone should be the official language forever and complain about the reign of terror let loose by the police on teachers and students. Had the Chief Minister met them and offered a few words of consolation, the uprising could have been quelled at the outset. However, the Chief Minister, who had the reputation of being indifferent, of ridiculing people and speaking arrogantly, refused to meet them. He apparently said, 'Why are they marching on the streets when they should be in class?' Reminding them of the prohibitory orders in force then, he indirectly threatened them.

Aristotle apparently said, 'Revolutions are not about trifles, but spring from trifles.' The Chief Minister soon realised how true Aristotle's words of wisdom were. When they were denied permission to meet the Chief Minister, the students raised anti-Hindi slogans and said firmly that they would not move unless he met them. The police started lathi charging them. Unable to bear police brutality and find any escape route, some of the fleeing students jumped into the stinking moat around the fort. The police pulled them out and beat them up again. The brutal attack on students angered people. Buses were attacked and their windows were shattered in stone-throwing. In Annamalai Nagar, Chidambaram, where the Annamalai University is located, 4,000 students took out a procession, indicating their resolve to defeat Hindi imposition even at the cost of their lives. When the procession reached Chidambaram town, the police stopped it, and reminded the students of the prohibitory orders in force. The students declared that they would defy the orders. The police tried to disperse them by beating them with lathis and lobbing teargas shells. The undaunted students tried to breach the police cordon and march forward. The police opened fire. One of the bullets felled Rajendran, a BSc student. He died on the spot. He was the first student martyr in the saga of the anti-Hindi struggle.

The killing of Rajendran sent shock waves across the State.

Students took this as a challenge from the government. They boycotted classes. They removed Hindi name boards from shops, sometimes using ladders. They brought down Congress flags in many places and burnt them. They made shop owners remove glass-framed portraits of Kamaraj, Shastri, Rajendra Prasad, Vallabhbhai Patel, Kakkan and Bhaktavatsalam and break the portraits in the shops. After they were broken, they forced shop owners to set fire to the shattered portraits. In the case of pictures depicting Gandhi and Nehru together, they set fire to them after cutting out Gandhi's image. They broke Hindi name boards in railway stations. Wherever they were unable to break the boards, they covered Hindi letters with tar. Students blocked cars and trucks on roads and raised anti-Hindi slogans. In some places, they wrote 'Down with Hindi' on uniformed policemen's caps and khaki shirts.

Instead of recognising the rising anger of the people and controlling them tactfully, the government increasingly relied on oppressive measures. On January 28, the police arrested 921 people, including 142 students. In Chennai alone, 468 people were arrested. Among the 219 arrested in Madurai, 110 were DMK members.

Speaking at the birth centenary of Lala Lajpat Rai in Delhi on January 23, Prime Minister Lal Bahadur Shastri had said: 'Some people are emotional to the extent of committing self-immolation. I don't know the reasons for the anti-Hindi agitations happening in Chennai. I don't want our people going through any hardship. It was agreed that Hindi would become the official language on January 26. We have confirmed it in our Constitution, and we are following what is laid down in the Constitution. Moreover, Parliament is aware of the problems of non-Hindi-speaking people. The states concerned can continue to use English as the official language. So, there is no issue. Why don't we resolve our differences through talks?'

On the same day, addressing the regional conference of Southern states, Home Minister Gulzarilal Nanda said: 'Now Hindi should be used commonly. India needs a link language. I am shocked and worried about the agitations happening in Chennai. There is no pardon, or even a half pardon, for the disturbances caused there.'

In the speeches of these mighty leaders in positions of responsibility, there was no sign of any legal assurance of justice to the demands of non-Hindi-speaking people. They spun the same old tales and conveyed an indirect threat couched in polite words.

The Madras government also resorted to divide-and-rule tactics and reduced the intensity of the anti-Hindi feelings among students. It ordered the closure of colleges and high schools until February 8 and asked the students to vacate hostels. The government thought that such measures would disrupt the students' unity and mitigate their anger. But, on the contrary, this enforced period of rest only helped the students to resume their agitation with renewed vigour.

On January 31, Congress president Kamaraj and Prime Minister Lal Bahadur Shastri met in Bangalore to find ways to handle the situation. The people who expected this meeting of two great leaders, the meeting of the South and the North, the meeting of the party leader and the government leader, to produce a just solution were disappointed.

Speaking at the 62nd birthday celebrations of Karnataka Chief Minister S Nijalingappa, Kamaraj said: 'Non-Hindi-speaking people are scared that if Hindi occupies the place of English, it will deprive them of their place in politics and other fields. In a democracy, people living in all the places and belonging to different sections have equal opportunities. If these opportunities are denied for whatever reason, it will weaken democracy. After Nehru, the assurance given will be binding on his successors in government. Hindi should be learnt in the interest of the nation.'

Kamaraj's words did not exude the sense of justice that non-

Hindi-speaking people expected. Beginning his speech like a fair-minded judge, he ended it like a Hindi fanatic. Speaking at the same conference, West Bengal Congress leader Atulya Ghosh pontificated on the need for Shastri and Kamaraj to handle the issue in such a way that non-Hindi-speaking people would not feel that an injustice was being done to them. Sanjeeva Reddy said: 'Non-Hindi speakers oppose Hindi because of the announcement of the Minister of State for Education that the Union Public Service Commission examination will be conducted in Hindi.'

Had these leaders spoken about the imperative of amending the Constitution to assure non-Hindi speakers of protection, students would not have continued with their agitation. The language agitation would not have happened.

Although the students' upsurge did not move the iron hearts of the rulers, it did strike a chord in the common people. Civil society, which had been extending moral support and offering their blessings to the protests until then, started speaking out vehemently against the government when its intransigence and brutality increased. Even the Bar Association of Chennai, a body of legal experts which is known to take decisions in a clear and calm manner, was forced to pass a resolution condemning the government's arrogant attitude. It pointed out that it was illegal to unleash special armed forces on students, entering hostels and beating up students lodged there. Its other resolutions were: 'The government should give compensation to the injured students. Lawyers should appear in courts without fees for teachers and students subjected to police violence. A retired High Court judge should be appointed to probe the police violence.'

The government increasingly used its iron hand to suppress the agitation, even as the people's support for the agitation increased. Political leaders condemned the government. Anna said: 'The police force's vengeful attacks on the students makes my heart writhe in pain. We have been shocked to read newspaper reports about midnight hunts, barbaric beatings, lathi charges, teargas attacks and firing. I need not defend the students, because they are capable of explaining their actions and defending themselves. I am happy to know that the student associations are acting on their own without incitement by political parties. They are fighting for their future. They have my sympathies, as do the intelligentsia of the State and other places. I am confident of achieving my objective of liberating South India from the grip of Hindi imperialism through the firm actions of a united front of progressive forces.'

Despite the condemnation of Arignar Anna and other leaders, the opposition of luminaries, the accusations of lawyers and the criticism of experts, the Chief Minister cackled like an angry dictator.

Colleges and high schools reopened on February 8. But the students' resentment had not subsided. In fact, their militancy had only increased. The holiday announced by the government had helped them to be better prepared for the struggle. They returned with increased resources.

Most of the students who returned to college refused to attend classes. In fact, they asked those students who were attending classes out of fear of the college administration to join them. In some colleges, they went on hunger strikes. In many towns, they took out massive processions and defied the police, who reminded them of the prohibitory orders in force. They were attacked with lathis and teargas shells. A large number of students were hurt in police violence.

The credit for making the nation aware of the general public's wholehearted support of the students' agitation in Tamil Nadu goes to the towns of Coimbatore and Pollachi. These towns organised complete general strikes. That was the first time that general strikes were organised as part of the anti-Hindi agitation. In Coimbatore, 600 hotels, 13 cinemas, and many industries, grocery shops, barber shops and laundries were closed. Students went on hunger strikes in front of colleges. Forty thousand textile factory workers and 20,000 workers from engineering and other industries struck work. They belonged to unions affiliated to the DMK and the Left parties. Lawyers boycotted courts.

Contrary to expectations, the student demonstrations were intense in Trichy. Students refused to enter colleges and went on hunger strike outside the premises. Another section of students held demonstrations inside the colleges. The District Collector and the State's Additional Director-General of Police rushed to the colleges to hold talks with them. The students concluded their fast at 5 pm and burnt Hindi books.

In Chennai, only a few women attended classes. Not a single student went to class in Pachaiyappa's College, Theagaraya College, New College, the Institute of Printing Technology and the Kilpauk Medical College. Students went on hunger strike in front of every college—100 students in Pachaiyappa's College, 60 in the Law College, 100 in the Veterinary College, 40 in the Institute of Printing Technology, 20 in Government Arts College, 14 in Theagaraya College, three women students in the Presidency College and 20 in the Government College of Arts and Crafts.

In the towns of Erode, Villupuram, Uthamapalayam, Madurai, Vellore, Thanjavur and Gudalur students boycotted classes and went on hunger strike with the support of the people. There was none who was not happy about the students' strong actions for the cause. The DMK extended its moral support to them. Lawyers' associations, trade unions, traders' associations, and farmers' unions, too, came out in support of the agitating students.

The students' anti-Hindi agitation committee met at the Madras Law College on February 8, 1965. It deliberated on the hardships the students would have to face when they resorted to direct action. Student leaders like P Sriniavasan, Naavalavan, and Ravichandran made it clear that a change in the government's language was not possible without direct action. Accepting their views unanimously, the committee announced the following agitation plan:

a) Students will picket post offices on February 9 and 10.
b) On February 11, they will stop trains all over the State.
c) On February 12, they will organise a general strike.

When these decisions were announced at a press conference, the reporters were shocked. They requested student leaders to review their decisions. The leaders told them that the decisions were taken after serious discussions and they would stand by them.

Dravidians have been protesting against the imposition of Hindi since 1938. Despite that, the government did not change its language policy. So, they decided to carry on the agitation, not just as an expression of resentment, but to force the government to accept their demands. While black flag demonstrations were necessary to express resentment, sacrificing of lives was essential to force the government to accept their demands. Tamil Nadu started preparing for this eventuality.

Chapter 18

I. Picketing

If the enemies can come with open hands,
tell us lies, shackle Tamil,
and proclaim this
Motherland is theirs,
Where is your traditional valour?
Where is your love for the language?
Awake and Arise

—Revolutionary poet Bharathidasan

Following the plans for agitation laid down by the committee, students swung into action, braving oppression, lathi charges, teargas attacks and firing. They set out with the attitude that come what may, they would drive away Hindi and save sweet Tamil.

The first batch of 13 agitators led by MN Ravichandran reached the post office on Anna Salai in Chennai at 10 am to picket it. The post office was cordoned off by a huge contingent of policemen. Thousands of people gathered on both sides of the road, waiting anxiously to witness the students' historic agitation. When the picketers raised slogans against Hindi imperialism, the massive crowd shouted 'Hindi Down Down' thunderously in unison. As soon as the first batch was arrested by the police, the second batch of 17 reached the post office. They were also arrested. The Chennai agitation gave a new momentum to the struggle across the State.

In Trichy, students announced their plan to picket the Teppakulam post office. Policemen surrounded the post office to protect it and arrest the picketers. The cordon had one policeman at every three feet. However, the agitators managed to break the cordon, enter the post office and break down a wall clock. They tore to pieces money order forms, telegram sheets and receipts. The entire office was ransacked. The police attacked the students with lathis and arrested 11 students, including Raghupathi. Another group of students attacked the Marakkadai post office. Then they marched to the Madurai highway and destroyed the banners of Hindi films. They broke down post boxes on both sides of the road. They scribbled on the road: 'This is the fate of whoever supports the imposition of Hindi'.

Students entered the State transport corporation's bus stand opposite Trichy Junction and requested the passengers to alight from buses. They tore down the cloth screens inside the buses and broke the windows. Finally, they set fire to a bus. In the face of this intensified agitation, the police also reacted strongly. Anti-Hindi demonstrations were held in Thanjavur, Coimbatore, Vellore, Tirupathur, Bangalore and Gudalore. Hoisting black flags, burning down Congress flags, blocking vehicles and pasting anti-Hindi posters on them, blacking out Hindi letters, burning Hindi books, defying prohibitory orders—these became commonplace.

In Chennai and Salem, 118 students courted arrest. In other towns, picketing programmes were not peaceful. As emotions ran high, the huge protests turned violent. The government was unable to control the agitators. Even deploying additional police forces from Andhra, Karnataka, Madhya Pradesh and Maharashtra proved no help. The government was reduced to requisitioning the Indian Army. In Tiruppur, the land where freedom fighter Tiruppur Kumaran shed blood, over 2,000 people, including students, tried to take out a procession. The police force's attempt to stop them led to clashes and widespread violence. A student was killed in police firing. Angered by his death, they attacked the police. Sub-Inspectors of police, R Ramasamy and NK Venkatesan, ran towards a ginning mill to save themselves from the crowd chasing them. They locked themselves inside the mill. The angry protesters broke open the mill gates and dragged them onto the road. They rolled a cart on them until they were almost dead. Even then, their anger didn't subside. They poured petrol on the police officers and set them on fire.

This gory tragedy shocked everyone in the State. People were alarmed that the situation was so out of control with emotions running high. Agitators, who were supposed to confront the government in a peaceful manner, succumbed to a wrong sense of vengeance. But Congressmen were the ones responsible for inflaming the agitators' emotions so much that they were provoked into killing officials. They had appreciated protesters who set afire 19 policemen in Chauri Chaura during the freedom struggle. When a judge was shot dead, they had hailed it as an act of courage. When Bhagat Singh had shot dead a police officer for having beaten up Lala Lajpat Rai, and when a student had killed a police commissioner in a case of mistaken identity, they had praised him. Vanchinatha Iyer had been celebrated as a hero after he killed Robert Ashe, the district collector of Tirunelveli. During the anti-Hindi struggle, Congressmen had to face the consequences of having encouraged and rewarded such acts of vengeance in the past.

In Manapparai near Trichy, students marched through the streets, defying prohibitory orders under Section 144 of the Criminal Procedure Code, to protect Mother Tamil. They broke down Hindi name boards, cut down Congress flag posts and burnt the khadi flags. A section of them laid siege to the railway station. Unable to stop them, railway officials fled the scene. The students took control of the station for about six hours. When the police force tried to regain control of the station, the students threw stones and chased them away. A contingent of armed police entered the scene and took control of the situation after opening fire. One student was killed in the firing.

Karur was an important centre of the agitation. When the police brutally beat up students walking in a procession, not sparing even schoolchildren, people were furious. They came like raging waves and attacked government offices. A section of the crowd entered the court and went on a rampage. Judges and lawyers had to run out. One of the protesters sat on a judge's seat and started hearing cases against detainees brought before him by other agitators. He declared that he was setting all of them free. The hearing went like this: 'Did you consume arrack? If you admit to it, you will be free. If you have not drunk arrack, six months' imprisonment.' By the time it all ended, the windows, shelves and documents were reduced to ashes. Insurance offices, municipal buildings and the district collector's office were also set on fire. The agitators ransacked the Karur railway station, brought down its roof and set the entire building on fire. The police opened fire, killing one person. As smoke engulfed Karur, it looked like a place ravaged by invaders. The razed railway station and burnt court building were testimonies to the valour of the agitators, much like the courage shown by Congressmen during the Quit India Movement of 1942.

The people of Kumarapalayam made enormous sacrifices. Over 5,000 of them took out a huge procession. When the police attacked with teargas and lathis without prior warning, the protesters retaliated by attacking government-run workshops and setting fire to public properties. Scared of the agitators, the owners of petrol stations allowed them to take any quantity of petrol they wanted. The agitators used the petrol to set fire to buildings all around. On the pretext of maintaining law and order, the police opened several rounds of fire indiscriminately, killing ten people. This incident shook the State. Kumarapalayam was engulfed in smoke. The blood-splattered streets were strewn with broken bricks and glass. It was horrific to see a free country filling graves with the bodies of people fighting to protect their own language.

In Tiruchengode, 5,000 protesters marched on, unmindful of the policemen's lathi blows. Even teargas could not deter them. Having failed to stop them, the police launched a brutal assault. Incensed by this, the agitators attacked the police station. The police opened fire, killing two and seriously injuring four. Even that could not restore peace in the town. The people regrouped and held a demonstration. The police opened fire again, killing one protester and seriously injuring two.

The railway stations at Trichy, Pudukkottai, Devakottai, Lalgudi, Vellore and Kanchipuram were attacked. In Ramanathapuram, Virudhunagar, Anbil, Poovalur, Tiruvannamalai, Thanjavur, Salem, Kallamangalam and Kurinjipadi, post offices came under attack. Hindi name boards were broken down. Students of the Sacred Heart College in Tirupathur conducted a novel agitation. They took out a procession with tonsured heads, taking the town by surprise. Large crowds gathered to see them. Police resorted to lathi charge to disperse them.

The agitation in Coimbatore was initially peaceful. However, clashes broke out between students and the police subsequently. Students removed Hindi name boards, hoisted black flags, and held demonstrations in front of a cinema showing Hindi films. A section of them entered the cinema hall and set fire to the screen and the film rolls. The police opened fire to disperse the demonstrators outside the cinema. Two people were killed in the firing and six students were injured. A seriously injured woman was admitted to hospital.

In Vellakovil, the demonstration was so intense that the police could not control the crowd. The protesters attacked the railway station, the post office and the telephone exchange. The police opened fire at three places. Eight students were injured in the firing. Two students were admitted to hospital in a serious condition.

II. Rail blockade

Every single resolution of the students' anti-Hindi agitation committee succeeded with overwhelming public support. The Ministers ensconced in the portals of power had not expected the agitation calls issued by the students to inflame people's sentiments about their mother tongue.

Every newspaper front-paged the students' call to block trains on February 11. Hundreds of policemen were deployed in every railway station to handle the situation. The agitators were undaunted by the police force's deterrent measures. They blocked trains in all the important stations and tied black flags to train engines. In some places, they set fire to compartments, shattered signals, brought down railway signal trees, set fire to rail godowns, broke Hindi name boards, as well as tables, chairs, fans and doors. They also delinked tracks and cut off telephone cables.

The protest was intense in Chennai, Coimbatore, Thanjavur, Chidambaram, Pondicherry and Trichy. As people surged ahead like a deluge, the police force was unable to control them.

The train blockade agitation in Thanjavur was historic. About 20,000 students and ordinary citizens gathered at the railway station. The police arrested 21 students who blocked a train by lying down on the tracks.

In Pondicherry, protesters stopped a train and damaged it. They set fire to the parcel office, a godown, tickets, ledgers and books. Three contingents of police rushed to the station and dispersed the students. A fire tender had to be brought in to put out the flames. In Villupuram, about 1,000 students stopped a train outside the station. They asked the passengers to disembark and then damaged the lights, water pipes and fans inside the compartments. They set fire to some of the compartments. They blacked out Hindi letters in the station and tied black flags to engines.

In Chennai, the protesters blocked trains at many places. They stopped a train in Kodambakkam and damaged it. They broke the chairs and tables in the retiring room of upper-class passengers and set fire to a first class compartment. Terrified railway officers locked themselves up inside the Station Master's cabin. When the agitators tried to set on fire the Indo-Ceylon Express, the police lathi charged them. A student was killed, and several others were injured in the police action.

Sensing that the situation was out of control, anti-Hindi agitation leaders Anna and Rajaji appealed to the agitators to stop the protests. But the agitators paid no heed to them. Realising that the agitation could not be controlled through lawful means, the Police Commissioner warned that he would impose a curfew. He stated: 'If our actions are unable to bring the situation under control by the dawn of tomorrow, we may have to consider imposing a curfew. However, it is not necessary at this stage. Generally, a prior announcement has to be made before imposing a curfew. But it is not possible in the present situation. This should be taken as a warning. A final decision will be announced on All India Radio. Curfew will be in force from 8 pm to 6 am I request parents not to send their children out.'

The flames of the volcanic eruption of the agitation reached Red Fort in Delhi. The Union Ministers were unable to ignore it any longer. Nor were they able to speak with the arrogance of power. They were in a predicament, lacking the courage to criticise the agitators or finding a way out. In order to appease the disappointed Dravidians, they were lavish with assurances.

Speaking to reporters, Home Minister GL Nanda said: 'The Centre is ready to meet the just demands of the people of the South. If the government's language policy is a hindrance to their job aspirations, we will make proper arrangements to set right the situation. However, experts will have to examine the issue. Nehru's assurance will be kept, whether it is part of the law or not. The issue is that Hindi should not be imposed on people who do not want it. The Constitution will not be an impediment. English will be used in every department as it was before. Hence, there is no need to amend the Constitution.'

But Dravidians had realised that the assurance of Nehru was itself a mirage, so they had no faith in other assurances. It was unfortunate that Nanda was not aware of this.

The Union Cabinet held an emergency meeting to discuss the situation. On the basis of its decision, the Prime Minister addressed the nation on radio. But his speech was like old wine in new bottle. People who expected justice from him were frustrated. Instead of paving the way for a solution, his speech rekindled emotions. Instead of calming people down, it agitated them further—to the extent that even two Union Ministers were incensed. Within minutes of the Prime Minister's address, the Union Ministers shot off their resignation letters to him. Their resignations imparted a new momentum to the agitation. The agitation committee of the students announced a general strike in the hope that it would open the gates of success.

III. General Strike

The agitation committee called upon the students to ensure a general strike all over the State. There was unprecedented response to their call. Factories, restaurants, shops, colleges and schools remained closed. The strike was total, even in hamlets. People ignored Union Finance Minister TT Krishnamachari's statement that the general strike was wrong and unnecessary. They held huge demonstrations. The situation in the towns was explosive. Demonstrations were held even in villages.

Demonstrations in Pollachi, Pondicherry, Trichy, Arcot, and

Tiruvottiyur created disturbances. Many places in Coimbatore emerged as centres of intense struggle. In Pollachi, about 50 kilometres from Coimbatore, the police used teargas shells and lathis to disperse militant demonstrators. The fleeing demonstrators set fire to government offices and schools while retreating. The town reverberated with sounds of gunfire as the Army's machine guns boomed to disperse the agitators. Many people were killed on the spot. No official figures of the number of casualties were released. Newspaper reports said two people were killed in two rounds of firing. But people alleged that the machine guns had killed about 100 people and that the dead were buried near the Army camp. The issue was raised in the Assembly. Pollachi was the only place where machine guns were used during the anti-Hindi agitation.

In Pondicherry, the general strike was complete. Transport services came to a standstill. Government offices were protected by a heavy police force. Under the pretext of bringing the situation under control and restoring peace, the police resorted to repressive measures. They did not spare even those who were out to buy groceries. Angered by this, people damaged and set fire to public properties. The Aurobindo Ashram was also attacked. The agitators broke down tables and chairs in the ashram. The railway station came under attack. When the police resorted to a lathi charge, the agitators retaliated by stoning them. They held torchlight demonstrations and used petrol bombs to set fire to public properties. The police opened fire in four places in which four people died and many were injured. Among those killed was a boy named Gandhi, barely six years old, who was watching the agitation from the doorstep of his house. A bullet fired at the agitators killed him instead. What was his sin? His death was proof of the indiscriminate fire opened by the police. Another victim was Innacimuthu, who did not have anything to do with the agitation. A courier with All India Radio, this innocent man was killed while he was passing by on a cycle.

In the Arni, Arcot, Jolarpet and Peranampattu towns in North Arcot, armed police opened fire to quell the agitation. In Jolarpet and Peranampattu, two persons were killed and many injured. In Arcot, a carpentry training workshop was set on fire. The agitators uprooted post boxes, lined them up in the middle of the road and held a demonstration. In Thanjavur district, police opened fire in Agaramangudi and Mannargudi.

In Tiruvottiyur near Chennai, the police used extreme violence to control the agitators, beating them up with the muzzles of rifles and jabbing them with bayonets. Booted policemen kicked the agitators. Incensed by these attacks, the agitators shattered streetlights and vandalised the railway station. They set fire to a train with eight compartments and uprooted railway tracks. In police firing, a DMK member was killed. Many people were seriously injured and some of them were admitted to hospital in a serious condition.

Chapter 19

The Defence of India Act Invoked

At about the midnight of February 16, 1965, the Congress government arrested Kalaignar Karunanidhi under the draconian Defence of India Act, because, in its view, it was his emotion-filled speeches that incited students to plunge into a militant battle against the imposition of Hindi. He was taken to the Palayamkottai jail on the same night. Kalaignar had unbearable chest pain because he was carried in a vehicle meant to transport vegetables. The accompanying policemen were ruthless and looked the other way as he writhed in pain. He fainted when the truck was nearing Madurai. It was only after he fell, unconscious, that he was taken to a hospital in Madurai for treatment. Then they proceeded to Palayamkottai Jail, hoping that he would not die since he had been provided with treatment.

Why was Kalaignar Karunanidhi singled out for arrest after the release of the other DMK leaders? And why was he arrested under the Defence of India Act? Why was he imprisoned under Section 30 of the Act, which bars legal remedy?

The advocate representing Kalaignar Karunanidhi argued in the Madras High Court that only two days after his arrest he was told that the Defence of India Act had been invoked against him and that it was the result of the political animosity between him and the Chief Minister. The court did not accept this argument. Angry MLAs belonging to the DMK fired salvos at the government. The

Chief Minister replied: 'We can't give the reasons for his arrest; the anti-Hindi agitation was not the only reason for his arrest, and we do not need to reply to your questions.' His attitude did not mean that he was hard-hearted. The reality was that he took refuge under the Defence of India Act out of cowardice.

Karunanidhi was already languishing in solitary confinement at the Palayamkottai jail when he was sentenced to six months' imprisonment in a case related to the burning of a copy of the Constitution. The government filed another case against him and Murasoli Maran and arrested the latter. Commenting on this, Kalaignar said: 'The first thing Anna told me when he visited me in jail was that my nephew had also been arrested the previous night. After saying this, Anna heaved a sigh. Was that sigh not a greeting for my family? It seems they have filed a case against me and Maran for writing something "wrong" in *Murasoli*. If a just argument is the new meaning given to the word "wrong," we will commit that "wrong" from generation to generation and attain glory.'

After Kalaignar Karunanidhi, the police arrested about 75 DMK cadre under the Defence of India Act. It then turned its attention to Tamil scholars, including KAP Viswanathan, and arrested them under the same Act.

The government was unhappy with the fair reporting of the agitation by newspapers. It despatched police and military officers to newspaper offices, asking them to censor reports of the government's reign of terror against anti-Hindi protesters. In some instances, these officers even stopped the press and removed the reports they did not like.

Newspapers had never faced this kind of harassment by British officials during the Quit India Movement. The government of free India, which prided itself on being a republic, stooped to curbing the freedom of the press, a cornerstone of democracy. It filed cases against dailies such as *Murasoli, Thamizhnadu, Dina Thanthi, Swadesamitran, Navamani,* and *Malai Murasu* and the weekly,

Malai Mani. *Dina Thanthi*, the highest selling daily in Tamil Nadu, published by SP Adithanar, who had led a life of dedication to Tamil, extensively reported on the anti-Hindi agitation. For this reason, Adithanar was arrested under the Defence of India Act on October 9, 1965, and kept in jail until January 7, 1966. This was his second arrest in connection with the anti-Hindi agitation. Earlier, in August 1960, the DMK had decided to show black flags to President Rajendra Prasad during his visit to Chennai. Adithanar had been arrested on October 11, 1960, when he was about to board a train at Madurai Junction, for having carried a story in his daily in support of the black flag demonstration. He was released only on October 16, 1960.

Even college professors, who educate thousands of intelligent people, who drive away the darkness called illiteracy with the light of knowledge, who lay the foundations for inventions and innovations, were beaten mercilessly by the police. This was another deplorable chapter in the history of the Congress. This happened on January 26, when hundreds of security personnel intruded into the hostel of Pachaiyappa's College and beat up the students in every room. On hearing the violence unleashed on students, Prof Sundaralingam and the assistant warden, Ramchandran, rushed to the hostel and requested the police to leave the place. The police ignored their pleas and instead attacked them. A bleeding Ramchandran fell unconscious. The Principal, Mr TS Sankaranarayana Pillai, issued a statement condemning the incident.

Police atrocities were not confined to Chennai. Their inhuman behaviour was repeated in Madurai. On February 10, students of Madurai Arts College burnt Hindi books. When they tried to take out a procession, the police attacked them with teargas and lathis. The students ran into the college campus to save themselves. The police entered the campus and attacked the fleeing students. The principal rushed to the college and asked the police to stop beating the students and leave the premises. He was 'rewarded' with beatings and kicks. He returned to his office, but the police did not spare him even then. An extremely patient principal endured the beatings stoically. The police also beat up Prof Varadachary, who came in to protect the principal. They entered the college's administrative office and beat him up again. This assault on the principal, despite knowing his official status, was not only a disgusting act of extreme cruelty but also an unpardonable sin. The police even filed a case against them and made them stand in the witness box like criminals.

Mr Arunachala Gounder, the principal of Madurai Diraviyam Thayumanavar Hindu College, was also arrested on the charge of inciting the students to fight against the imposition of Hindi. And the only evidence they had against him was that he was a professor of Tamil. When would Hindi imperialists cease to consider one's love for the mother tongue a crime? When would this come to an end?

Another Tamil professor arrested by the police was Dr Ilakkuvanar of Madurai Thiagarajar College. The police refused to release him on bail initially. His crime was that he had announced that he would walk from Madurai, the headquarters of the Tamil Sangam, to Chennai, the administrative headquarters of the State government. He planned to meet people along the way and explain the importance of making Tamil the medium of instruction in schools. The government, which cites college students' lack of interest in learning their subjects in Tamil as the reason for not making it the medium of instruction, should have welcomed Ilakkuvanar's initiative. But it arrested and jailed him under the Defence of India Act.

Having arrested Tamil professors under the Defence of India Act without respect for their worth, the government went on to invoke the law against students as well. It arrested student leaders P Srinivasan, K Raja Mohammad, Na Kamarasu, K Kalimuthu,

N Naavalavan, P Jeyaprakasam, Sethu, R Subramanian and Duraikannu and incarcerated them in the Palayamkottai Jail.

During the freedom movement, Pandit Nehru had said that law and order was the refuge of dictators and reactionaries who did not respect the law. Would he have anticipated that the very dictators and reactionaries nurtured by the Congress would be prostrating before the sanctum sanctorum of the law?

Chapter 20

In Other States...

Let you be free soon, let you succeed,
Life doesn't know heat or cold,
And a fighter doesn't know fatigue or fall,
Says he,
Nurturing his motherland's agitation
without malice

—Poet Bharathiyar

Anti-Hindi agitations had been spearheaded by Tamil Nadu from the very beginning. Bengal was like the right hand in the struggle. Hindi fanatics have often claimed that those who oppose Hindi are few and they are confined to Tamil Nadu and Bengal. These fanatics do not know that when the fight for noble ideals begins, very few lead from the front; but, as the days go by, they gain the strength to challenge and defeat imperialism. Bengal was the guide for non-Hindi-speaking people in the North as Tamil Nadu was to Dravidians in the South. The anti-Hindi sentiment in these states awakened the non-Hindi-speaking people of other states.

The simultaneous development of anti-Hindi sentiments in the non-Hindi-speaking states shocked Hindi fanatics. They hoped to create a permanent charter recognising Hindi as the official language by using Gandhi's name, enforcing the Congress' organisational discipline, cleverly citing the threat from China, emphasising the importance of national unity and arguing that English was an alien language. But the anti-Hindi agitations that arose in the non-Hindi-speaking states evoked the fear of losing political power.

Although Hindi was imposed in Kerala under the three-language formula, no political party in the State came forward to make Hindi fanatics aware of the anti-Hindi sentiment that prevailed among students and parents. The Congress and the communists in Kerala, where the level of unemployment among the educated is very high, spread the wrong idea that if the people of the State learnt Hindi, they would have an edge over the people of other non-Hindi-speaking states in capturing jobs at the all-India level. Instead of creating a movement that would defeat Hindi fanatics, they nurtured the slavish attitude of garnering jobs by bowing down to Hindi. On the other hand, the student army of Kerala was up in arms against this slavish mentality and rose to assert their linguistic rights. They pasted posters and pamphlets on cars, bikes, buses, trucks and in trains hailing Malayalam, rejecting Hindi and demanding English.

When Lal Bahadur Shastri visited Ernakulam in February, hundreds of law students gathered in front of their college holding black flags to show the Prime Minister their opposition to the imposition of Hindi and condemning the crowning of Hindi on January 26. The police rushed to the venue, snatched the black flags and arrested 15 students.

The anti-Hindi protest in Ernakulam spread and intensified in other parts of Kerala from February 10. On that day, college and school students in Kottayam boycotted classes and took out a huge anti-Hindi procession. On February 12, student representatives from the district of Ernakulam met and issued a statement calling for a general strike in Kerala on February 12 as it was done in Tamil Nadu. They called upon students to boycott classes and hold anti-Hindi demonstrations. Koresan, a student of CMS

College in Kottayam, went on a fast-unto-death protest. His health deteriorated on the third day of his hunger strike. Expressing their solidarity with him, four students of Baselios College and two students of BCM College for Women went on a hunger strike. When Koresan's condition deteriorated further on February 12, the police admitted him to a hospital. But another student named George Kurien started a hunger strike at the same venue.

In response to the call by their leaders, students of Kerala boycotted classes and held demonstrations on February 12. The agitation intensified in the major towns of Kerala. A group of writers and journalists undertook a one-day fast in front of the Kottayam post office. Students from the Regional Engineering College also joined the agitations and raised slogans against Hindi. They shouted slogans demanding the resignation of AV Thomas, a Union Minister from Kerala, in line with the example set by two Union Ministers from Tamil Nadu.

The anti-Hindi agitation committee of students in Kerala met again on February 16 and reviewed the dangerous situation prevailing in Tamil Nadu. It strongly condemned the Union government's intransigence despite the supreme sacrifices made by anti-Hindi agitators in Tamil Nadu. It issued a statement calling for a general strike at the all-India level on February 18 and appealed to students to boycott schools until February 23. Sensing that the protests were spreading, the government ordered the closure of schools for five days. However, despite the closure of educational institutions, students participated in the demonstrations held in front of their colleges and schools on February 18. Palakkad witnessed a clash between the demonstrators and Jana Sangh volunteers supporting Hindi. The agitators brought down the Jana Sangh's flag poles and tore up the flags.

In the State capital, Thiruvananthapuram, demonstrators gathered at important road junctions. They stopped cycles, scooters, trucks, and buses and pasted anti-Hindi posters on them. This was done in Kollam, Kottayam, Ernakulam and Changanassery as well.

It may be thought that the anti-Hindi agitations in Kerala were not as intense as they were in Tamil Nadu. It should be remembered that students in Kerala fought without the cooperation of any political party and without the moral support of any political leader. All they had was the support of the common people. Conducting a struggle peacefully without support from a political party was a turning point in the history of the anti-Hindi agitation.

Karnataka, too, contributed to the anti-Hindi movement. Along with fraternal states that raised their voice against the imposition of Hindi, Karnataka clearly demonstrated its anti-Hindi stance to Hindi imperialists. In response to the DMK's call to observe January 26 as a day of mourning, the party's Karnataka wing swung into action in Bangalore. On learning of its plan, the State government arrested many DMK volunteers and councillors. However, black flags were hoisted, and black festoons were hung in many parts of the city.

Anti-Hindi feelings grew, leading to demonstrations in Bangalore on February 9. Thousands of students sporting black badges gathered in the streets and raised anti-Hindi slogans. They removed Hindi sign boards along the procession route. In some places, they broke the boards. The police resorted to lathi charge to disperse the protesters, which resulted in clashes. Undaunted by the lathi charge, they resumed the procession and reached the Town Hall, where they passed a resolution against making Hindi the official language.

Anti-Hindi protests broke out again on February 10 with the participation of thousands of students and citizens. When a section of the protesters held a demonstration near a school in Vannarapet, the police lathi charged them. The students, who were chased away by the police, entered a school in Cox Town and asked the students to join their agitation. The police dispersed them again with a lathi charge. Some of the students gathered at the Vidhana Soudha (State Assembly) and started a hunger strike. Sensing that the situation was turning volatile, the District and Sessions Judge issued prohibitory orders under Section 45 of the Mysore Police Act.

In the demonstrations held all over Bangalore, students raised anti-Hindi slogans in Kannada. In Sivaji Nagar, the police could not disperse the protesters. They chased them away with a lathi charge and two teargas attacks. The government announced the closure of all schools and colleges in the city for two days. Despite that, a huge protest broke out on February 12. Students from 10 colleges and nine high schools went on a hunger strike in front of the Vidhana Soudha. They raised slogans against making Hindi the official language and demanded that Kannada be given that status. Expressing solidarity with the fasting students, hundreds of engineering college students took out a procession. At the Indian Institute of Science, 230 students and research scholars undertook a 12-hour fast.

On February 11, Kolar saw a huge, unprecedented demonstration. Thousands of students and workers of the Kolar Gold Fields marched in a procession through the streets of the town. They removed Hindi sign boards on the way. As the crowd remained unmoved even after a lathi charge, the police threw teargas shells at them.

Chief Minister S Nijalingappa, who had been speaking in support of Hindi, changed his stance after realising the justness of non-Hindi speakers' protests. Addressing a public meeting, he said: 'We can defer the language issue for some time. There are more important issues that need to be addressed now. The government will see to it that Hindi is not imposed on anyone, especially on students. There are some basic reasons for popular apprehensions about Hindi. But violence is not the way to express them.' Thus, the demonstrations in Karnataka succeeded in changing the attitude of some persons in power.

Historically, Bengal has been hailed as the land of the brave. Hindi fanatics knew that Bengal, like Tamil Nadu, had long opposed Hindi. All the political leaders, scientists, litterateurs and other experts had been voicing their opposition to Hindi from the beginning. When the Assembly debated the question of the official language, the Bengali representatives asked why Bengali could not be given that status. They never approved of Hindi as the official language. Thus, in Eastern India, Bengal was at the forefront in opposing Hindi. When Bengal stands up and protests, it is like the roar of a lion. A massive procession of students was held in Calcutta on February 11, which drew the common people into the struggle. Anti-Hindi slogans reverberated all over the city like the death knell of pro-Hindi politicians. The procession was welcomed by people, who lined up on both sides of the route. When it reached the Bhawanipore School, the agitators asked the students to come out of their classes and join them. Some students stayed put in the classrooms, and the agitators entered the rooms to persuade them to leave. A security guard stabbed three school students and seriously injured them. As the news of the stabbing spread, thousands of students moved to Bhawanipore and laid siege to the school. The police lathi charged and teargassed the protesters. They arrested four students. The entire city seethed with rage. To control the situation, the government ordered the closure of all schools in Calcutta until February 15.

Fearing that the students' protests would attract other citizens, as it had in Tamil Nadu, the State government moved an unofficial resolution in the Assembly demanding equal status for all the national languages. Jyoti Basu, the Leader of the Opposition, proposed the resolution, which was seconded by Congress member Prathap Chandra Chunder. It was passed by the House unanimously. However, it did not have the desired impact on the city. Agitations broke out again on February 13 and 14. Thousands of students and ordinary citizens participated in the demonstrations, which were intense in Northern and Central Calcutta. Screening of Hindi films was stopped in four cinema halls.

In Baranagar, Barasat and Khardaha in Bengal, Hindi sign boards were broken down. Cinema halls screening Hindi films were blockaded. Alarmed, theatre owners stopped screening Hindi films in 40 theatres. Although the agitations in Bengal lasted only a few days, they made clear the people's hatred of and opposition to the imposition of Hindi.

The credit for forcing the State government to convey to the Centre the people's reasonable opposition to Hindi should go to the brave Bengali protesters.

In Andhra, the speakers of sweet Telugu were prepared for any sacrifice in the fight against Hindi. The struggle there was as intense as it was in Tamil Nadu. Initially, these protests in the form of processions were confined to towns such as Tirupati and Visakhapatnam. They gained momentum after the agitation intensified in Tamil Nadu. On February 10, thousands of students from Venkateswara University marched through the streets of Tirupati wearing black badges and holding black flags. They raised slogans against Hindi, praised Telugu, and demanded that English be the official language. They held a demonstration inside the Tirupati railway station. The police lathi charged and teargassed them. In the brutal attack, six students were seriously injured and 14 were arrested.

The agitation spread to the Kurnool and Nellore districts and Madanapalle in the Chittoor district. Hindi sign boards were removed from post offices, railway stations, telephone exchanges, courts and police stations. On February 12, the struggle intensified in Tiruttani, the hometown of President S Radhakrishnan. When the police lathi charged the protesters, about 500 of them broke into the library in the President's house. They brought the books out and burnt them. They also damaged a portrait of the President.

In Anantapur, about 2,000 students marched in procession on February 14. They either blacked out or broke Hindi sign boards in public places and private establishments. When the police lathi charged them, they retaliated by throwing stones. Many people, including the Sub Divisional Magistrate, were injured.

A general strike was observed in Cuddapah. Not a single shop was open and transport services came to a halt. The protesters took out a procession and shouted slogans hailing Telugu and rejecting Hindi.

On February 15, there was a turning point in the struggle. A complete general strike was observed in Nellore. About 10,000 students and other citizens organised a massive procession, stunning the town. The slogan-shouting demonstrators laid siege to the Nellore North railway station. Armed policemen lathi charged and teargassed them. But the protesters did not retreat. They attacked the station from different directions. The police opened fire. Many were seriously injured. One of them succumbed to his injuries in a hospital.

The police's violent retaliation angered the people. They gathered again in the evening and uprooted rail tracks and cut off communication lines. The police opened fire again, which injured many more people. A section of the crowd attacked the post office while fleeing. When they tried to set fire to the post office, the police dispersed them with a lathi charge. The situation turned volatile due to police brutality. The government imposed a curfew. The fearless anti-Hindi protests of the people of the town, during which a person lost his life, gave a special place to Nellore in the history of the agitation.

On February 17, thousands of students held huge demonstrations in Cuddapah, Proddatur and Kadiri. The agitation in Andhra reached its climax at Hindupuram on February 18. When about 1,500 agitating students ransacked the railway station, the police beat them mercilessly. Angered by this attack, other citizens also joined the protest. The police opened fire when the situation went out of control. A few protesters were injured. The protesters fleeing the scene attacked the police station. The police opened fire again, killing one person. This death led to riots, prompting the police to open fire again. One protester lost his life in the shooting.

Even if the government had apologised for the Hindupuram atrocity, God would not have accepted it, since the police fired on a peaceful, unarmed group of protesters. The people of the town condemned the police brutality and observed a total bandh the following day.

If Hindi fanatics fail to acknowledge the just struggles of the people of Bengal, Andhra, Karnataka and Kerala, which they conducted without the encouragement or support of any political party, those who truly wish to protect national unity should begin to worry and wonder which direction the Indian subcontinent is going to take.

Chapter 21

After the Storm

The intense involvement of ordinary citizens, the protest methods they adopted, the loss of lives, the destruction of property, transport disruptions and the administrative crisis were unprecedented in the history of Tamil Nadu. The emotions that had built up for 25 years since 1938 burst out in a deluge during the anti-Hindi struggles. Tamils fought against the imposition of Hindi, proving that the valour reflected in literary works like *Kalingathu Parani* and *Purananuru* had not died.

It was only after the situation had turned grave with reports of police firing and blood-stained streets in every city and town that Union Ministers Indira Gandhi and D Sanjivayya[79] rushed to Tamil Nadu to offer their condolences. The Prime Minister hurriedly convened a Cabinet meeting and reviewed the situation. He announced that he would convene a meeting of Chief Ministers on February 23 and 24 to hold consultations on the language issue. He briefed the President about the precarious situation prevailing in Tamil Nadu. On radio, he appealed to the people to maintain peace.

Congress president Kamaraj, who was camping in Kochi for an election campaign, rushed to Tamil Nadu. At Coimbatore, when he was asked to give his opinion on the Prime Minister's address on radio, he said: 'I've not heard it; so, I cannot say anything about it.' This was a matter of shame for Tamils. Kamaraj was not ashamed of it because he took pride in being a nationalist.

Telegrams carrying news of police oppression, the fiery consequences of the agitators' response to it, and police firings and lists of people killed in them poured into the agitators' camps. The protesting students were stunned and extremely saddened at the growing list of martyrs. They were fighting for a just cause. Their intent was pure. And they were determined to carry on the struggle. Their methods were not new, but the intensity of the agitation and its consequences were unexpected and ominous.

The agitation committee held long deliberations on the consequences of oppression, the resignation of Ministers, the Chief Ministers' conference, the appeals of Rajaji and Annadurai and the indescribable grief that had engulfed Tamil Nadu. Although the government had not accepted their just demands, it had at least decided to reconsider the language issue and find legal ways to ensure the continuance of English as the official language. Taking this into consideration, the committee decided to suspend the agitation. In an appeal to students, it said: 'With the successful observance of a general strike today, we will end our protests. We request students not to continue the struggle. In a few days, the general council of the agitation committee will meet. A final decision will be announced. We appeal to the government to release all those arrested in connection with the anti-Hindi agitation.'

Only after this announcement did the government breathe easy.

Arignar Anna said: 'The students have taken an intelligent decision. We are proud of them. By deciding to suspend the agitation, they have created a situation conducive to finding a solution. The government should release the arrested students unconditionally and restore peace.'

Union Home Minister Gulzarilal Nanda[80] said: 'The students' decision will prevent others from creating trouble. A new chapter will begin now.'

Although the students' decision was welcomed unanimously by political leaders, a small section was disappointed.

Despite the Tamils' heroic sacrifices, which were unheard of even during the freedom struggle, the government refused to amend the Constitution to change the language policy. It did not accept the demand to make official all the 14 national languages. Many people were unhappy with the suspension of the agitation and wondered whether the agitation would later get the kind of massive support that it now had. Was it not the duty of the protesters to take advantage of the unprecedented unity among people on the language issue and their readiness to make any sacrifice, and carry on the agitation bravely? Was it right to refrain from giving a final blow to the poisonous snake when it was on the verge of death? Was it right to drop the gun when one more bullet would have killed the tiger?

Thus, the agitation continued despite its formal suspension. It ran like a driverless vehicle. Though the situation was not as volatile on February 13 as it was on February 12, agitations continued in many places. The places that did not witness protests looked like graveyards. At Gudiyatham and Arni in the North Arcot district, police fired on protesters to disperse them. Many were injured in the firing. At Namakkal in the Salem district, about 3,000 protesters carrying petrol cans and stones rained stones on the police station and threatened to burn it down. The police opened fire six times to disperse the huge crowd.

Gingee in the South Arcot district had been ruled by brave kings and the rock fort of Raja Desingu is a standing testimony to valour. It was no surprise that people of the town protested strongly against the imposition of Hindi. They set fire to the office of the Archaeological Survey of India and attacked the panchayat office and the police station. The police force's lathi charge and teargas-lobbing failed to disperse the protesters. Oppression was a blunt knife for people who were ready to sacrifice their lives.

Unable to bring the situation under control, the police opened fire, killing two persons.

In the Gudalore and Cumbum areas in Madurai district, the protesters fought bravely against the imposition of Hindi. In the police firing to disperse a crowd attacking the Gudalore post office, three persons were killed. Angry protesters attacked the police station and killed two policemen guarding it. They hauled the dead body of one, dumped it in a truck and set it on fire. When the post office was attacked in Cumbum, the police fired on the crowd, killing two persons.

To restore peace in these two areas, a 1,500-strong army contingent was deployed. The army committed innumerable atrocities—beating up people mercilessly, chasing and attacking people on the streets, entering homes and harassing even children and bed-ridden patients, kicking even the aged with booted legs, breaking vessels, abusing and beating up women, raping young women and so on. All these atrocities were committed in retaliation for a mob having killed two constables. If the government thought that the army was justified in perpetrating violence on innocents on the pretext of avenging the death of the policemen, time would make it realise how people were forced to fight back when hundreds of innocent unarmed agitators were shot down mercilessly by the security forces.

The police arrested many people on charges of inciting the Gudalore riots and abetting the killing of the two policemen. Among the arrested was the DMK legislator, M Rajangam[81]. While in custody, the police tortured him and even administered electric shocks to him. He was so brutally beaten that he started bleeding all over the body. When a thirsty Rajangam asked for water, the police gave him urine. Though he was accused of committing murder, the court acquitted him.

The government was shocked when there was no normalcy despite the formal suspension of the agitation. It censored news of the continuing agitation lest it encouraged those who wanted to resume the struggle. Fearing government action, newspapers themselves blacked out the news of sporadic agitations. They were forced to carry only the information provided by the Chief Secretary to the Government. Freedom of expression was reduced to the status of a government dole.

The students' agitation committee met on February 18, deliberated on the prevailing situation and the assurances given by Ministers. It took the following decisions:

1. The committee reiterates its demand to scrap Part 17 of the Constitution dealing with official language.
2. Students will not be satisfied unless English is restored to its pre-1950 status as the only official language.
3. The government's inefficiency and diplomacy deficit were responsible for the disturbances in Tamil Nadu. We don't believe in the government's assurances.
4. The decision of Union Ministers C Subramaniam[82] and OV Alagesan[83] to withdraw their resignations is disappointing. Their resignation and the withdrawal of resignation were mere 'stunts'.
5. When the Chief Ministers of non-Hindi-speaking states meet, they should demand scrapping of the constitutional provision on the official language.
6. The recruitment exams for Central government jobs should be conducted in all the 14 national languages.
7. In order to create a harmonious situation in Tamil Nadu, the government should release the arrested students unconditionally.
8. The government should pay compensation to the families of the students who were killed and those who lost their limbs in the course of the agitation.

The students' decision on language-related issues were based on the DMK's language policy.

All the arrested students were released unconditionally and the government withdrew the cases against them in order to restore peace in the State and prevent a recurrence of the agitation. Exams that were to take place in March and April were postponed to May.

Many Chief Ministers publicly urged the government to amend the Official Languages Act to ensure the continuation of English as the official language and give legal status to Nehru's assurance. Karnataka Chief Minister S Nijalingappa[84] said that amending the Act would satisfy people. Andhra Chief Minister K Brahmananda Reddy[85] said that it would be good to give legal status to Nehru's assurance in the interest of national unity.

After consulting his Cabinet colleagues and the opposition leaders, Chief Minister PC Sen of West Bengal issued a five-point plan to resolve the language issue. It said:

1. Hindi should not be imposed on non-Hindi-speaking states unless their Assemblies accept Hindi by a three-fourths majority.
2. All-India recruitment exams should be conducted only in English. If Hindi is imposed, the government should allow use of all the 14 national languages. Government posts should be allotted on the basis of population-based reservation.
3. Parliament members should be allowed to speak in their respective State languages.
4. Centre-State communications should be in English. If any communication is in Hindi, it should have an official English translation.
5. The government should extend to all State languages the financial assistance it gives to Hindi.

In his inaugural address to Parliament, President S Radhakrishnan had said that English should continue as the additional official language as long as non-Hindi-speaking people wanted it.

The great revolution initiated by students and supported by the common people forced the government to change its language policy. It could not evade the issue by giving lavish assurances or through oppression. It had to come to a legally binding agreement. Although people were not fully satisfied with the changes the government had agreed to make, they considered it a temporary victory and decided to be patient. And Hindi fanatics worried that the flagpole of dominance they had established would fall.

Chapter 22

The January Revolution

'Revolution can never be forecast; it cannot be foretold; it comes by itself. But when it comes, nobody can stop it'.[86]

—VI Lenin

Dravidians and Bengalis are the only people in the world who created a revolution to protect their mother tongue. No other country in the world has such a long list of people who sacrificed their lives for the sake of their language. The January Revolution, as it is called since it began in Tamil Nadu in January, is often referred to as an 'agitation' or a 'riot' only by those who lack knowledge of their own language, who are not angered by its destruction, who do not love their language, who are slaves of Hindi imperialism and who keep their eyes shut in the dark room called united India.

Revolution does not consist only in opposing foreign rule and fighting for freedom. Its goal varies with time and the situation prevailing in a country. The Quit India Movement of August 1942 was a revolution for freedom from alien rule. The French Revolution, which had the goal of establishing 'Liberty, Fraternity, Equality', was against the King. The Russian Revolution, which was aimed at establishing socialism, was against the Tsar. The American Revolution was the result of a conflict between the white settlers and the British rulers. The Industrial Revolution was a turning point in the history of England, which brought about great technological changes. When new ways of practising agriculture emerged, it was called the Green Revolution.

The May Day revolution ensured eight-hour workdays for the working class. Similarly, the January Revolution was a historic struggle to protect the mother tongue.

The world always remembers and praises those who take part in revolutions and sacrifice their lives, because it is their martyrdom that paves the way for a life of freedom for crores of people. Non-Hindi-speaking people have a duty to hail those who took part in the January Revolution and fell victim to the bullets of oppressors, committed self-immolation, lost their legs, arms and eyes, underwent torture and shed blood. It was the martyrdom of those spotless souls that brightened the future of non-Hindi-speaking people.

History hails people who fight for a noble cause, even if they commit mistakes. As an English writer-philosopher said, every revolution in the world has seen some untoward incidents, but history does not underestimate it because of that. Even some horrible incidents that have happened because of the force of circumstances are seen as typical instances of courage.

The reign of terror unleashed by the Tamil Nadu government during the January Revolution will never be forgotten by the younger generation. Its oppressive ways created killing fields. It took pleasure in killing hapless people and even fleeing students. The army went around the State with murderous intent, like vultures circling in the sky looking for dead bodies. Newspapers released lists of martyrs like election results. *The Hindu* carried the following details of people who were felled by police bullets in various districts:

Chengalpet
Tiruvottiyur 1
North Arcot

Arcot 1
Aarni 6
Jolarpet 1
Pernambut 3
Walajabath 1
Pondicherry 5
South Arcot
Gingee 1
Chidambaram 1
Coimbatore
Kumarapalayam 6
Pollachi 10
Tirupur 4
Sennimalai 1
Ukkadam 2
Vellakovil 3
Salem
Tiruchengode 4
Madurai
Cumbum 2
Trichy
Karur 3
Trichy town 4
Manapparai 1

According to *The Hindu*, the total number of deaths was 60. But the official count released by the government was 50. It played many tricks to hide the real figures. It forced newspapers to publish false figures furnished by it. In some places, it set fire to trucks carrying the dead bodies of people killed in police action. In other places, it secretly buried the bodies. Neither the government nor the newspapers presented the real figures. It is estimated that the number of casualties was around 150.

Nanjil K Manoharan, the DMK's Parliamentary Party leader said: 'I have been informed that 150 people were killed in firing by the police and the army. The government arrested about 30,000 DMK cadre all over Tamil Nadu. I have sent telegrams to the President and the Prime Minister asking them to dismiss the bloodthirsty Chief Minister of Tamil Nadu, and also asked the Prime Minister to order a judicial probe into what happened during the agitation. If the judicial probe proves that the extremely brutal oppressive measures taken by the Chief Minister are justified, I am ready to resign as a Member of Parliament.'

However, the government refused to order a judicial probe.

The members of the DMK in the Assembly condemned the government for having unleashed terror on people who were conducting a democratic struggle and demanded the Chief Minister's resignation. In his speech in the Assembly, DMK leader KA Mathiazhagan narrated with evidence how members of the intelligentsia were tortured by the police. Pointing out the injustice of invoking the Defence of India Act against people fighting for their mother tongue, he reminded the rulers of how empires that relied only on the law came crashing down in history. He said: 'What is the Defence of India Rules (DIR)? What a terrible weapon it is! Is it not a law to be enforced in a jungle raj? Doesn't it look like the Star Chamber law of 15th-century England? What was the fate of the royal family of Stewart of Scotland? The Tsar of Russia imprisoned people's leaders in Siberia. What happened to his Duma (Parliament)? Didn't the Tsar and his empresses disappear from history without a trace? Irish nationalist leader Charles Stewart Parnell was incarcerated in Ireland. Didn't the youth of Dublin rise in revolt after that? The Nazi dictator, Hitler, vowed to reduce London to a heap of ashes. Ultimately, he committed suicide in an underground chamber. We have similar histories of Italy and Spain.

'How is the DIR used today? It is used as the Defence of

Congress Act and the Defence of Bhaktavatsalam Act. Consider the opinion of the people. Don't run your government at knife point. If you invoke the DIR against us today, what is the guarantee that it will not be used against you tomorrow? Go and meet the people. We'll also come with you. We'll either live with the three and a half crore people of Tamil Nadu or die with them. Realise the blunder you have committed in this issue and correct yourself. We'll lend you a helping hand.'

Communist Party of India leader M Kalyanasundaram[87] and Swatantra Party leader S Ganesan[88] also condemned the government's oppression. Ira Nedunchezhiyan, Leader of the Opposition in the Assembly, said: 'If the government thinks these incidents were instigated by someone, we should say that its attitude is wrong. The situation continues with no hope of any solution. The government is entirely responsible for this. The Chief Minister's speeches and the tyranny of the police sowed the seeds. Sporadic riots occurred as a consequence of the anger generated by oppression. One instance of violence led to another like a chain reaction. Tamils do not trust the Indian government. Had the Central Ministers resigned as a way of conveying the wishes of the people and the importance of the issue to the government, the situation would have been different. It might have been simpler and easier to handle. Had they resigned, it would have been a shock to the government. But the Ministers do not wish to lose their posts.'

The DMK legislators' speeches were stormy, devastating and volcanic. Their words fell like bombs on the imperialists' ears. But what would verbal bombs do to a Chief Minister who was unmoved by the deaths caused by the real bombs hurled at Tamils at his behest? He justified the government's oppression on the pretext of maintaining law and order. He spoke in favour of acts of injustice in the name of restoring peace. He did not realise his mistakes, nor did he own up to them. He did not mourn the dead, nor sympathise with them. He interpreted atrocities as acts of duty and said killing was inevitable.

The Chief Minister said: 'Winning a battle by instigating anarchy will never succeed in a democracy. Anarchy is completely alien to democracy. One can get votes once in five years by explaining to the people one's principles and philosophy. If one resorts to anarchy, it will not be tolerated. Some fear has been created. And we are involved in allaying that fear. But I conclude my speech by saying firmly that if someone uses a few people to create hatred out of that fear and pave the way for anarchy, we will not allow that in our democracy.'

A Chief Minister who says anarchy cannot be accepted in a democracy has not understood that riots and confusion happen when people lose faith in democratic ways. It is repression by the government that leads to anarchy.

Like in all revolutions, there were some unpalatable incidents in the January Revolution, too. There were instances of arson, damage and destruction of public property and murder of police officers. Why did Dravidians, who believe in values such as love, morality and culture, resort to such unprecedented political violence? Why were they forced to indulge in such violence? Such questions were raised in political circles after the January Revolution. At a function in New Delhi in February, the President regretted these incidents and said: 'Did we take all possible actions within our powers to pre-empt such happenings? Political wisdom consists in anticipating dangers and taking measures to prevent them as far as possible. We should try to implement our principles with the cooperation of a majority of people.' This should have told the entire country what mistakes the ruling party had made.

If we examine the incidents that occurred during the January Revolution, the people's uprising, and the government's oppression, it is evident that the State and Central governments were entirely responsible for them. We arrive at the following conclusions:

1. The Union government worked overtime to establish Hindi imperialism.
2. The Congress government's non-Hindi-speaking members failed to convey to the Centre the real, reasonable feelings of the non-Hindi-speaking people and help it to take a positive stand. Even while speaking of the need for the continuance of English as the official language, they were in favour of Hindi. They gradually reduced the use of English in administration.
3. The Tamil Nadu government instigated the police force and the Congress to defeat the DMK's observance of January 26 as a day of mourning all over the State.
4. The Chief Minister refused to meet student representatives and hear out their stance on the language issue. Moreover, he abused them.
5. The State government imposed prohibitory orders under Section 144 of the Criminal Procedure Code to deny the people their fundamental right to take out processions and hold public meetings to express their opposition to the enthroning of Hindi.
6. When people marched out in processions, it attacked them brutally with lathis and teargas shells and opened fire on them.
7. Congressmen organised rival processions in some places to prevent the agitators' march and thus provoked riots.
8. Even when the list of martyrs was growing long, Prime Minister Lal Bahadur Shastri spoke on radio in support of Hindi without respecting their feelings or consoling them.
9. The Tamil Nadu government requisitioned non-Tamil-speaking police and personnel from other states and let loose a reign of terror through them.
10. The Chief Minister's short-tempered nature, intransigence and tyrannical attitude ensured that the January Revolution spread far and wide.

If the State and Central governments evade these issues and try to blame others, it will only pave the way for another revolution.

Although the January Revolution did not write the epitaph of Hindi imperialism, it achieved some victories that gave hope of establishing the linguistic rights of non-Hindi-speaking people. The following were the victories:

1. It tore to pieces the claims of Hindi imperialists that the Centre's language policy enjoyed people's support. It made clear to the world that Dravidians and Bengalis would not accept Hindi as the only official language.
2. The revolution forced the government to accept that they would have to incorporate Nehru's assurance into the Official Languages Act and it agreed to amend the Act.
3. It made the government accept the use of all the 14 languages mentioned in the Eighth Schedule of the Constitution in the recruitment exams for Central government jobs.
4. It succeeded in creating a storm within the Congress vis-a-vis Hindi.
5. The revolution created a firm belief among non-Hindi-speaking people that the government's efforts to make Hindi the official language will be defeated and eventually, it will accept their mother tongues, too, as official languages.
6. It created a new interest in the development of national languages. Thus, it marked the beginning of the first phase of a renaissance.

It is true that these are significant victories. But non-Hindi-speaking people should beware that if they remain content and become complacent with these victories, Hindi imperialism will resort to new modes of deception and enslave them again in the future.

Chapter 23

The Two Language Formula

'This House refuses to accept the Union government's Hindi language policy. By refusing to implement the Centre's language policy and respecting the views of the Tamil people, including students, this House resolves to do away with the three-language formula, include Tamil and English and remove Hindi completely in all the schools in Tamil Nadu.'

—Tamil Nadu Chief Minister Arignar Anna

The language revolution of 1965 did not achieve complete success in eliminating Hindi, but the movement against Hindi's dominance had a great impact in Tamil Nadu. Supporters of Hindi were described as frauds and equated with Vibhishana, Ravana's brother who defected to Rama's side and opponents of Hindi were respected as idealists and as brave, self-respecting soldiers and protectors of Tamil. This public mood was the reason for the DMK alliance's historic victory in the 1967 election. In the general election of 1957, the DMK had won 15 seats with a vote share of 12.8 per cent. In 1962, it won 50 seats with a vote share of 27.1 per cent. In the general election of 1967 that was conducted within two years of the language revolution of 1965, the DMK won 138 seats with a vote share of 41.21 per cent. The Congress was routed and lost power.

The DMK formed the government and Arignar Anna assumed

office as Chief Minister. Tamils were overjoyed; as the revolutionary poet Bharathidasan said: 'Only a Tamil who has researched Tamil should become the Chief Minister of Tamil Nadu.'

That was the beginning of a new history and a golden age.

The defeat of the Congress in Tamil Nadu in the general election of 1967 stunned nationalists, because the party was known for its belief, bordering on arrogance, that it was invincible. So much so that Kamaraj had declared that he could win lying down. Rajaji's repartee was: 'No doubt you'd lie down, but you can't win.' The Congress' hopes tumbled like a house of cards.

The DMK, which rode to power on the anti-Hindi and pro-Tamil wave of 1965, enacted laws and implemented plans encouraging the movement against the imposition of Hindi and initiatives to protect and develop Tamil. On the Tamil Nadu government's emblem, the words 'Satyameva Jayate' were replaced with their pure Tamil equivalent, 'Vaaimaiye Vellum'. 'State Secretariat' became 'Thalaimai Seyalagam'. Parry's Corner became Paari Munai. Kellys, a Chennai locality, became Killiyur. 'Express Bus' became 'Viraivu Vandi'.

The Second World Tamil Conference was held with a lot of fanfare, taking the entire country by surprise. A postage-stamp honouring Thiruvalluvar was released on the occasion. Statues of great Tamil writers and poets were erected on the Marina. Verses from Tirukkural were painted inside State Transport Corporation buses. The Anna government introduced the practice of reading out one Tirukkural every day to mark the beginning of the State Assembly's proceedings. It encouraged the principle of making Tamil omnipresent in Tamil social life with the slogan 'Engum Tamil, Edhilum Tamil' (Tamil Everywhere, Tamil in Everything). Above all, the State's name was changed from Madras State to Tamil Nadu (Tamil country)[89], which was considered the crowning of Tamil nationalism.

The Indian government was forced to amend the Official

Languages Act, 1963, as a result of the success of the anti-Hindi movement in Tamil Nadu, the DMK's rise to power, and the rapid spread of anti-Hindi feelings among the non-Hindi-speaking people in other states. Fearing loss of support among non-Hindi-speaking people and worsening of the situation unless it amended the Act to ensure the continuance of English as the official language, the government introduced a Bill seeking to amend the Act of Parliament on November 27, 1967.

Hindi fanatics opposed the Bill, arguing that they did not have the power to amend the Act in such a way as to ensure continuance of English as an official language and that such a move was unconstitutional.

Speaking on behalf of the DMK, Nanjil K Manoharan said: 'The government has the power to make that amendment. I want to make it clear that as far as the DMK is concerned, it will not accept any legal measure other than a constitutional amendment in this regard.'

Home Minister YB Chavan[90] replied saying that the introduction of the Bill was just and legal, because it was not a new Bill, but one seeking to amend an earlier Act. The Hindi fanatics in the House did not relent and demanded a division. The Bill received 181 favourable votes and 25 opposing votes. Among those who voted against it were MM Joshi[91] (Jana Sangh) and Madhu Limaye[92] (Socialist Party).

The parliamentary debate on the Bill began on December 7, 1967. The Hindi fanatics opposed the Bill, arguing that it was unnecessary to allow English to continue as the official language, that it would harm national unity, and that everyone should accept Hindi as the official language as it was recognised as such by the Constitution. The members from non-Hindi-speaking regions welcomed the amendment. The Congress members spoke in favour of the Bill in line with the party's whip to maintain organisational discipline. Although Communist leaders such as SA Dange[93] supported the Bill, they spoke strongly against English. The DMK was the only defender of the interests of non-Hindi-speaking people. Its members made forceful speeches with evidence.

Supporting the Bill, AK Sen made a nuanced point: 'The Constitutional provision on the official language says Hindi in Nagari script is the official language. It uses the word "shall". Had the word "is" been used instead of the word "shall" an amendment of this type could not have been made. The word "shall" has been used, implying that there can be a change in the Official Language Act in future.' As soon he said this, the Hindi fanatics raised a hue and cry.

In his speech, Acharya Kripalani strongly criticised the supporters of Hindi and English equally. He said Hindi supporters were enacting a deceptive drama in the language issue and that they spoke frenziedly in this House. He accused them of enrolling their children in English medium schools.

Many said at the time that English had developed as a national language like all other the Indian languages. Communist Party of India leader, SA Dange, argued against including Sanskrit in the Eighth Schedule of the Constitution. He said: 'Why was Sanskrit, which was not spoken in any part in India, and not even by a large part of the intelligentsia, added in the Schedule? Was it for your communication with God? Communication with God in this country is carried on in other languages as well, in English in the Bible, in Arabic in the Quran, in Sanskrit in the Gita, and the Gita reader does not understand the Sanskrit of the Gita at all. Then why was it incorporated? Because that is an expression of the Hinduism that dominates the framers of the Constitution.'

The debate continued for three days. Although many members took part in it, it was K Anbazhagan, Leader of the DMK Parliamentary Party, who spoke at length on the issue, giving a satisfactory explanation of his position. He said: 'Hindi is the common language of North India. It is not the common language of South India. I do not want to be cowed down before Hindi imperialism in any shape or form. I want to make people understand this: whatever is the position of Hindi in this country, the same position should be given to our language, Tamil. As my friends from other linguistic regions would agree, Bengali, Marathi and all the regional languages should get equal opportunity and parity in this country. I suggest our language(s) should become the official language of this country right up to the Centre. Till then, the Hindi people should wait. If they want to take us with them, if they want to create confidence in us, if they feel that all belong to the same Bharat Mata, if our blood is the same as theirs, if our aim is the same, they should wait and accommodate us. You accommodate Tamil also with Hindi, you accommodate Telugu. You accommodate Kannada, you accommodate every other regional language which will play the role of official language.' His speech took the House by storm.

The Languages (Amendment) Bill, which was passed by Parliament in December 1967, and which got the Presidential assent on January 8, 1968, did not really meet the long-term demands of non-Hindi speakers. It was not against Hindi's domination; nor did it give equal status to English or the other Indian languages. It just allowed the continuance of English as the official language even after 1965. Under the amended Act, the use of English for official purposes was not mandatory. What it did was to weaken the important provisions of the original Official Language Act of 1963 and thus support Hindi.

When the House was debating the Draft Bill, the Home Minister proposed a resolution on the language policy on behalf of the government on December 7. He requested members to discuss the Draft Bill and his resolution together. The following resolution moved by Chavan had four aspects: 'Whereas under Article 343 of the Constitution, Hindi shall be the official language of the Union, and under Article 351 thereof it is the duty of the Union to promote the spread of the Hindi language and to develop it so that it may serve as a medium of expression for all the elements of the composite culture of India.

'1. This House resolves that a more intensive and comprehensive programme shall be prepared and implemented by the Government of India for accelerating the spread and development of Hindi, and its progressive use for various official purposes of the Union, and an annual report giving details of the measures taken and the progress shall be laid on the Table of both Houses of Parliament, and sent to all State Governments;

'2. Whereas the Eighth Schedule to the Constitution specifies 14 major languages of India besides Hindi and it is necessary in the interest of the educational and cultural advancement of the country that concerted measures should be taken for the full development of these languages;

This House resolves that a programme shall be prepared and implemented by the Government of India, in collaboration with the State Governments, for the coordinated development of all these languages, alongside Hindi, so that they grow rapidly in richness and become an effective means of communicating modern knowledge.

'3. Whereas it is necessary for promoting the sense of unity and facilitating communication between people in different parts of the country that effective steps should be taken for implementing in all states the three-language formula evolved by the Government of India in consultation with State Governments;

This House resolves that arrangements should be made, in accordance with that formula, for the study of a modern Indian language, preferably one of the Southern languages, apart from Hindi and English in the Hindi-speaking areas, and of Hindi along with the regional languages and English in the non-Hindi-speaking areas.

'4. And, whereas it is necessary to ensure that the just claims and interests of persons belonging to non-Hindi-speaking areas in regard to the public services of the Union are fully safeguarded;

This House resolves (a) that compulsory knowledge of Hindi shall not be required at the stage of selection of candidates for recruitment to the Union services or posts, excepting any special services/posts for which a high standard of Hindi knowledge may be considered essential for the satisfactory performance of the duties of the service or post; and (b) that all the languages included in the Eighth Schedule to the Constitution and English shall be permitted as alternative native media for the All India and higher Central Services examinations after ascertaining the views of the Union Public Service Commission on the future scheme of the examinations.'

This resolution was against the interests of non-Hindi-speaking people and it ignored Nehru's assurance on the continuance of English as the official language. It did not give any right to the speakers of regional languages in the recruitment for Union government jobs. Nor did it accept the demands that arose during the anti-Hindi agitation of 1965.

The first aspect of the resolution made it clear that Hindi alone would be the official language and the government was committed to encouraging it. The second aspect was an eyewash. The government did not treat regional languages as equal to Hindi. The three-language formula was a deceptive way of imposing Hindi. We exposed it irrefutably. The fourth point says that Hindi was not compulsory in the first stage of recruitment to Union government jobs. But it made Hindi compulsory for continuance in service and for promotions.

Stating that the resolution was unnecessary because it went against the interests of non-Hindi-speaking people, Kamaraj pleaded with the government not to adopt it. The government ignored his request.

The government's amendment to the Official Languages

Act and its resolution on the language policy not only greatly disappointed non-Hindi-speaking people, but also created unrest again in Tamil Nadu. Students and citizens protested and prepared for another round of struggle. Protest marches and meetings were held in important towns. A meeting of the Assembly was hurriedly convened on January 23, 1968, to condemn the government's attitude, to make the government realise the sentiments of the Tamil people on the language issue and to clarify the State government's language policy. Nedunchezhiyan moved the following resolution on behalf of the State government: 'The serious situation arising out of Parliament adopting the Official Languages Amendment Act and the related resolution must be discussed.'

The Congress, the Communist Party of India (Marxist), the Swatantra Party, and the Thamizharasu Kazhagam moved amendments. On behalf of the government, Anna proposed a historic amendment. It said: 'The Constitution should be amended in such a way as to recognise Tamil and other national languages as the official languages. Until then, English should continue as the official language. The Official Languages (Amendment) Act adopted now is not conducive for this objective to be achieved. Since the resolution adopted along with the Official Languages (Amendment) Act has done injustice to the people by causing hardships to them and imposing new burdens on them, that resolution should not be implemented. In the view of this House, the resolution, by stressing on adoption of the three-language formula, aims to impose Hindi and make it the official language eventually. This House refuses to accept the Central government's plan to impose Hindi...this House resolves to reject the three-language formula and introduce in its place a two-language formula under which Hindi will be completely removed and Tamil and English will be accommodated.'

The house erupted with joyful applause when this resolution was read out—a scene unprecedented in the history of the Tamil Nadu Assembly.

Tamil scholars, students and political parties had been at the forefront of the anti-Hindi movement so far. But after the DMK government took office under the leadership of Anna, the Tamil Nadu government itself helmed it. The DMK government passed this resolution not out of its fear of or subservience to the Union government. It boldly declared that the House refused to accept the Centre's policy of imposing Hindi. It put an end to the three-language formula and brought in the two-language formula. It drove away Hindi from all the schools, much to the joy of students, who had fought against Hindi and even sacrificed their lives.

The Assembly debated the resolution moved by the government and the amendments proposed by the political parties. Indirectly pointing out that Anna was being guided by Rajaji in the language issue, Congress member G Bhuvaragan said: 'There is widespread talk among people that somebody is helping the Chief Minister.' Anna replied: 'I admit that someone from the top is helping me. Help comes from here (pointing to his head).' The House roared with laughter. Forward Bloc member PK Mookiah Thevar said: 'This meeting is considered the most important event in the history of India. We need only two languages. One of them is Tamil and the other, English. Mother tongue Tamil comes first; then only English, for communication with the rest of India. After meeting Chief Minister Anna, honourable Jayaprakash Narayan told Rajaji: 'Before the meeting, I thought the Chief Minister was a tough person, who would be quick to anger and would be impatient. But when I met him, I was reminded of Gandhi.' The House welcomed his remarks with a loud cheer. Mookiah Thevar said: 'Even if Anna, people like me and all the Ministers present here have to spend 15 to 20 years in jail and die in captivity, we will oppose Hindi strongly.' CPI(M) member A Balasubramaniam[94] said: 'Hindi has been given a high place. We can't allow this. We must change this. As far as we are concerned, we say that all 14 national languages should have equal status. Until then, in my view, English should continue as the second official language. There is no need for a compulsory official language. As Lenin said, nobody can be sent to heaven by the force of a stick.'

Swatantra Party leader HV Hande[95] said: 'What we want to say, specifically, what our leader Rajaji says, is that Tamil must be safe, English should be a protective fence around it. Kamaraj, the former president of the All India Congress Committee, had asked the party to stop with the amendment and not to impose the resolution. But Congressmen in the North did not accept his advice.' In his speech, MP Sivagnanam, who was known as Silambu Selvar (one who is well-versed in the Tamil epic *Silappadhikaram*) recounted how the Congress took disciplinary action against him for joining Annadurai's struggle against Hindi in an earlier phase of the agitation. He said: 'Giving Hindi the status of official language at a time when it has not become the official language in the Prime Minister's own State scares us. Naming Hindi as the official language and imposing it on Tamil Nadu, where Tamil is not given the status of the official language or made the medium of instruction, only goes to prove the imperialistic thinking behind the move. Tamil Nadu should demand official status for all the 14 national languages and talk to the Central government on that basis. In the meantime, English also should continue as the official language at the Centre.'

PG Karuthiruman[96], the Leader of the Opposition in the Assembly, said: 'The government's resolution will confuse the already volatile situation. It will not solve the issue. The resolution is worded in such a way as to disrupt national integration, and not aimed at preserving national unity. Through this resolution, the DMK has only revived the plan it had given up earlier.'

Anna's reply at the end of the debate was momentous and served as the final warning to Hindi imperialism. He described how the anti-Hindi struggle had taken different forms from 1937 to 1967. He pointed out how the questions of language had been resolved in various countries and explained the reasons behind the party's support of English. Laying bare the fraudulence of the three-language formula, he pointed out that Hindi was divisive and English helped the cause of unity.

Anna gave a withering reply to the Congress members' charge that the DMK was encouraging separatism and acting against national integration and that those who took the help of Rajaji would never develop politically. Explaining his relationship with Rajaji, he said: 'Rajaji said then (in 1937) that Hindi should be learnt compulsorily. We opposed it then, as suggested by honourable Ma Po Si [MP Sivagnanam]. It was Rajaji who sent me to jail for the first time in my life. And I am happy to say that it was the same Rajaji who created a conducive situation for me to become a Minister for the first time in my life. In this very House, our friends said in 1958, "Don't follow Rajaji. He is a tamarind tree under which nothing grows." Now, after I've grown into such a big teak tree under his shadow, they are asking me not to follow him. Somehow, I went ahead and I grew well.' The House burst into laughter.

Responding to the Congress' charge that he was instigating separatism by using the language issue, Anna said: 'What I am doing is highlighting how the Centre's language policy will pave the way for national disintegration. If I had to encourage separatism, I could do that with just one sentence, which would find a place in the history books. I could convene this House and declare, 'Tamil Nadu will be a separate country, Long Live Tamil!' There were loud cheers in the House. 'All the national languages of India should be made official languages,' Anna added. 'Until then, English should continue as the official language. This is Kazhagam's stand. We will not be fully satisfied with the language policy until this becomes a reality. Now, through our language policy, we are using English to prevent the entry of Hindi. This is like using the upper garment to avoid getting drenched in the rain when we cannot find an umbrella.'

After Anna's resounding reply, the other parties withdrew their amendments. The Congress decided not to take part in any voting on the issue. The House adopted the resolution unanimously. Thus, the two-language formula came into practice. Hindi was removed from all the schools in the State.

The two-language resolution adopted by the Anna government shocked the nation. Several questions were raised: How can one adopt a resolution rejecting Hindi, which has been accorded constitutional sanction as the official language? Is it not against the Constitution? Is it not a challenge thrown at the Central government? After adopting such a bold resolution, will the DMK government survive? But Anna was not fazed by such questions. He answered them with his characteristic courage and clarity at a public meeting held to salute the martyrs of the anti-Hindi struggle. He said: 'The experts in Delhi are wondering whether the resolution aimed at abolishing Hindi will harm the relationship between the Centre and Tamil Nadu and what action could be taken against us. I am ready to face the Centre's action, however stringent it may be. What can they do? Prison is not new to me. I went to jail when I was a student. I went to jail when I was a member of the State Assembly and the national Parliament. If, as a Minister, I get an opportunity to go to jail again thanks to my Congress friends, I will accept it happily. It will be the most interesting chapter in my entire life. Imprisonment does not intimidate me.

'The two-language resolution has been adopted in the Assembly as a culmination of the peaceful anti-Hindi struggle that began in 1937. We do not have to write a new chapter. I have done whatever is possible. Now, let the Delhi government do what it can. As I have said earlier, one loses one's life only once. Not twice. If we are going to lose our lives for this cause, we will certainly be happy.'[97]

Anna's rule established that the DMK would stand firm like the Himalaya in opposing Hindi and that it would not bow down to any force.

Chapter 24

Constitution Burning...Again!

'It is with selfishness and greed that I am going to participate in this struggle which has been on for about 50 years, since 1937. I wish this struggle would end in my lifetime. I want to close my eyes for the last time after a solution is found. I want to see these words: "Hindi's dominance has died and Tamil has become the official language. Hindi imperialism will not enslave Tamil hereafter. Tamils will not be reduced to the status of second-class citizens. Nehru's assurance has been incorporated in the Constitution." If I close my eyes for the last time after seeing this amendment, I will be a thousand times happier than a person who writes his will and hands it over to his grandson before he dies.'

—Kalaignar Karunanidhi

'Unity in diversity' was the motto of Pandit Nehru. But his grandson, Rajiv Gandhi, who became Prime Minister in 1984, considered this motto dangerous and talked about unity and integration. To take forward this slogan, he formulated a new education policy in 1986. This policy was of no help to the State governments. It didn't help the Union government to start new engineering and medical colleges, nor did it give any assurance on improving the salaries of teachers and enhancing their quality. On the contrary, the government planned to open Navodaya schools all over the country with Hindi as the medium of instruction. The

Union Budget increased the allocation for education manifold and most of it was spent on Navodaya schools.

The DMK, which created history by conducting a valiant struggle against the imposition of Hindi, accused the Union government of launching a new war by imposing Hindi through this education policy. Resolving to mobilise people and launch a struggle again, it organised an anti-Hindi conference in Coimbatore on November 8 and 9. A reception committee under the leadership of M Kannappan made the arrangements, L Ganesan inaugurated it and P Srinivasan hoisted the party flag at the venue, while S Kandappan presided over the conference. With lakhs of people participating in it, the conference venue was a sea of humanity.

Addressing the conference, DMK general secretary K Anbazhagan said: 'When we oppose the dominance of Hindi, it means we are opposing the North's deceit, opposing the force that wants to enslave Tamils, opposing Delhi's authoritarianism. To emphasise that, we are going to set on fire Part XVII of the Constitution. If anyone says it is wrong to burn Part XVII, then we'll look forward to burning the entire Constitution.'

Kalaignar Karunanidhi's special address at the end of the conference ignited the hearts of the participants, especially the youth. It was a warning to Hindi imperialism. He said: 'In the Ramayana, Rama kills Vaali indirectly by hiding behind a tree with the help of Sugriva. Similarly, the Northern Rama is afraid of imposing Hindi directly. Lacking courage, he thinks he can shoot the arrow and kill Vaali with the help of the Sugriva (MG Ramachandran) in Tamil Nadu. The DMK is waging a war to prove that Rama cannot kill Vaali from a hidden spot in the present times.'

This was greeted with loud and long applause.

The speakers at the conference gave evidence of how the MGR government vacillated and went off-track on the language issue. The resolution adopted at the conference not only clarified the DMK's language policy, but also made it clear that the party was prepared to make any sacrifice to implement it. It stated: 'The DMK, which follows Anna's principle that all the national languages, including Tamil, should be made official languages of the Union government, urges the government to stop imposing and propagating Hindi, and to find ways and means to incorporate Nehru's assurance in the Constitution. This conference resolves to set aflame Part XVII of the Constitution that lays down Hindi as the official language at public meetings all over Tamil Nadu in order to reiterate our demand and prevent the establishment of Hindi imperialism in India.'

The DMK president, Kalaignar Karunanidhi, appealed to volunteers to be ready to dedicate themselves to the cause of protecting Mother Tamil and face imprisonment, however prolonged it would be. A list of courageous volunteers was prepared. The resolution of the Coimbatore conference, Kalaignar's letters to partymen in *Murasoli* explaining its importance, and the fiery speeches made at public meetings evoked tremendous response from the people. Even before the Rajiv Gandhi government at the Centre, the MGR government shuddered with fear. It was also forced to oppose the imposition of Hindi, just as the DMK did. The State government adopted the following resolution: 'According constitutional recognition to Nehru's assurance, which has been endorsed by Indira Gandhi and Rajiv Gandhi, will not only allay the real fear among non-Hindi-speaking people, but also help avoid the confusion, disruption and law and order issues arising out of Hindi imposition. So, Part XVII of the Constitution relating to the official language should be immediately and necessarily amended in such a way as to ensure continuance of English as the official language with a constitutional guarantee.'

This was a sign of victory for the DMK's Coimbatore conference. Pointing this out, Kalaignar Karunanidhi wrote in *Murasoli*: 'Such a change, such a revolution has come about suddenly. Dear Brother! Who can deny that it is the result of your war cry?'

Although MG Ramachandran passed this resolution as a tactic to retain public approval, Kalaignar did not attribute any ulterior motive to the Chief Minister because he did not want anti-Hindi forces to be divided. Addressing a press conference, he said: 'The resolution passed by the Assembly is what the ruling party could do in expressing its opposition to Hindi. As a party of the opposition, the DMK's struggle to urge the Union government to implement the resolution passed by the State Assembly will strengthen the resolution.'

Had MG Ramachandran followed Kalaignar Karunanidhi's example of opposing Hindi by rising above political boundaries? No. As soon as the DMK prepared the ground for a battle, MG Ramachandran had a change of heart. His government unleashed oppression against the agitators.

The DMK had asked its cadre to burn a copy of Article 343 of the Constitution laying down that Hindi in Devanagari script should be the official language of India. Kalaignar Karunanidhi chose November 17, 1986, as the day of the agitation, because it was on the same date 23 years ago (1963) that Anna had led the agitation in which a copy of the Constitution was set aflame. As planned, the first phase of the agitation began under the leadership of the DMK general secretary, K Anbazhagan. At a function organised to send Anbazhagan to the agitation venue, Kalaignar said: 'This peaceful struggle led by Professor Anbazhagan, the lieutenant of our self-respect movement, is another milestone in the 50-year-long language struggle of Tamils.'

At the Sami Pillai Street in Chennai's Park Town, Anbazhagan declared, 'This is an agitation of sacrifice to which we have dedicated ourselves to get rid of the injustice meted to out to Tamils through the Constitution,' and he burnt a copy of Article 343 of the Constitution. A thousand-strong crowd loudly cheered him. Among the other leaders who joined the agitation were S Ganesan and KV Parthasarathy.

The agitation was organised in many parts of Chennai. Party MLAs P Ponnurangam, A Selvarasan, S Balan, Parithi Ilamvazhudhi, 'Misa' Ganesan and N Balaraman participated in them. In Coimbatore, it was led by district secretary M Kannappan, M Ramanathan, R Mohan, MLA, M Thamizh, Rasammal, and Ramayya. The lists of volunteers who participated in the agitation in each district were released by the party headquarters.

On November 11, V Krishnamurthy, S Padmanabhan, T Killivalavan and K Jayabal led the agitation.

Unmindful of the rigorous punishment mentioned in the Prevention of Insults to National Honour Acts of 1957 and 1971, thousands of people plunged into the protests, posing a challenge to the Centre. The MGR government, which was bound by its own Assembly resolution on the language issue, took advantage of the fact that it was the main opposition party that was organising the protests, and went all out to suppress the agitation. Worse, it conspired to disqualify the legislators who burnt copies of Article 343 of the Constitution. As part of the conspiracy, Congress member NSV Chiththan moved a motion calling attention in the Assembly to the participation of some of the legislators in Constitution-burning. Pointing out that five MLAs from Chennai and one from Coimbatore had been jailed for burning copies of a section of the Constitution, he said (addressing Speaker PH Pandian): 'I want to know whether these six persons continue to be members of the Assembly after burning the Constitution? Will you allow them to function as MLAs here? Or, are they going to take the oath of allegiance to the Constitution again? I would like to hear your explanation.'

In response, the Speaker read out Article 188 of the Constitution. It says: 'Every member of the Legislative Assembly or the Legislative Council of a State shall, before taking his seat, make and subscribe before the Governor, or some person appointed in that behalf by him, an oath or affirmation according to the form set out for the purpose in the Third Schedule.' That is, they should declare their belief in and allegiance to the Constitution, sovereignty and national unity. This is a political ritual or custom imposed during British rule. No law says that violating this oath is unlawful. Political leaders all over the world have violated their oaths in one way or another in public interest. Yet, the Assembly Speaker chose to cite Article 188, as if some big crime had been committed. Interrupting him, Nedunchezhiyan, the Leader of the House, said (turning to Chiththan): 'Some members of this House are involved in an agitation and they have been jailed for 15 days under certain sections of the law. A trial will ensue. The House or others can take action only on the basis of the verdict in this case. It depends on the sections under which the verdict will be given. Until the verdict is out, we are not supposed to take any action. We should decide only after the verdict is given.' DMK member A Rahman Khan tried to speak on behalf of the jailed legislators, but Nedunchezhiyan said: 'Chiththan raised a doubt. The House need not take it into consideration. The issue is sub-judice. The Speaker can act on the legal question only after the arguments in court and the verdict. There is no need to raise the issue again.'

However, Speaker Pandian clarified that he did not have the power to act on a development outside the House and that the House would have to wait for the verdict. He confined himself to reading out Article 188 of the Constitution. The conspiracy had not taken full shape then. It was in the making through serious consultations among MGR, Speaker Pandian, and Minister Panruti S Ramachandran and S Thirunavukkarasu. It came to light on November 24 when the House met. At the end of Question Hour, Chiththan reminded the House of the 'important issue' he had raised and wanted to know whether those who had burnt copies of a section of the Constitution continued to be members of the House and whether the Speaker would allow it.

Immediately, the Speaker said, 'The burning of the Constitution by members of this House cannot be tolerated. It is unconstitutional and unnecessary.' He read out his decision: 'We've got information from the Chennai Commissioner of Police that the Assembly members K Anbazhagan, S Balan, Parithi Ilamvazhudhi and P Ponnunrangam have been arrested on the charge of burning Part XVII of the Constitution at a public place. A similar piece of information has it that M Ramanathan, a member representing Coimbatore (East) and R Chinnasamy, a member from Dharmapuri, have been arrested on the same charges. I want to reply to Chiththan's question whether the House should wait for the court verdict before taking any action against them. It is the Speaker's responsibility to take action against members who violate the oath of office. The executive will take action on the basis of the case. But this House is duty-bound to take action against them. As one who acts in accordance with the Constitution, I cannot be a mute spectator to the public burning of the Constitution. Every member is bound to act according to Article 188 of the Constitution. By setting aflame a copy of the Constitution, they have indicated that they don't have faith in the Constitution.

'I did not expect the lawmakers themselves to burn the Constitution. As there is no legal provision dealing with this issue, I have no option but to take action against them as per the residuary powers granted to the Speaker by Assembly Rule No 312 in order to protect the Constitution. Hence, I declare that K Anbazhagan, S Balan, A Selvarasan, Parithi Ilamvazhudhi, P Ponnunrangam, M Ramanthan and R Chinnasamy are not eligible to continue as members of the House as they have violated the oath of office they took under the Constitution. I will send the notes in this regard to the Governor and the Election Commission in New Delhi.'

The Speaker's decision led to noisy scenes in the Assembly.

His decision was unfair, undemocratic and dictatorial. It was an injustice that shocked the entire nation. Even the Hindi fanatics had not betrayed the Tamils like this; they had not disqualified Anna and others for burning copies of the Constitution. But the MGR government, which claimed to follow the footsteps of Anna, betrayed not only Anna but the entire Tamil community.

On hearing Pandian's decision, the DMK Legislature Party sprang up like a wounded tiger. The Speaker refused to allow Nanjil Manoharan and Rahman Khan to speak, shouting that the Speaker alone was the guardian of the Constitution. However, Nanjil Manoharan started making sharp remarks that pierced through the din and bustle. 'You give your reply after allowing me to speak. I categorically say that the Constitution is for the people and not the other way around. When Anna tried to burn a copy of the Constitution, he was only jailed for six months.' The ruling party members raised a hue and cry, preventing Manoharan from continuing with his speech. Declaring that the DMK did not accept the Speaker's decision, he staged a walkout along with his party colleagues. The members of the CPI(M) and the CPI also walked out in protest.

Nedunchezhiyan, who had said clearly and firmly on November 21 that the Speaker should act only after the court gave its verdict on an issue that happened outside the House, spoke in support of the Speaker's dictatorial decision on November 24, dishonestly and timidly throwing to the winds his assurance and showing his gratitude to the rulers. Arguing foolishly, he said: 'When Anna burnt a copy of the Constitution, there was no practice of taking oath. Nor was there a law on disqualification. The law on disqualification came only after all those developments.'

This was not true. The Constitutional provision making it mandatory for an elected member of the Assembly to take the oath has existed for a long time. The Government of India Act of 1935, too, had this provision.

The provisions on disqualification of members had been incorporated when the Constitution was framed. Nedunchezhiyan seemed to be unaware of these facts. Pointing out that Periyar and Anna were prepared to accept any punishment, he sermonised that the DMK should follow their example. The DMK had plunged into the agitation without bothering about the possibilities of getting imprisoned, facing hardships, being subjected to the security forces' oppression, or losing positions of power. Its members were prepared to sacrifice their youth and lives. Nedunchezhiyan had no reply to the DMK members' question that whether those who claimed to be 'the real younger brothers' of Anna could resort to such acts of betrayal.

Indian Union Muslim League leader AKA Abdul Samad and Congress leader Kumari Anandan urged the Speaker to reconsider his decision and wait for the court verdict. Refusing to heed their advice, the Speaker said: 'This is not a hasty decision. I pondered over the issue for two or three days. It is my independent decision based on my concern that those who come to the House as people's representatives are indulging in such acts. This is my decision and there is no question of reconsidering it.'

However, the MGR government seriously doubted whether the court would accept the Speaker's decision based on his residuary powers. In order to present before the court the argument that Tamil Nadu had disqualified them on its own, Nedunchezhiyan moved a resolution in the House on December 22, disqualifying the DMK members concerned for burning copies of the Constitution. Interrupting him, Manoharan said: 'This resolution should not be moved by the Leaders of the House. The issue is sub judice. Hence, the House should not discuss it.' When Pandian refuted him, saying that this issue was not a legal issue to be settled in a court of law and it was one concerning the violation of the Constitution, Manoharan hit back, saying that it was the issue of violation that was sub judice. Panruti Ramachandran tried to divert the issue by saying that the resolution was about the conduct of Assembly members.

The Speaker does not have the power to take action against members for their actions outside the Assembly. It was not as if Pandian or Panruti Ramachandran or Nedunchezhiyan were not aware of this fact. There is no rule or ethical principle for those who are bent on revenge. In the arrogance born of their majority in the House, they claim for themselves a non-existent power. Pandian argued that the House could take action against members for their conduct inside and outside the Assembly. Manoharan accused him of arriving at this decision by converting his residuary power into an extraordinary power. IUML's Abdul Samad said (addressing the Speaker): 'Anna himself had once burnt a copy of the same constitutional provision. It was only after the incident that he became the Chief Minister of the State... you should create conditions conducive for the return of these members to the House.'

CPI member K Subbarayan said: 'Had the members insulted the nation, the [Prevention of] Insults to National Honour Act is in place to punish them. Hence, it is not proper for you to appropriate that Act's provision and take action in this House.' Condemning the ruling party's adamant attitude, CPI(M) member K Ramani said: 'The Constitution does not say anywhere that the Speaker has the power to expel an elected member. Articles 191 and 192 clearly define disqualification. Article 192 lays down five reasons for disqualification. Those reasons do not apply in this case. So, this resolution has to be dropped. It is wrong and undemocratic. In such situations, the opposition parties should not be punished.'

When Nanjil Manoharan got up to speak, the ruling party members raised a hullabaloo. Ignoring them, he said (addressing the Chair): 'You don't have the power to expel or disqualify members elected by the people for whatever reason. You can't disqualify them except under the five reasons mentioned in the Constitution. As I said at the outset, you have misused power by converting your residuary power into an extraordinary power. The DMK respects the Constitution. Setting aflame a paper on which Part XVII of the Constitution that declares Hindi in Devanagari script as the official language is printed is not tantamount to insulting the Constitution. Moreover, we did that to attract the attention of Rajiv Gandhi to this issue and strengthen the hands of the Chief Minister. I do not want to plead with you to reconsider your decision. The DMK will not be weakened by the reduction of its numbers in the House. You and the Leader of the House have given a verdict which is improper and unconstitutional, and which cannot be accepted by right-thinking people. You should not bring into force this strong decision, whatever your reason may be. Anna was sentenced to six months' imprisonment for trying to burn a copy of the Constitution; no one told him that he should not continue as a Rajya Sabha member. No one moved a resolution for that.'

Nedunchezhiyan replied to the debate on the resolution, but did not give an honest, acceptable answer to the questions and doubts raised by the members on behalf of the DMK and the other parties. He made a speech on December 22 which was completely contradictory to the stand he had taken on November 21. His explanation invited the country's ridicule. He said:

'On November 22, the honourable member Chiththan suddenly raised a question regarding this issue. I said a decision could be taken after the cases relating to this issue came to an end. I said this only casually. As the Leader of the House, I could not have given a decision. Two days later, on November 24, the Speaker announced his decision. This House has the responsibility to accept that decision.' He concluded his speech thus: 'We took this decision in the case of three members. After reconsidering the decision, if you apply this to all the ten members, it will create a conducive situation for this House to decide.'

This was the last stage of the conspiracy. On November 24, the Speaker had disqualified seven members. In the agitation that followed, three more DMK legislators, M Abraham, Madurantakam C Arumugam, and VK Raasu had participated in the Constitution-burning. But the Speaker did not disqualify them. The House discussed the issue of disqualifying them through a resolution. But Nedunchezhiyan said that he was adding the seven members disqualified previously to the new resolution on the three members, taking the total to 10. This announcement created an uproar in the House. The opposition parties argued that since the ruling party was trying to disqualify seven members who had already been disqualified, it amounted to the government accepting indirectly that the Speaker's November 24 decision was wrong and illegal. The Speaker, who had disqualified seven members claiming that he had the power to do so, was trying to disqualify them again through another resolution! The opposition condemned it as a clownish, dictatorial move. But the Speaker refused to allow the opposition members to speak, throwing the House into disorder. An angry Pandian declared: 'The sky is the limit of my powers. The power of this House is my power. You can't even reach that. Neither you, nor those around you can do it. I am saying this again: The sky is the limit of my power. The power of this House is my power.'

Did even dictators anywhere shout like this, drunk with power? It was condemnable that an Assembly Speaker spoke thus, and a ruling party encouraged it.

Eventually, Nedunchezhiyan announced the decision of the House that the ten DMK legislators, including Anbazhagan, were not qualified to continue as its members, that they were removed from the House and that their seats would be vacant. He requested the House to accept the resolution. The members of the Congress, which had initiated the process of disqualification through Chiththan, also walked out, saying that the punishment meted out to those who burnt the Constitution amounts to punishing the voters. Rahman Khan demanded a division on the resolution so that history would note down the list of traitors. The resolution was accepted by 131 members and rejected by 24.

Thus, the MGR government's conspiracy succeeded in the Assembly.

Political leaders, intellectuals and newspapers condemned the MGR government's autocratic act of disqualifying the DMK members elected by the people. Newspapers condemned the government's Hitler darbar. In an editorial, *The Hindu* expressed concern over the Speaker's action. 'While the question of its constitutional validity remains, its implications for the democratic structure are worrying,' it said, adding, 'The Speaker's action may be brushed aside as an individual's authoritarian act, but the wholesale disqualification proves the lack of tolerance on the part of the AIADMK.' 'If this attitude grows,' it said, 'it will end as a dictatorship of a party with a majority in the Assembly.'

The Tamil weekly, *Kalki*, said: 'It will be appropriate if the MGR government expresses regret over the action and moves another resolution in the Assembly withdrawing its earlier resolution. But such generosity cannot be expected from the present ruling dispensation. When a ruling party becomes arrogant and when we cannot expect fairness from it, only the judiciary can protect democracy and public interest—we hope it will.'

The English weekly, *India Today*, published an article unmasking MGR. It said that driving Karunanidhi and the DMK away from politics seemed to be the only desire of MGR. The resolution disqualifying DMK members, it said, was one more instance of this attitude.

Explaining how appalling Pandian's decision was and how it ran counter to parliamentary rules and practices, Kalaignar wrote a letter to his cadre (*udan pirappu*, meaning sibling) titled 'Two Pandyas—Two Verdicts' (Irandu Pandiyargal-Irandu Theerpugal) in the party organ *Murasoli*. In the article, he cited Dr Nanjudaara's privilege motion and Speaker S Chellapandian's honest verdict:

1. In 1939, a privilege motion was moved against the Congress legislators violating their oath of allegiance to the King (British) by their participation in the freedom movement. Citing Professor Keith, an expert in constitutional law, he ruled that there was no privilege issue in that case.
2. The act of burning copies of the Constitution, said to have been committed by some members, did not come under the grounds for disqualification defined in the Constitution.
3. The House cannot take into consideration members' activities outside the House which are not related to their duties inside the Assembly.
4. In the British Parliament, a point of order was raised against a member ridiculing the practice of taking oath on June 16, 1952. The Speaker ruled that it was not an issue to be raised as a point of order.
5. Even if the burning of the Constitution was a crime, it was taken care of by the existing laws. So, it is not a privilege issue of the House.
6. S Chellapandian respected, nurtured and protected democratic rules and practices. PH Pandian stomped on them and cut them to pieces.

The DMK was not scared by Pandian misusing his residuary powers as Speaker and taking revenge on the party. Nor did it give up its Constitution-burning agitation. DMK president Kalaignar Karunanidhi declared: 'We are not going to be cowed down even if our positions of power are snatched away. Our sword will not be blunted. I say this again—'Let Tamil Live Even If We Fall Down and Die.' I don't know if you will write this slogan on the walls or not. But do write it in your hearts.'

The burning of the Constitution in protest continued as planned.

When a gooseberry was given to King Adhiyaman, he passed it onto Avvaiyar, the grand old lady of Tamil poetry, as it was believed to give a long life to one who eats it. It would be a matter of pride for Tamil if Avvaiyar had a long life, he believed. In Dharmapuri, which had been ruled by Adhiyaman, the agitation was held on November 23. The legislators R Chinnasamy and M Kamalanathan participated in it and courted arrest.

In Kamarajar district, which was named after the great freedom fighter Kamaraj, a team of party cadres led by district secretary V Thangapandinan, VP Rajaan, S Amudhan and P Srinivasan were arrested for setting a copy of the Constitution on fire. On November 27, the agitators led by Veerapandi Arumugam, GK Subash and Kamalam Manikkam were arrested and jailed. In Chengai Anna district, which takes pride in being the birthplace of Anna, an agitation was organised on November 29 under the leadership Madurantakam C Arumugam, MLA, and V Narasingha Murthy. Over 1,500 people participated in it and courted arrest.

On December 1, agitations were held in the North and South Periyar districts and the Nilgiris district. At the same place where Periyar led the first anti-Hindi agitation of 1938, the Periyar district secretary A Ganesamurthy, NKK Periyasamy, Subbulakshmi Jagadeesan, P Balasubramanian, and Bakkiam Pazhaniappan were jailed for burning copies of the Constitution.

In Nilgiris district, LS Raasu and P Pushpavathi led the agitation. Though it is a hilly area, a large number of people participated.

On December 3, the agitation was held in Pasumpon Thevar district and in the Ramanathapuram district. In Sivaganga, home to the Marudhu brothers, the agitation was led by district secretary T Krishnan.

The agitation was led by M Gandhi in Kadaladi; in Paramakudi by Sakthi Kothandam; in North and South Arcot districts by Pulavar Govindan, TS Mohammed Sakhi, VK Raasu, MLA,

K Venugopal and MG Venkatakrishnan; in Madurai by SS Thennarasu, S Kaverimaniam, P Kamatchi and Mayathevar; in Thiruvidaimaruthur by Thanjavur district secretary Ko Si Mani; in Mannargudi by Mannai P Narayanasami; in the Union Territory of Pondicherry by S Muthu, S Narayanan, G Pugazhendhi, S Rajamanikkam and A Thangavel; in Karaikal by VMC Sivakumar and Seeni Thriumalai.

On December 8, a copy of Part XVII of the Constitution was set on fire by K Chozhan and VT Shanmugam.

The last phase of the agitation was held on December 9. Many DMK members participated in Chennai, Trichy, Pudukottai and Tirunelveli districts. In Tirunelveli, it was led by V Gopalsamy, MP, district secretary DAK Ilakkumanan, P Thambidurai, CK Shahul Hameed, V Aazhvar and K Sami; in Thoothukudi by Nellai Buhari and A Ayyasami; in Pudukottai by district secretary A Periyannan, S Raja and P Sezhiyan; in the important of towns of Trichy district by Anbil Dharmalingam, Kulithalai Muthukrishnan, Porselvi, Ilamurugu and SK Vadivelu.

When it was announced that the agitation would be led by Kalaignar Karunanidhi at about 10 am on December 9 in Chennai, the entire city was thrilled. In his letter to the party cadre, Kalaignar said: 'I will be entering the battlefield along with you as the student of Periyar, the younger brother of Anna, and a sibling of Perasiriyar (Anbazhagan), the veteran who weathered many a storm, with the pledge not to be cowed down by the mean-minded rulers.'

On December 9, a meeting was held under the leadership of Sadik Pasha to send off Kalaignar Karunanidhi to the battlefield. Addressing the crowd, he said: 'I don't know how many times I've gone to jail. I am ready to go to jail whenever the rulers want me to and, when I stand before a judge, I'll repeat revolutionary poet Bharathidasan's lines, "The jail that wants to trap us is like a garden where the kuyil sings."'

On the next day, he arrived at Valluvar Kottam standing atop an open vehicle. When he climbed on to the stage erected near Anna's statue, thousands of people who had gathered there greeted him with rousing slogans: 'Long Live Doctor Kalaignar, Long Live Doctor Kalaignar.' After garlanding Anna's statue and taking a pledge to follow in his footsteps by opposing Hindi domination and protecting Mother Tamil, he set fire to a copy of the constitutional provision relating to the official language. Joining him in this agitation were Arcot N Veerasamy, Minor Moses, SP Sargunam, SAM Husain and R Kennedy. The police arrested all of them and took them to jail.

Unable to bear the shock of Kalaignar Karunanidhi's arrest and imprisonment, the DMK members Needamangalam Govindarasan and Kulithalai Srinivasan killed themselves by consuming poison. Students and the DMK cadre took out processions condemning his arrest. Some tender-hearted young volunteers—Kovai Balasubramaniam, Bodi Murugan, Allur Muthu, Ariyalur Pugazhendhi, Ulundurpettai Pugazhendhi and Porur Jagajivan Ram, committed self-immolation.

About 20,000 DMK members, who had been jailed on charges of insulting the Constitution, assembling illegally and hatching a conspiracy, refused to come out on bail. They fought the cases from inside the prisons. Even those who fell ill chose to stay back in jails. Kaliyaperumal of Kattumannar Kovil, Subramanian of Guduvancheri, Arunachalam of Salem, Mookan of Marudur and Kalaignar Piththan died in jail.

After the trial, they were acquitted by courts, which treated the days they had spent in jail as term served. In some cases, they were released on the grounds that the charges against them had not been proven in court. A Ramamurthi, Additional Judge at Tirunelveli, acquitted 71 people, including V Gopalsamy, on the grounds that their objective was to oppose Hindi and not to insult the Constitution. At the Sengottai court, the judge acquitted DMK cadre, accepting advocate Pandi Valavan's argument that writing down the words of a constitutional provision on a piece of paper and burning it did not amount to insulting the Constitution itself.

The cases against Kalaignar and Perasiriyar Anbazhagan came up for hearing at the 11th Madras Metropolitan Court where Muthusamy was the judge. In his affidavit, Anbazhagan said firmly: 'Honourable Sir! We indulged in this struggle because there was no other way to protect Tamils' rights and attract the attention of the nation. We are prepared to accept any punishment awarded by the court.' The court sentenced him and nine others to nine weeks of imprisonment. Since the days he had spent in jail before the verdict were counted as part of the term of punishment, he was released on the day of the verdict.

On December 26, 1986, Kalaignar appeared in court and read out his affidavit denying the charges against him. In his affidavit, he elucidated the dangers of Hindi imperialism and its consequences for Tamils if it was not resisted. Pointing out that he was standing up not only for himself but for others as well, including the judge, he said his objective was to fight for linguistic right and not to insult the Constitution. 'If Hindi fanatics and the governments supporting them try to impose Hindi imperialism, treating Hindi as the queen of all languages, giving constitutionally-mandated equal opportunity only to the people of Hindi-speaking states and refusing to pursue the good objective of unity in diversity in an India of many nationalities, languages and cultures, it is they who are insulting the Constitutional principles... Hindi imposition was indirect so far.... Now, Hindi has started invading every department. The DMK was forced to launch a war out of fear that if Hindi imperialism was not resisted, it would reduce non-Hindi-speaking people, especially the people of Tamil Nadu, to the status of second-class citizens.

The DMK has concluded that it should no longer delay its decision to launch a peaceful agitation to prevent darkness from engulfing the future of five crore Tamils. It is not for ourselves that we are launching this agitation. As a Tamil who has been involved in this language war for 50 years, since my youth, I would like to state that this war is being fought for the sake of all sections of Tamil people, including those instigating the authorities to arrest us, those who have arrested us, those who have made accusations against us, and those who have come forward to bear witness against us and those itching to punish us.

'In order to press our demand for the necessary amendment to the Constitution, we are writing "Hindi is the official language of India" on a piece of paper and setting it aflame. Let this fire spread... not as a destructive conflagration, but as one that ignites minds. As has been mentioned in the charge sheet, this was not an act done on the sly. It was done openly in front of thousands of people, hundreds of police constables and officers, after explaining in detail what we were going to do and why we were doing it. Hence, there is no conspiracy here. There is no cause for the charge of insulting the nation. A farmer who removes the weeds in a field is not insulting the field; he does it to nurture the crops. Similarly, we, who respect the Constitution, are not only raising our voice in support of other languages and the rights of other language-speakers, but also keenly focussing on protecting the good crop called national integration.'

There was pin-drop silence in the courtroom when Kalaignar read out this statement in his characteristic metallic voice. The court was surprised to note that his argument was not only that of an ideologically committed political leader, but also that of a constitutional expert. The hearing was postponed to another day. On December 30, the judge sentenced Kalaignar and his co-agitators to ten weeks' imprisonment. Kalaignar smiled, implying that he was prepared to spend even 10 years in jail for the sake of sweet Tamil. He was led off to jail amid rousing slogans hailing him raised by the thousands of supporters who had come to court.

Although the punishment given to Kalaignar Karunanidhi was expected, processions, demonstrations and hunger strikes took place in important cities and towns of Tamil Nadu as a mark of protest against the guardian of Tamil and Tamils being unfairly punished. In the past, people had committed self-immolation for the sake of Tamil. It was only for Kalaignar that self-immolations were committed in support of a leader.

The government was not content with taking pleasure in hurting, insulting and taking revenge on Kalaignar. Ignoring the fact that he was a former Chief Minister, Kalaignar was made to wear the prison uniform. He was not bothered in the least. Making his enemies hang their heads in shame, he said: 'During the Congress rule also they gave me the prisoner's uniform. Even under this government, which claims to be opposed to Hindi, I've been made to wear that uniform. We regard this as our service to our language.' Newspaper reports of Kalaignar having to wear the prison uniform shocked the State. Mariappan of Aruppukottai and Vedhamanikkam of Chatrapatti died of this shock. The people of Tamil Nadu believed that this was uncivilised behaviour on the part of the State government. Peaceful protests threatened to take a more serious turn. Realising that it was impossible to run the administration smoothly by keeping Kalaignar Karunanidhi in prison, the MGR government unexpectedly released him and his co-agitators at about 10 am on February 2, 1986. Here was proof of the fact that the State, the law, the police and the judiciary would bow down before idealists.

There is a basic difference between the anti-Hindi agitations of earlier years and the one that took place in 1986. In the past agitations, the Kazhagam confronted the enemy in the battlefield—the enemies who had brazenly declared that Hindi was the official language and learning it was essential to get jobs. However, in 1986, it faced not enemies in the battlefield but traitors who claimed to be opponents of Hindi while backstabbing them. The

North was happy at this scenario. Congress cheered; the heart of Hindi imperialism brimmed over with joy.

In the Constitution-burning agitation that lasted from November 17 to December 9 in 1986, as many as 19,314 people were imprisoned; of these, 1,642 were arrested as a preventive measure; 17,627 volunteers were punished for reducing a constitutional provision to ashes. This was a historically unprecedented method of struggle which attracted global attention, including a special mention in the internationally acclaimed *Time* magazine.

In the Quit India struggle launched by Gandhiji, only 1,586 were jailed in South India. But the number of people imprisoned in the anti-Hindi struggle led by Kalaignar Karunanidhi was 17,672. Is there a parallel to this history of sacrifices?

It is this struggle which proved to Hindi imperialists that the DMK was like an army always in a state of preparedness to save Tamil and the Tamil race. The 1986 struggle produced four beneficial outcomes:

1. It prevented the MGR government that swore by Periyar and Anna from impairing the Tamil consciousness and self-respect nurtured by those leaders, revived the passion for Tamil and the ideas rooted in rationalism among the Tamil people.
2. It made the world realise that it was impossible to split the DMK with the help of the Centre, crown members of one faction as traitorous Vibhishanas and thus destroy the Dravidian traditions of Tamil Nadu; and that the DMK was an army of soldiers who were prepared to make any sacrifice to protect those traditions.
3. This struggle succeeded in preventing the MGR government from opening the Navodaya schools which the Rajiv Gandhi government proposed to set up under its new education policy.

The participation of about 20,000 volunteers in the struggle, despite knowing that strong punishment awaited, and their unparalleled sacrifice was the reason behind the DMK returning to power in 1989.

Chapter 25

The 14 Language Formula

'While demanding that Tamil, the State's official language and the foremost Dravidian language, should be accepted as the official language of the Centre, this general council wants English to continue as the official language until the official languages of the states are accepted as the official languages of India.'

—Dravida Munnetra Kazhagam

Hindi fanatics believe that the language issue has come to an end. However, the January revolution of 1965 created a heightened awareness among non-Hindi-speaking people. There is a consensus across political divides that this issue has to be reviewed again to find a solution acceptable to all. Opinions are divided along the following lines: 1. The language issue can be resolved by amending the Constitution; 2. Both Hindi and English should be accepted as the official languages; 3. English should be accepted as the second official language as long as non-Hindi-speaking people want it that way; 4. English alone should be the official language; 5. While making Hindi the official language, the Centre should help in the development of the other major languages by recognising their rights and extending full cooperation; and 6. All the 14 languages listed in the Eighth Schedule of the Constitution should be accorded the status of official languages.

At the height of the struggle, it was suggested that since this was a national issue, a solution had to be found by an analysis that considers factors such as national unity, administrative efficiency, approval of an overwhelming majority, protection of the minority communities' languages, development of dialects, the rights of regional-language speakers and prevention of dominance of any one language. However, owing to the failure of those who had agreed to find a solution with these factors in mind, Hindi ascended the throne.

A country with a population of 100 crore has only 14 developed languages. It is through them that various cultures, customs and civilisations have been nurtured traditionally. In the present situation, no one will accept the decision to accord the official status to one language by ruining these traditions. The Congress thought it would successfully implement its one-language formula, taking advantage of anti-British feelings and the thirst for freedom. Had the Congress respected rich, ancient languages such as Tamil, Malayalam, Bengali and Telugu, recognised their rights and accorded official status to many languages, it could have pre-empted these language agitations. The Congress was not afraid of recognising many languages as official languages; rather, it did not wish to do so.

It is not that recognising many languages as official languages had not been considered. It had been accepted by the Constitution as a policy for the states. Article 345 of the Constitution says: 'Subject to the provisions of Articles 346 and 347, the Legislature of a State may by law adopt any one or more of the languages in use in the State or Hindi as the language or languages to be used for all or any of the official purposes of that State.'

The very same rulers who had accepted the concept of having many official languages at the State level, gave Hindi monopoly rights at the Central level. Only after overcoming the hangover of freedom did some Congressmen realise the dangerous consequences of accepting one language as the official language in the subcontinent which is home to many developed languages. Speaking on the language issue in the State Assembly, Bengal Chief Minister BC Roy said: 'It is true that the constitutional experts were also discussing the question of having one official language for the country. They forgot that this is a country of many languages. It has people whose culture and traditions developed based on the Aryan language; people who have progressed based on the Dravidian languages; and people who speak languages that have significant Mongolian influence. So, in such a country, it is possible to have many official languages.'

On the need to accept more than one language as the official language, the Tamil Nadu government said: 'In fact, the practice of using many languages simultaneously for many administrative functions could be established at the Central or the State level.'

Many countries have recognised more than one language as official languages. In Canada, English and French are the official languages. Flemish and French are the official languages of Belgium. Finland has accepted Swedish and Finnish as the official languages. In South Africa, English and many African languages enjoy the status of official languages. Switzerland has German, French and Latin as its official languages. English, German, French and Russian are the administrative languages of the United Nations. The European Common Market has Dutch, French, German, and Italian as administrative languages. Accepting more than one language as the official or the administrative language has not affected the administration in any way in these countries and institutions. When speakers of many languages live under a single political system, the administration can benefit people by accepting their languages.

Many support the idea of recognising the State or regional languages as official languages. This concept has gained new strength among the intelligentsia and in political movements. Even those who oppose it cite only administrative glitches as the reason. They do not find fault with the justness of the practice.

In his message to the Language Development Board, reputed Indian scientist, Sir CV Raman, said all the 14 languages listed in the Eighth Schedule of the Constitution should be accorded equal respect in all the branches of the government, including Parliament.

Sri Prakasa, one of Gandhiji's close friends and former Governor of Maharashtra, said: 'I state this again boldly: Either English or Hindi or any one domestic or foreign language cannot be the official language of India. All the state languages should be accorded equal status. English also should be added to them.'

Addressing a public meeting at Varanasi, Praja Socialist Party leader, SM Joshi, said that the only way to avoid the danger of making Hindi the official language is to give equal status to all the 14 national languages.

Recognising the sentiments of Bengalis regarding their language during the January revolution, the Bengal government passed a resolution in the Assembly demanding equal status to all the 14 national languages.

Hindi fanatics maintain that it is a sin to give the status of national language to other languages and refuse to find a solution based on the experiences of other countries. They believe that they can establish Hindi's dominance through the Constitution and the Congress' parliamentary majority. Responding to Nanjil Manoharan's plea to recognise all the 14 national languages as official languages of the Union government, Home Minister Lal Bahadur Shastri said that it was not practical to accept Manoharan's demand. When the experience of other countries in the language issue was cited, he said: 'That may be true. But there is no need to follow other countries in every issue.' He did not explain what harm could befall by adopting the practices of other countries. In fact, he had no explanation because he was afraid that adopting those practices would uproot the dominance of Hindi and destroy the rulers' long-term imperialistic plan. The issue is complex, indeed. But other languages need to be respected and given their fair due and accepted happily.

Some critics say that while it was possible to accept two or three languages, how can 14 languages be recognised? They say rhetorically: where is a country with 14 official languages? Canada and Belgium have recognised only two official languages. But they did not choose these two out of 20 languages in their respective countries. Switzerland, which has three languages, has made all three of them official. In short, they have given official status to all languages in use in their countries. In a family of two children, the father's property is divided into two; in a family of 10 children, property is divided among the ten. Can we divide the property among two in this family and send the remaining eight children out with begging bowls? The demand to give official status to all the 14 national languages is aimed at not only defeating Hindi but also getting due share in the Central government.

In India, speakers of the States' languages are not small in number. Nor are they vagabonds. They are great people living in this country for thousands of years with distinct languages and cultures. Compared to each language group in the European countries, the population of speakers of each language in India is much bigger. The population of Belgium, which has two official languages, is 97,27,000. In Finland, which has two official languages, it is only 49,35,000. The population of Switzerland, which has three official languages, is only 66,00,000. But the population of Telugu speakers in the Indian sub-continent alone is 6.6 crore. There are 6.96 crore Bengali speakers and 5.3 crore Tamil speakers. In Kashmir, apart from Kashmiri and Sanskrit, each dialect is spoken by more than a crore people. How can people bear to be denied their due in the matter of the official language at the Centre? They cannot be the yes-men of Hindi imperialism. They are great people who want to march ahead in the present-day world.

It is true that there is no country in the world with 14 official languages. But it is unfair to argue that all the 14 national languages need not be given the status of official languages. Is there any other democratic country like India which has multiple, and sometimes mutually contradictory, languages, cultures, traditions and customs? India happens to be a nation that is contradictory to the very definition of 'nation' given by thinkers ranging from Aristotle to Appadurai. We have followed a new grammar in constituting the nation. Hence, we must follow new methods of deciding its official language. We have created a country which is the first of its kind in the world. Therefore, we have to accept its 14 languages as official, unlike anywhere else in the world. A man who rears a goat has to buy fodder according to its need. Can a man rearing an elephant buy fodder that would satisfy a goat? Similarly, official languages are determined based on the needs of respective nations.

Some people are afraid that if 14 languages become official, each department would have to be run with 14 languages in which notes, orders, definitions, explanations, and replies would have to be written. Contrary to their thinking, all the departments of the Union government need not use all the 14 languages. Nor is there need for officials to learn all the 14 languages. Knowledge of English and their respective mother tongue is sufficient.

If the languages of all the states are accepted as official languages, there is no need for a link language. The argument that India needs a link language is as dangerous as the argument that it needs only one official language. If one language is accepted as the link language, that language will become dominant. Hence, all the state languages should be made the official languages and link languages. When needed, English translations will be of use to all Central government departments.

To implement the 14-language formula, a big change needs to be made in the Indian political structure. In the existing structure,

State governments depend on the munificence of the Union government. This has to be changed by granting autonomy to the states so that they can meet the needs of each citizen. The Union government has monopolised many rights that are unnecessary for it. The situation is so pathetic that from those seeking scholarships for education to those needing industrial licences, all are forced to knock the doors of various Central departments. People's lives based on rights and entitlements will be protected only by reducing the powers of the Union government.

A translation department will have to be set up in the Central government's secretariat. Every letter written in a regional language must be translated into English. The Central Secretariat should send replies in officially approved English translations. In Parliament, members should be allowed to speak any of the 14 state languages. As in the United Nations, facilities should be created for simultaneous translations of their speeches. Except writ petitions, cases relating to constitutional issues, politically important cases and social reform-related cases, no cases should be allowed to go to the Supreme Court as an appeal. The Supreme Court verdicts should be in English. Lawyers should be allowed to argue their cases in their own languages, if the judge permits it. In cases filed on the basis of laws enacted by State Assemblies, the decision of the respective high court should be final. In cases filed against the State on the bases of laws enacted in state languages, the high court should give its verdict in the language of the State concerned. Along with it, an official translation should also be provided.

In communications with foreign countries, English alone should be used.

In the recruitment exams held for Central government jobs, only the state languages should be the medium. Every candidate should write replies in English in some exams. A person who wants to work in the government of another state should learn the official language of that State.

State languages should be the medium in the exams for Indian Administrative Service, Indian Foreign Service and Indian Police Service. In some subjects, answers should be written in English. Successful candidates should be given priority to serve in their respective states.

The states can communicate with the Centre in their official languages. But such communication should have an English translation attached to it. Between the states, communication should be in their respective official languages with official English translations. The Union government's offices in every State should use the official language of the State in administration. For instance, post offices, railway stations, income tax offices, port-related institutions should conduct their business only in Tamil. When these offices want to communicate with the Central government Secretariat or Union Ministries, they can use the State's language along with an official translation of the text.

Communist Party of India leader M Kalyanasundaram moved a resolution that said: 'The businesses of Central government offices functioning in states should be conducted in the respective state's languages and English. The Union government is requested to give equal status to all state languages.'

In its report, the Official Language Commission recommended: 'These institutions with governmental responsibilities should consistently function bilingually. That is, for internal communication, they should use Hindi. For communication with the people of the State concerned, they should use the State language.' If the State language is used along with English translation and avoids Hindi, the communication between the administration and the people will be smooth.

Opponents of the 14-languge formula cite two reasons for their objection:

1. If all the 14 languages are given official status, every State would appear to be functioning like an independent nation.

2. This will greatly harm national integration leading to the waning of the all-India sentiment.

These two reasons are cited not out of any love for national unity. This is a statement of imperialists who want to enslave the states in the name of national unity. Similar objections were raised when the nation debated the linguistic reorganisation of states. Now that Indian states have been demarcated on the basis of language, it is evident that national unity has not been harmed.

National unity and national integration should not be used to show off one's political ingenuity. They should serve the interests of the states. The creation of a new imperialism was not why the states came together to constitute the Central government. It was to protect their lives, rights, languages and cultures through the power of unity. If those advocating the idea of 'all-India' unity expect every State to give up its linguistic rights, change its culture, homogenise traditions and reduce its powers, people will look at national unity and the Central government as parts of an imperialist conspiracy. The unity of all of India is only for protecting the states' rights. National integration is only for nurturing the states' languages. It is not for sacrificing languages and rights. Saying that the 14-language formula will give India the appearance of a combination of many nations is part of false propaganda. If all the 14 languages are accepted as national languages, it will prevent India from being dismembered by the domination of Hindi—the domination of a single language will end, paving the way for equal status to all the national languages.

- All these languages will develop without any hindrance, according to the abilities of the people who speak them.
- As the State and Central government offices would conduct their affairs in the language spoken by the people of the respective states, they will become people's administrations.
- The pathetic situation of non-Hindi-speaking people being considered second-class citizens will be averted.

The DMK passed a resolution demanding official status to all the 14 national languages keeping in mind all these interests and benefits. But Hindi imperialists refuse to accept it. They are planning to convert India into their own land. They don't want to accept that others too have a share in it. Seeking their approval for the language issue will not work in practice. There is no historical proof of imperialists respecting people's voices. But the Hindi chauvinists have not realised that people have succeeded in bringing imperialists down on their knees.

Although anti-Hindi struggles since 1937 have not fully succeeded, the bloodshed by Tamils and their sacrifices have not been in vain. It was because of their struggles that the invasion of Hindi imperialism has been stalled. Those struggles have ensured that non-Hindi-speaking people will never accept Hindi as the official language. Nehru assured the nation that English would continue to be an official language. It was with the promise of fulfilling that assurance that the Official Languages Act was enacted. It has been recognised that the 14 languages listed in the Eighth Schedule would be national languages. Candidates have been allowed to write Central recruitment exams in their respective state languages. Hindi has been completely removed from Tamil Nadu schools with the implementation of the two-language formula. The assurance that Hindi will not be imposed on non-Hindi-speaking people has been accepted in principle. The people of Tamil Nadu have been defeating the pro-Hindi Congress in elections held since 1967. However, the constitutional recognition of Hindi as the official language remains.

All the 14 languages, including Tamil, should be accepted as official languages of the Central government. Until then, English should also continue as an official language. The Union government has not come forward to accept these demands put forth by us and amend the Constitution accordingly. So, we should continue our struggle.

We should remember Anna's words:

'Don't stop sounding the bugle. Don't bring down the hoisted flag. If Hindi imperialists throw 10 dead bodies on the path to Hindi's domination, we should show that hundred people will die for the sake of Tamil. Without such determination, it will be impossible to achieve success.'

Afterword: Reflections by a Granddaughter

Kavya Balaji

Launched within the confines of a humble cinema hall and blessed by three prominent Chief Ministers—Arignar Annam, Dr Kalaignar, and Thiru MGR—this book holds significance in shaping the political landscape of Tamil Nadu. It extended the discourse initiated by my grandfather, Aladi Aruna, a young author at the age of 31, and the wisdom embedded in its pages, integral to its essence, resonates across generations through family conversations.

My grandfather's resistance against the imposition of Hindi and attempts to Sanskritise and sanitise the South Indian cultural landscape, mirroring its Northern counterparts, related to a pivotal issue—the erosion of our democratic system and its impact on economic progress.

The present Central government's coercive push to promote Hindi in all social media posts, renaming Teachers' Day as 'Guru Utsav' and introducing celebrations like 'Sanskrit Week' echoes historical patterns reminiscent of past initiatives to influence language and cultural practices. In these trying times, the lessons from this book are of great value, as our forefathers also faced similar challenges. By learning from their experiences, we can unite against common obstacles, transcending divisions such as unionists vs separatists, men vs women, the educated vs uneducated, religious individuals vs atheists. Together, we must preserve the Tamil language with determination, courage, perseverance and resilience for the sake of our unique cultural, linguistic, and political heritage.

Resisting the imposition of Hindi and opting for Tamil is an act of democracy, empowering people to determine what they believe is right for them and to shape their destiny. Choosing and respecting the differences in our language and culture emphasises that it is not just about linguistic preferences but also a democratic expression. Any erosion of the Tamil language in favour of another suggests a democratic erosion.

While the argument from political leaders in the North emphasises the need for Hindi as the sole language to unite us under the banner of 'One Nation, One Language,' my grandfather's perspective, shaped by the early years of India as a fledgling nation and democracy, reveals that the true unifying language has always been democracy. Despite the forces of Hindutva attempting to erase our Tamil identity in the name of 'unity,' they, in reality, push for 'uniformity'. The book demonstrates that my grandfather, along with many others, undertook the challenging task of keeping this passion for democracy and diversity alive. While Hindutva forces may attempt to dampen these flames, it is our responsibility, as it was for those before us, to keep the embers alive and preserve federalism, democracy, and the Tamil language.

Periyar EV Ramasamy with CN Annadurai and M Karunanidhi.

குடி அரசு

"KUDI ARASU"

வீழ்க இந்தி!

Front page of the Tamil Magazine *Kudiyarasu* (3 September 1939), run by Periyar. It carried an editorial titled 'Veezhga Indhi' (Down with Hindi).

Periyar and Annadurai with black-shirt volunteers.

Black flag hoisted on DMK headquarters
during the anti-Hindi agitation in 1938-39.

Ramamirtham Ammaiyar and Kumarasami Pillai
leading a procession from Trichy to Madras.

Women staging a black-flag demonstration in Erode against Premier Rajaji.

Anti-Hindi demonstration by black-shirt volunteers in Kumbakonam in the late 1930s.

Students in Madras come out into the streets to join the anti-Hindi agitation as protests erupt in January 1965 after two ministries of the central government issue circulars for replacing English with Hindi in official communications.

Demonstrators set fire to effigies of the 'Hindi demon'.

SUBRAMANIAM, ALAGESAN RESIGN

Arson spree in city: suburban station sacked

CURFEW ALERT

Statutory effect for Nehru pledge sought

More Ministers back South's stand on language issue

EXPRESS NEWS SERVICE

NEW DELHI, Feb. 11

We stand by Nehru assurance

Schools, colleges closed till Mar. 1

Premier's dilemma

Governor appeals

Two more 'harakiris'

23 KILLED IN POLICE FIRINGS

Army rushed to riot-torn towns

Two Tamil ministers in the Lal Bahadur Shastri government resign on 11 February 1965, as the protests in Tamil Nadu against the imposition of Hindi escalate.

Students of Presidency College, Madras observe a day-long public fast.

Students of Fatima College in Madurai on an indefinite fast.

Students of Pachaiyappa's College on hunger strike in Madras.

A 1,000-strong crowd of students entered the Egmore railway station and held up an electric train.

'Tamil vazhga' (Long live Tamil); 'Hindi or India?' —women in a protest march.

M Ramanathan setting fire to a copy of Part XVII of the Constitution. (Part XVII of the Constitution contains provisions for an official language for the Union, the states, the judiciary and to be used in inter-governmental communication.)

Soldiers of the Seventeenth Madras Battalion patrol Pollachi town.

Annadurai declaring in the State Legislative Assembly, in January 1968, that his government will follow the two-language formula (mother tongue and English).

Anti-Hindi protest in Madurai by the DMK youth wing on 15 October 2022.

A memorial in Chennai for those who died in the Anti-Hindi agitations of the 1930s and 1960s. (Photo by Surya Prakash SA; Wikimedia Commons.)

Natarasan and Thalamuthu, who died in police custody during the anti-Hindi agitation in 1939. They are considered the first 'Tamil martyrs'.

Tamil scholars Thiru Vi Ka, Ramamirtham Ammaiyar, K Appadurai and Navalar Somasundara Bharathi.

Tamil scholars and activists Pattukottai Alagirisamy and S Dharmambal; revolutionary poet Bharathidasan; and founder of *Dina Thanthi*, SP Adithan.

Tamil maryrs of the 1960s: A Chinnasamy, Sivalingam, Veerappan, Aranganathan, Shanmugam and Sarangapani.

Notes

Chapter 1: A Definitive Purpose in the History of Tamils

1 Éamon de Valera, an Irish political leader and statesman.
2 Bharathidasan wrote the song '*Sange Muzhangu*' under a collection of poems titled *Sanga Nathan* to sing the praises of the Tamil language.
3 Arnold Toynbee, an English Historian.

Chapter 2: Hindi, Urdu, Hindustani

4 Gandhi in *Young India,* 2-2-1921. For Gandhi, Hindustani should neither be Sanskritised Hindi nor Persianised Urdu but a combination of both. It should freely admit words, whenever necessary, from the different regional languages and also assimilate words from foreign languages as long as they can mix well and easily with our national language. Gandhi wanted a national language which is rich and powerful, capable of expressing the whole gamut of human thoughts and feelings. He felt that confining oneself exclusively to Hindi or Urdu would be a crime against the intelligence and spirit of patriotism.
5 In the Karachi session of the Indian National Congress in 1925, it was decided that Hindustani should be the lingua franca of the independent nation. Due to the influence of the Hindi Sahitya Sammelan and the Bharatiya Sahitya Parishad, they modified the resolution in a few years to say that Hindi should be the national language. It left many members of the Congress disappointed and created communal tensions.
6 Rajendra Prasad was the first president of independent India (1950-62).

7 Purushottam Das Tandon was a freedom fighter from Allahabad, Uttar Pradesh. He was known for his efforts to promote Hindi as the official language. Despite many leaders advocating for Hindustani as the national language, Tandon insisted on the usage of Devanagari script and rejected Urdu script as well as words with roots in Arabic and Persian.

8 In 1945, Gandhi wrote to Purushottam Das Tandon that he intended to resign from the Hindi Sahitya Sammelan because it preached that only Hindi in the Devanagari script could be the national language. Tandon replied that he could not agree that all Indians should learn Urdu and Hindi and he believed instead that it was more important to oust English from its position and to convert the speakers of regional languages to Hindi. Several days later, Gandhi resigned from the Sammelan, saying, 'My definition of Rashtra Bhasha (national language) includes a knowledge of both Hindi and Urdu and both the Nagari and Urdu scripts. Only thus can a happy fusion of Hindi and Urdu take place.' Gandhi in *Young India*, 23 August 1928; cited in *Gandhi, Thoughts*, p. 30.24 Gandhi to Tandon, May 28, 1945. See *Gandhi, Thoughts*, p. 133.

9 As India's partition became imminent in 1946, Urdu—perceived as aligned with Pakistan—was discarded from among the national language contenders of newly independent India.

10 Govind Ballabh Pant was appointed Minister of Home Affairs in the Union Cabinet on January 10, 1955 by Prime Minister Jawaharlal Nehru. He was also responsible for establishing Hindi as an official language of the central government and a few states.

11 Seth Govind Das, parliamentarian and independence activist. Das, a Hindi author, supported Hindi as the national language of India.

12 In speech to the Hindi Sahitya Sammelan at Indore; reproduced in *Gandhi, Thoughts on National Language*, p. 14. Gandhi used the words Hindi and Hindustani at different times for several reasons, but he was always speaking of the same tongue, that is, broad Hindustani, written in both the Urdu and Devanagari scripts.

13 Raghunath Vinayak Dhulekar, also known as RV Dhulekar, brought an Amendment Bill in Parliament to work and speak in Hindi, which could then be translated in English language for all Members

of Parliament. On December 10, 1946 he delivered his first major speech in Hindustani. In his speech, he said that people who do not know Hindustani have no right to stay in India.

Chapter 3: The First Language War

14 Navalar Somasundara Bharathiar, Tamil scholar, writer, professor and lawyer. He participated in the anti-Hindi agitations of Tamil Nadu. He also headed the movement for the abolition of untouchability in Madurai.
15 Ku Ma Balasubramaniam, famous lyricist who wrote the song '*Singaravelane Deva*' for the film Konjum Salangai.
16 TV Uma Maheswaran Pillai, president of Tamil Sangam, Karunthattankudi, which is also known as Karanthai.
17 KAP Viswanathan, Tamil scholar, writer and social activist.
18 WPA Soundarapandian, a famous leader of the Nadar community, who was also a member of the Madras Legislative Council from 1920 to 1937.
19 Bharathidasan's poem, *Senai ontru thevai; perum senai ontru thevai.*
20 Palladam Ponnusamy, leader who threatened to observe fast-unto-death in front of Rajaji's house.
21 Shanmuganada Adigal, one of the three sanniyais [sanniyasi: monk] who participated in anti-Hindi agitation.
22 CD Nayagam, a close associate of Periyar. It was at his house that the marriage of Periyar with KA Mani Ammaiyar, took place.
23 AT Panneerselvam, one of the leaders of the Justice Party and Minister.
24 Rajah Sir Muthiah Chettiar, industrialist, philanthropist, also the first Mayor of Chennai.
25 Eezhathadigal, one of the three sanniyasis who participated in the anti-Hindi agitation. His original name was Sivananda Adigal. Since he was from Sri Lanka, he was called Eezhathadigal.
26 Arunagiri Adigal of Saadhunarayana Desigar Madalayam. He was one of the three sanniyasis who participated in the anti-Hindi agitation.
27 Tiruvarur Balasundaram, poet.
28 Khan Bahadur Khalifullah of the All-India Muslim League served

as Minister of Public Works in the Kurma Venkata Reddi Naidu Cabinet from April to July 1937.

29 Dharmambal, social activist who was given the title 'Veera Tamil Annai' (Heroic Tamil Mother) for her contributions to anti-Hindi agitations.

30 Ramamirtham Ammaiyar, leading woman activist of Self-Respect Movement, social reformer.

31 Malarmugathammaiyar, eminent woman leader of Dravidian movement.

32 R Narayani Ammaiyar, prominent Tamil woman organiser in Self-Respect Movement.

33 In 1924-25, the Vaikom Satyagraha was a non-violent agitation for access to prohibited public environs of the Vaikom temple in the Kingdom of Travancore. Periyar was a key figure in this struggle.

Chapter 4: The Satyagraha of 1948

34 Kuthusi Gurusamy, writer and journalist, who was also the editor of *Viduthalai*, founded by Periyar.

35 NV Natarajan, one of the founding members of the DMK and one of the Aimperum Thalaivar—one of the five big leaders of the DMK.

36 KK Neelamegam; the executive committee member of the Dravidar Kazhagam under whose chairmanship dissidents of the organisation met to discuss the 'autocratic ways of Periyar'.

37 TM Parthasarathy, author of *History of DMK—1916-1962*, published by Pari Nilayam, Madras, pp 640.

38 Omandur Ramasamy Reddiar, Chief Minister of Madras Presidency.

39 Dhanalakshmi Ammaiyar, social reformer, Self-Respect activist.

40 K Appadurai, multilingual scholar, linguist.

41 Alamelu Appadurai, severely beaten during the anti-Hindi agitation of 1948. Took a leading part in several agitations against Hindi imposition.

42 Kanchi Manimozhiyar, a leader who ran the magazine Porvaal to propagate the ideas of Dravidian Movement.

43 N Jeevarathinam, prominent leader of the Dravidar Kazhagam. There is a manimandapam in Chennai in his name.

44 Sathiyavani Muthu, DMK's first woman MLA, its first woman

Minister and the first Union Minister representing a Dravidian party.

45 On July 9, 1949, 70-year-old Periyar married 32-year-old Maniammai. This marriage caused outrage and is one of the reasons that caused a split in the organisation and paved the way for leaders such as Annadurai and Karunanidhi to form their own party, the Dravida Munnetra Kazhagam (DMK).

Chapter 5 The Constitution and the Official Language

46 K Santhanam, Congress leader and Minister.

47 Draft of the Indian Constitution, 1948: '99(1) In Parliament, business shall be transacted in Hindi or English: Provided that the Chairman of the Council of States or the Speaker of the House of the People, as the case may be, may permit any member who cannot adequately express himself in either language to address the House in his mother tongue. (2) The Chairman of the Council of States or the Speaker of the House of the People may, whenever he thinks fit, make arrangements for making available in the Council of States or the House of the People, as the case may be, a summary in Hindi or English of the speech delivered by a member in any other language and such summary shall be included in the record of the proceedings of the House in which the speech has been delivered.'

48 Lakshmi Kanta Maitra, Congress Nationalist Party leader, Constituent Assembly Member (elected on Indian National Congress ticket) from Bengal, Member of Provisional Parliament of India.

49 N Gopalaswamy Ayyangar, Prime Minister of the princely state of Jammu and Kashmir and later a Minister in the first Cabinet of independent India.

50 Muhammed Saadulah, British India's Prime Minister of Assam.

51 Mahavir Tyagi, a prominent freedom fighter and a parliamentarian.

52 'Quaid-E-Millat' (Leader of the Nation) M Muhammad Ismail, founded the Indian Union of Muslim League (IUML), and was a Member of Constituent Assembly, the Lok Sabha, Rajya Sabha, and Madras State Legislative Assembly.

53 Tiruppur Angappa Ramalingam Chettiar, Member of Constituent Assembly from Madras Province, parliamentarian elected from Coimbatore in 1951.

54 PT Chacko, former Minister from Kerala.

55 Maulana Hasrat Mohani, freedom fighter and poet who coined the slogan 'Inqilab Zindabad'.

Chapter 6: The August Agitation

56 KR Ramasamy, noted theatre and film personality.

57 TP Vedachalam, well-known advocate and close friend of Periyar.

Chapter 7: The Imposition of Hindi

58 The 1951 Census of India reported that nearly 150 million or about 42 per cent, have as their native tongue Eastern and Western Hindi, Urdu, Hindustani, collectively known as Hindustani.

59 Rahul Sankrityayan, author of *From Volga to Ganga* and many other books.

60 Sitaram Chaturvedi, scholar of Hindi and Sanskrit language and literature from Banaras, Uttar Pradesh.

Chapter 8: The Devanagari Script

61 MK Gandhi, 'Thoughts on National Language', *Young India*, 27-8-1925.

62 'The Dravidians, being in a minority, should learn the common language of the rest of India than the rest should learn Tamil, Telugu, Kanarese and Malayalam in order to be able to converse with Dravidian India... Let no Dravidian think that learning Hindi is at all difficult. A little time taken from the recreation hour daily and in a systematic manner will enable an average man to learn Hindi in one year'. Further, 'our greatest assembly cannot be a real object lesson to the masses unless it speaks to them in a language which the largest number can understand. I appreciate the difficulty of the Dravidians, but nothing is difficult before their industrious love for the Motherland.' (MK Gandhi, *Young India*, 1921)

Chapter 11: The Official Language Commission and the Parliamentary Committee

63 Paramasivan Subbarayan, fourth Prime Minister of Madras Presidency from 4 December 1926–27 October 1930.

64 Suniti Kumar Chatterji, Padma Vibushan recipient, linguist, educationist.

65 Dr Raghu Vira, linguist, politician, member of the Constituent Assembly.

Chapter 12: Black Flag

66 'Kalingathu Parani', 12th-century Tamil poem by Jayamkondar, which describes the victory of Chola King, Kulottunga I.

Chapter 13: The Official Languages Act

67 Swami Rameshwaranand, Jana Sangh leader elected to Parliament from Karnal in undivided Punjab (present-day Haryana), frequently demanded Hindi be accorded sole national language status.

68 Mani Ram Bagri, a parliamentarian and social activist who joined the parliamentary socialists like Rammanohar Lohia and Jayaprakash Narayan.

69 Hukam Chand Kachwai, freedom fighter, BJP leader, and Member of Parliament from Madhya Pradesh.

70 Section 3 of The Official Languages Act, 1963: '3. Continuance of English language for official purposes of the Union and for use in Parliament—(1) Notwithstanding the expiration of the period of fifteen years from the commencement of the Constitution, the English language may, as from the appointed day, continue to be used, in addition to Hindi, a) for all the official purposes of the Union for which it was being used immediately before that day; and b) for the transaction of business in Parliament.'

Chapter 14: Setting Aflame the Constitution

71 Kanchi Kalyanasundaram, DMK Member of Parliament in the Rajya Sabha from 1969–1976.

72 C Neelanarayanan, treasurer of DMK, who was severely beaten during Emergency.

73 TK Ponnuvelu, DMK leader, member of the Tamil Nadu Legislative Council in 1968. The State subsequently adopted a unicameral legislature.

74 VR Periyannan, MLA from Senthamangalam, Tamil Nadu from 1962-77.

75 A Muniyandi, DMK leader and MLA from Tamil Nadu from the Nilakottai constituency, elected in 1967 and 1971.

76 Jagadambal Velayudham, member of Tamil Nadu Assembly, 1962-67, Jayankondam Constituency.

Chapter 15: Self-immolation

77 Gogineni Ranga Nayukulu, also known as NG Ranga, founding president of Swatantra Party, Padma Vibhushan awardee.

Chapter 16: January Revolution and a day of mourning

78 Bharathidasan poem.

Chapter 21: After the Storm

79 Damodaram Sanjivayya, Chief Minister of Andhra Pradesh, 1960-62; president of Indian National Congress 1962-64; Union Minister of Labour and Employment 1964-66.

80 Gulzarilal Nanda, twice sworn in for short stints as Prime Minister of India; after the death of Jawaharlal Nehru on May 27, 1964, and after the death of Lal Bahadur Shastri at Tashkent on January 11, 1966.

81 N Rajangam, DMK MLA and Minister.

82 Chidambaram Subramaniam, Congress Minister who spearheaded Green Revolution, Bharat Ratna awardee.

83 Ozhalur Viswanatha Mudaliar Alagesan; Member of Constituent Assembly, Member of Parliament and Union Cabinet Minister; opposed Central government's language policy.

84 Siddavanahalli Nijalingappa, Chief Minister of Mysore State (now Karnataka) from 1956 to 1958 and 1962 to 1968.

85 Kasu Brahmananda Reddy, Chief Minister of Andhra Pradesh 1964-71.

Chapter 22: January Revolution

86 Address at a Meeting in the Polytechnic Museum. From *Lenin, A Revolutionary Life* (Taylor & Francis, 2013) by Christopher Read, p. 224.

87 Meenakshisundaram Kalyanasundaram (1909-88), state secretary of

the Communist Party of India (CPI), legislator from Tamil Nadu, Member of Parliament.

88 Kamban Adippodi Saw Ganesan, former Mayor of Chennai, Tamil writer and historian.

Chapter 23: The Two Language Formula

89 On July 18, 1967, Chief Minister Anna prepared a resolution to change the name of Madras State to Tamil Nadu in English and Tamil languages. Speaking on the debate, Opposition Leader PG Karuthiruman said, 'Madras is a name in world history; Tamil Nadu will take time to reach the same heights.' So, he suggested that the name ought to be 'Tamil Nadu-Madras State'. However, Tamil Nadu was accepted and the resolution passed unanimously. Anna uttered 'Tamil Nadu' three times, loudly cheered by legislators. Anna recognised the contributions of Thiyagi Sankaralinganar, who died after going on a hunger strike, and MP Sivagnanam, in the formation of Tamil Nadu.

90 Yashwantrao Chavan, also known as YB Chavan, the last Chief Minister of the Bombay State. He was Home Minister under Prime Minister Indira Gandhi.

91 Murli Manohar Joshi, former BJP president and former Union Minister.

92 Madhu Limaye, socialist and follower of Rammanohar Lohia. He was active in the Janata Party government which came to power following Emergency.

93 Shripad Amrit Dange, founder of the Communist Party of India (CPI) and its chairman from 1962-81.

94 A Balasubramanian, state secretary of the Communist Party of India (Marxist).

95 HV Hande, Swatantra Party leader who later joined AIADMK and became Minister in MG Ramachandran's Cabinet.

96 PG Karuthiruman, Congress leader; the last opposition Leader of Madras State and first opposition leader of Tamil Nadu.

97 CN Annadurai's speech during Two Language Policy Resolution in the Tamil Nadu Legislative Assembly, 1968.

ALSO FROM SPEAKING TIGER

VIDEO MARIAMMAN

Stories

Imayam

Translated by Padma Narayanan

In his pathbreaking fiction, the acclaimed Tamil writer Imayam has written about the brutal complexities of the caste system and patriarchy in unadorned, powerful prose. *Video Mariamman* is a collection of fourteen of his finest stories.

Poonkothai goes looking for her daughter who has eloped with a 'low-caste' man, hoping to give the daughter her certificates and some money so that she can lead a decent life. The 'Stolen Girl', born into a family of black magicians and abducted when she had barely reached puberty, grows up to be a tough survivor who lives life entirely on her own terms. Srinivasan, a police constable, tormented after being a pallbearer for a Dalit corpse and horrified by its implications for his social status, decides to quit his job. Chandravadanam, a music prodigy, dies, and Kalaiammal, who brought her up without ever entering her house, mourns her death and curses the man for whom she gave up her youth and music.

In these and ten other stories—translated by Padma Narayanan with great skill and sensitivity—Imayam proves why he has been hailed as a writer with few equals anywhere, for his deep humanism and fierce sense of justice.